D0293049

Advance Praise for

ESCAPE FROM MANUS PRISON

'Stunning. This book should be on every reading list in the country. Stateless, without papers and too often without a drop of water to drink, Jaivet Ealom escapes Myanmar and the Rohingya genocide that continues to destroy his people. From Jakarta to Manus Island, Papua New Guinea, in sinking boats and cargo planes, he lives by his wit. In this world, babies drop to the bottom of the ocean and men are caged, beaten, numbered. A chance reading of Viktor Frankl's *Man's Search for Meaning* restores his soul enough to get him, still undocumented, to Toronto. Ealom writes, "The choice of how I responded, or who I wished to be, was still my own to make." We share Ealom's world, and this choice is ours too. Read this book. Know who you wish to be.'
—**Kim Echlin, award-winning author of** *Speak, Silence*

'An inspiring, eye-opening, harrowing, heartbreaking and triumphant journey that is testament to the resilience of the human spirit. The raw and vulnerable storytelling will touch you to your core and keep you spellbound till the last page. This book will restore your faith in the power of humanity that makes Canada the True North Strong and Free!' —**Samra Zafar, bestselling author of** *A Good Wife: Escaping the Life I Never Chose*

'This incredible, heart-stopping escape story is about shameful truths and spiritual authenticity; it's about government sanctioned torture and it's about redemption. Thank God Jaivet Ealom recorded his saga. From the merciless tactics of a government to the lyrical writing of a man who finds goodness in the face of evil, this book astonishes because it exposes the secret deals countries make to deny justice, and it takes you into the heart of a decent man. I couldn't put it down and was almost breathless when I read the last page. My only unanswered question: Who will play Jaivet in the movie?' —**Sally Armstrong, bestselling author of *Power Shift: The Longest Revolution***

'Jaivet's memoir has all the taut propulsion of a thriller, yet devastatingly, this is a story all too real. *Escape from Manus Prison* offers a first-hand account of the brutal treatment of refugees at every turn, from exploitative smugglers to the xenophobic policies of foreign governments.' —**Camilla Gibb, bestselling author of *Sweetness in the Belly* and *The Relatives***

'Art, culture and writing: these are gifts and they are weapons. I'm proud of Jaivet for speaking out—for history, and for all of those whom history would silence.' —**Behrouz Boochani, award-winning author of *No Friend But the Mountains***

ESCAPE FROM MANUS PRISON

It matters not how strait the gate,
How charged with punishments the scroll,
I am the master of my fate,
I am the captain of my soul.

William Ernest Henley, 'Invictus'

ESCAPE

ONE MAN'S

FROM

DARING QUEST

MANUS

FOR FREEDOM

PRISON

JAIVET EALOM

VIKING

VIKING

an imprint of Penguin Canada, a division of Penguin Random House Canada Limited

Canada • USA • UK • Ireland • Australia • New Zealand • India • South Africa • China

First published in Australia in 2021 as Escape From Manus by Viking,
part of the Penguin Random House group of companies
Published in Viking paperback by Penguin Canada, 2022

www.penguinrandomhouse.ca

LIBRARY AND ARCHIVES CANADA CATALOGUING IN PUBLICATION

Title: Escape from Manus Prison : one man's daring quest for freedom / Jaivet Ealom.
Names: Ealom, Jaivet, author.
Identifiers: Canadiana (print) 20210394757 | Canadiana (ebook) 20220132097 |
ISBN 9780735245198 (softcover) | ISBN 9780735245204 (EPUB)
Subjects: LCSH: Ealom, Jaivet. | LCSH: Rohingya (Burmese people)—Biography. |
LCSH: Rohingya (Burmese people)—Social conditions. | LCSH: Refugees—Burma—
Biography. | LCSH: Refugees—Canada—Biography. | LCSH: Escaped prisoners—
Australia—Biography. | LCSH: Escapes—Australia. | LCGFT: Autobiographies.
Classification: LCC HV640.5.B93 E25 2022 | DDC 305.89140591092—dc23

Map of Jaivet's journey by James Rendall
All photos courtesy of the author unless otherwise stated.
Cover design by Talia Abramson
Cover image © Cole Burston
Co-writer Craig Henderson

Printed in Canada

10 9 8 7 6 5 4 3 2 1

Penguin
Random House
VIKING CANADA

PROLOGUE

'I'm going to die tonight. I'm going to die *tonight*.'

I was sad to realise I'd never feel the sun again. Most likely none of us would. It was past midnight and I'd had time to think things through. I accepted the finality. I was at peace.

Crouched around me in the darkness were a hundred men, women and children. The wind howled, and the air grew louder with the cries of desperate souls. Like me, they could see the world ending. Young families prayed together, united in their terror and grief. A mother clutched a baby close to her chest, looking at her child for perhaps the last time. A silent farewell.

Next to her, a group of men – fathers, sons, survivors – tried to project strength and calm. Others wept loud and long. They had made it this far, only to die on the relentless waves. Lost to history, soon to be forgotten. Their stories would never be written.

For all the desperation and pleas for help from God, it had fallen strangely quiet inside my head. I'd somehow managed to turn down the noise and switched off the lights, so I could have a final, frank conversation with my soul.

'Have I been a good person? What is the measure of goodness?'

Staring straight at death made me look at my life. Twenty-one years on earth, and what had I done with them? Were my days just a waste of effort, or had I been a contributing member of the human race? Did I use my time here wisely? Had I made any difference at all?

I lifted my eyes to search for comfort in the permanence of the stars, but heavy clouds had muted the sky. The only light came from the wavering glow of a kerosene lamp and the glare of a couple of flashlights from the depths of the boat, where people took turns bailing out the rising water. They were fighting a losing battle. We were far from land on an angry sea and our broken vessel was sinking fast.

It had been three days since we'd all scrambled aboard the old fishing hulk off a far-flung beach near Kendari, Indonesia. The crew was supposed to sail us to Darwin, Australia where, according to a rumour that everyone had heard at one time or another, Australians opened their hearts and their country to people like us – those on the run from torture, persecution and death. We thought they were good and caring people, so different from the ones we were fleeing from.

The final maritime push in our gruelling odyssey toward salvation had been an almost comical study in human error. The agents we'd put our trust in turned out to be sneaky and unreliable. Alarmingly, they appeared to be incompetent as well.

The rickety boat they surprised us with – so unprepared for a long sea voyage – had bled oil and breathed smoke from the moment it departed. There was precious little food or water onboard, no navigational equipment beyond a compass, no radio and no life jackets. Now, seventy-two hours later, the hull had ruptured and we were sliding into the watery abyss.

That so many people – all of us strangers from different lands – would wager their lives on such a hopeless journey testified to our shared desperation. Each of us was fleeing conditions we considered harder to bear, on balance, than the possibility of death by drowning. When the only choice is between a murderous homeland and the cruel sea, it's not much of a choice at all.

Panic had swept across the deck earlier that afternoon when the bilge pump failed and the engine sputtered and drowned. An army of green waves pushed the boat sideways to the wind, and rocked it savagely. When word spread that its belly was filling with water, our belongings were dragged from the hold below and hurled into the sea.

Everything we owned, all the possessions we hoped to carry into our new life, was tossed out on the faint hope that we might survive the ordeal. My backpack was out there somewhere, bobbing along in the sad slick of our last worldly possessions. Not that mine amounted to much: some spare clothes, a few toiletries, and documents from Burma, the only place I'd ever known. Once my homeland, now the stage of a bloody genocide. It was with mixed feelings that I was leaving that life behind.

Whatever wasn't nailed down eventually joined the sinking trail of luggage. Even the remaining diesel was drained from the fuel tanks and tipped overboard. The men took turns descending in small groups to bail sea water out of the hold using plastic containers. During my first shift, the water sloshed up to my knees. The next time I went down, at dusk, it lapped at my hips.

When night fell, our fears grew. It seemed the habit of the ocean to grow more combative once the sun had turned its back. Our timber hulk twisted in the peaks and valleys of unseen waves, each new swell promising to throw us overboard once and for all. We clung to the bucking, waterlogged boat with cold and aching fingers.

It was the end of our second day without food or water, and those of us who'd been scooping up buckets of the oily sea were worn out, as weak as kittens. It was around 11 pm when I last went below to help. Now the water was chest high. While I tried to stay strong, eventually my body gave out. As I dragged myself back to my place on the roof of the doomed boat, I knew what would happen next. 'I'm going to die tonight.'

As someone who had always been a good believer, I was surprised the fear of God didn't stir in me as I sat among the others and waited

3

for the end. My shipmates were a mystery to me, and their hopes and the dreams they'd had would remain unknown.

For myself, I was fairly certain that death would come swiftly. Although I'd grown up near the coast I'd never learned to swim. I might have made peace with dying but I dreaded the thought of water pouring into my lungs. My only prayer was to ask God for a gentle end.

My thoughts turned homeward to Burma, where my younger brother Shahed would be waiting for an update on my journey to Australia. My cell phone hadn't been in range of a signal for days, but I typed a message anyway: 'Dear brother, tell Mom and Dad that I love them, and forgive me if I was not a good son. The boat is sinking. I didn't make it. I'm sorry. Goodbye.'

I saved the message and pushed the phone into the pocket of my jeans. I hoped if my body washed up on the shore that maybe someone would find it, and somehow retrieve my dying words. Hungry, exhausted and balanced on the precipice of my remaining moments, I felt a wisp of sleep wrap around me like a blanket. As my eyes closed, I reminded God of my final wish.

'Please let me die in my sleep.'

It wasn't to be the last time I recited that prayer. On many a night in the years that followed – after I had finally made it to safety, and started an unexpected new chapter in my life – I begged God over and over again, 'Please, kill me before I wake up.'

Eventually, the prayers would stop.

ONE

'It will come: Humanity must perforce prey on itself.
Like monsters of the deep.'

William Shakespeare, *King Lear*, Act 4, Scene 2

'You young guys are like tadpoles swimming in the hoof print of a bull.' I'm not sure if it was my mother or grandmother who first explained my world to me in those terms. They were members of Burma's Rohingya Muslim community, with the good fortune of being born in an earlier era of relative security. They remembered being able to travel wherever they liked, and live a life of freedom and choices. My brother Shahed and I – also born in Burma – did not.

Our world, growing up, was actually a roofless prison. Its boundary was a circle of land five kilometres wide and ringed with army check-points. My hometown was in the far north-west of the country, in Rakhine State (formerly known as Arakan and still referred to in that way by the Rohingyas). Maungdaw was a coastal trading city of about 400,000 – the majority of whom were Rohingyas – located near the border with Bangladesh. I was born a decade after Burma's ruling military junta had stripped the Rohingyas of our legal existence and introduced increasingly draconian controls on our movements.

That town, just a dot on the world map, was the limit of my earthly existence. It was all I knew. I'd never seen a building higher than a two-storey village house, let alone a university or an airport. Not even the next town. Until I was seventeen years old I spent my entire life

5

hemmed in, save for one emergency trip across the border to Bangladesh to see a doctor when my nose wouldn't stop bleeding.

Our lives weren't just constricted in a physical sense. Although it was a relatively busy trading hub, Maungdaw was anything but modern. A hostile government and inadequate planning had left us without the basics that other people might take for granted. Civil services were thin on the ground and households had to make do with just two hours of electricity every second day.

The region had been contested territory for generations. The Buddhist majority who controlled the country considered the Rohingyas to be illegal immigrants from Bangladesh, although our roots in Burma dated back centuries. The myth of our foreign origins, once invented and shared, was a sharp blade used to cut us from the national fabric.

By the time I was a toddler, the military rulers were well advanced in a focused, long-term program of oppression and harassment. Their campaign would eventually lead to the deaths of tens of thousands of my people, and the expulsion from our homeland of hundreds of thousands more.

Persecution and ethnic cleansing follow a cruel logic that is familiar from the history books. Now it was our turn. We lived under a kind of apartheid: our communities were segregated from Buddhist ones, and there were rules that applied only to us. We were forced to live in specified wards, register our houses with the regime and report how many people lived in each dwelling. Rohingyas were prodded, hounded and controlled. We couldn't have an extra person stay as a guest in our home without written permission. Soldiers thought nothing of dragging terrified families out of bed in the middle of the night for a surprise head count.

We had our own language and customs, and the regime, eager to shore up its claim to legitimacy, used culture as a wedge to deepen the gap between the minority and majority. Our access to education was blocked through a government tactic of placing schools in Buddhist neighbourhoods and staffing them entirely with Buddhist teachers. School was a staging ground for abuse, and Rohingya kids wept with fear at the mere suggestion of leaving home for lessons. Children either didn't attend or were so marginalised in classes that they were better off at home.

At school, as in the wider community, the Rohingyas were faced by a presumption of guilt. When a transgression or a perceived crime occurred, especially in a case of a Rohingya against a Buddhist, no investigation was required – the Buddhist always won.

There was no need to kill us outright, not at that point. The system was stacked against us: the laws, the media, the culture and the way people understood the world. It was the birthright of the Rohingyas to carry the blame and the shame.

Rohingyas of my generation were forbidden from joining the public service. In a nation entirely dominated by the government, this meant we were reduced to lives of menial employment: manual labour, fishing, farming or working in small shops.

To rise any higher was to ask for trouble. A Rohingya who swam against the tide and managed to become educated might be a target of the government and be thrown in jail on spurious grounds. I happened to be one such creature, a tadpole that managed to leap out of the bull's hoof print and into a decent school.

Ours was, remarkably perhaps, a relatively middle-class family. My hard-working dad was fortunate to run a small shop in Maungdaw where he sold household appliances. Jobs were scarce for most men, let alone for women, so my mom stayed home to manage the house and look after Shahed and me.

My mother was from a family that believed in the value of higher education. Back in the days when Rohingyas were full citizens, my uncles had stood for local elections, served in public office and worked in banking and medicine. One even ascended to become head of a hospital.

My mother, also remarkably, was well educated herself. Her fluency in Burmese was a rarity for a woman of her background.

7

Burmese was the tongue of the ruling junta, and calling it the official means of communication was an understatement. It was the only language allowed in the newspapers, the courts, the schools – you name it.

While most Rohingyas, especially the men of my parents' generation, were literate and had a place in the national order, the practice ended before I was born. By the time my brother and I came onto the scene, the regime had taken steps to put us in a linguistic and socio-economic ghetto.

One way it did this was through an attempt to wipe out the writing and literature of our people. It was a crime, for example, to be caught holding a book in our native script. By debasing Rohingya and turning it into the language of the street, the law blocked the intellectual progress of our community, and ensured our rich heritage would not easily be passed down to the next generation. It was an act of cultural genocide that opened the door to the campaign of physical violence that was to come.

For those of my generation, to be literate implied the ability to read and write in Burmese, since it was the only language in which reading and writing were possible. Even in Rohingyan, the word 'literate' suggested a full meaning of 'literate *in Burmese*'.

Speaking Burmese signalled you were educated and capable of grasping how things worked, and my mother believed our mastery of this language would give me and Shahed a fighting chance in this country, or at least enable us to glimpse what lay beyond the limits of our little world in Maungdaw.

In this, she cut a lonely path. Other parents inadvertently passed down their fears and warnings to the next generation on the pretence of safety. To stop their children straying into danger in Buddhist neighbourhoods, they spooked them by saying the Mog (meaning 'Buddhist people') were coming to get them. Other times they simply scared them by saying, 'The police are coming to get you if you don't stop crying.' The police, needless to say, were Mog too.

Naturally the Buddhist parents told their little ones similar stories about Rohingyas lurking in our neighbourhoods. These cautionary tales only reinforced the government's social and cultural separation, and helped maintain our lesser status.

My mother didn't subscribe to the Mog myth. If anything, it was our fellow Rohingya kids she tried to shelter us from. While other boys were out in the fields, flying kites and running wild, Shahed and I were at home, reading books. There were Rohingya games I never played and turns of phrases I never learned.

Instead, my brother and I developed our own language, which conveyed as much through silences as words. Even today, when we talk about our parents or other delicate topics, our deepest thoughts and feelings are shared in the pauses between sentences.

In our family, we kept to ourselves, staying in a protective bubble of privacy and reflection that I have never truly left, no matter how far I've travelled. When I was four years old, my mother sent me to a pre-school deep inside Maungdaw's Buddhist neighbourhood where I was the sole Muslim and Rohingya student. My mother was set on exposing me to the country's language and culture from an early age. She was determined that I also learn to not fear Buddhist kids.

Her progressive parenting introduced me to a whole other world that few children from my neighbourhood had glimpsed. Even Shahed, who is only two years younger than me, missed out on the gift. By the time he was old enough to attend pre-school, the government had closed them to the Rohingyas.

As I grew older and shifted into elementary school, I found the religious divide between me and my fellow students hard to cross, despite my slowly broadening horizons. My parents were devout Muslims, as I was. I spent a lot of time worrying that my Buddhist friends, as non-believers, were headed for a punishing afterlife. This was both confusing and upsetting, since I loved my classmates and I didn't want them to suffer. We had such good times together and they never made me feel like I was any different or the odd one out.

Under my mother's influence I came to understand that, as a Rohingya, we did not have the luxury of being merely ordinary. We had to be well educated to counter the racism and oppression the government was using to stunt our lives.

In Arakan, privilege was 100 to one in favour of Buddhists. My mother stressed we must try to always be better than them – not just academically, but in terms of human decency. If we didn't, we would forever become just two more of Arakan's disposable people, trodden under the heel of the regime and its supporters. Education wasn't just the key to success, it was vital to our very survival.

It was difficult to keep up with my fellow students, let alone outperform them. Burmese had a grammar that was pretty much the opposite to that of our own Rohingyan language. The education system was underfunded for Buddhist and Rohingya alike, and teachers made an effort with us that was so weak as to be worthless. The only reason I managed to persevere, and even rise to the top of a number of my classes, was through home-schooling, with my mother as my instructor.

The biggest roadblock to Rohingya progress came in 1982, with the passing of the notorious Citizenship Law. This legislation replaced the concept of 'indigenous races' with that of 'national races' – and then omitted the Rohingyas from the list of ethnic groups. Since the law entirely defined citizens in terms of their ethnicity, it meant that the government no longer recognised our claim to being Burmese. At a stroke, we ceased to exist in any official sense in our own country.

The oppression we encountered was more than just the invisible, thread-of-a-spiderweb-on-the-face variety. Our town, like every Rohingya community in northern Arakan, was patrolled by a paramilitary unit of the Burmese armed forces. The Na-Sa-Ka (later rebranded as Border Guard Police, or BGP) brought together police, intelligence, immigration and border guards. It had been established solely for the purpose of subjugating our people, by enforcing the country's apartheid-like policies, and its lopsided laws.

These shock troops paid regular visits to our villages, turning our houses upside down in a display of power. Under the guise of enforcing law and order, they released their animal spirits. Robbery, forced labour and sexual assault were common.

When soldiers pounded on our door, my mother had to rise above her fear of what was coming. 'Okay, what is it you need?' she would say in Burmese, with a cutting fluency that could awe and placate, bringing a measure of calm to the situation. Her ability to speak their language implied she might know the limits of their power under the law.

In Burma, English instruction begins in middle school, a legacy of the colonial days, since the British only left the country in 1948. In my parents' time, the ties to England were still strong: the University of Rangoon, for example, had been established by the British and modelled on Oxford and Cambridge. By my time, the junta had put the Burmese language in the top spot, but English was still heard in the classrooms, and to me it sounded like magic, a song played on a musical instrument, calling me away to a grander and better world than the one I knew.

By this point, the truth of my life in an open-air cage had started to become clear. While our town was majority Rohingya, I realised we were a minority in the country, and an unpopular one. Classmates who had once been friendly had learned of my otherness from their parents, whose motives were murky. Did they support the persecution, or were they just wary of the ruling regime? Were they brainwashed? Probably a mix of all those factors. More than anything, they knew where their interests lay.

I graduated high school with strong grades. When Rohingyas were stripped of citizenship rights, we were also banned from attending what were considered Tier One universities, which were the only way to study subjects like medicine, engineering, economics and aeronautics.

This ensured most professions were the exclusive domain of Buddhist Burmese. By the time I graduated, the ban had been extended to law school, leaving just non-specialised liberal arts degrees open to us.

The allegory of the frog in the pot of slowly boiling water was well known in our culture, for good reason. To avoid attracting too much criticism, the changes enacted by the junta were made incrementally, one edict after another. Our freedoms were reduced so gradually as to quell any dissent. We did not know any better than our very circumscribed ring of rights and opportunities, and by the time we did, we were too weak and hemmed in to find a way out.

The first travel restrictions were introduced during my parents' time when they were told they could go anywhere they pleased – as long as it was inside Burma. Next they were banned from travelling outside Arakan State, and later from outside one of the state's five districts. Since almost all Tier One programs were offered at the universities that were interstate, mostly located in Burma's largest city, Yangon (formerly known as Rangoon and still referred to in that way by the Rohingyas, just as we still refer to Burma, rather than Myanmar), the policy managed to stifle both movement *and* education.

By the time I was born, the ring had grown tighter still, and we were largely prevented from leaving our town – a semi-rural universe that could be traversed in about half an hour. If we wanted to go further, we had to apply to the Na-Sa-Ka for permission, and they loved to refuse the requests, both out of cruelty and hope of a bribe.

Over the course of two generations Burma's military regime had thoroughly boiled the frog and drained the puddle. Problem was, I still had my dreams. I wanted to attend university, to acquire knowledge, learn about the world, have a career, contribute to the human race and build a more prosperous life for myself.

Foolish hopes. I was imprisoned in a port town, basically an overgrown fishing village. What future did I have other than to sell things or catch fish?

The introduction of a national ID required us to explicitly state our faith and our race – something we had to repeat whenever we filled in the endless forms required to get anything done officially. As for our supposed race, we had one option, to classify ourselves as 'Bengali', as if we were foreigners who had recently wandered in from the country next door.

Restrictions were put on places of worship as well. At first it was a general embargo on new buildings, then extensions of existing mosques were outlawed, followed by a ban on repairing ones that had started to fall apart. Eventually Maungdaw's central masjid, which had stood for centuries, was taken over by the Buddhist regime and rebadged as a fire station – a cruel joke considering how soon agents of this same regime took to setting our homes ablaze.

While the Na-Sa-Ka weren't necessarily a feature of our day-to-day lives, their menace hung over our communities like a thundercloud. One instrument of control was the so-called census. As a boy I was never more humiliated than on the days we were summoned, family by family, to a makeshift barracks and grilled about our personal lives: 'How many people live in your house? How many children are there? What are their names? Their ages? Are there any new children?'

They'd ask other questions as well, designed to humiliate: 'Who is sleeping with whom?'

Women who observed purdah were ordered to remove their scarves and other covering garments on these occasions. I watched all of my aunts, my mom and even my grandma traumatised and humiliated in this manner. If a woman was attractive, the Na-Sa-Ka would make her stay uncovered for longer so they could leer at her in a sordid quasi strip-show. In the West it would be considered sexual violence on a systematic, government-sanctioned scale.

Before being released from the interrogation, we were photographed in a group mugshot, as we held a plate with digits that both identified our household and the number of family members in it. We were then sent on our way until our next intimidation session. It was my first taste of being reduced to a number by a sadistic regime, but it would not be my last.

The regular census-taking also set the scene for the impromptu military intrusions in the dead of night, when squads of soldiers battered on doors and demanded families line up to be checked against the records. If you were found where you shouldn't be, you were taken back to the police station or the military barracks, where you had to either find family members to produce the ransom or face jail time.

The raids themselves were punishment enough. If they wanted, the soldiers would violently assault the women present. If they were hungry, they'd take your food. If they saw something they liked, they would take that too.

Rape was a preferred weapon among the Na-Sa-Ka. It not only crushed and traumatised the victim but, in a society where dignity and collective family values were more important than individual pride, it stabbed at the heart of the community.

The regime had other weapons at its disposal. When I was finishing high school, Rohingyas were forbidden from marrying without permission. To apply, couples had to front up to an army barracks and be interrogated separately about their plans, before being strip-searched and ogled. Any couple who could stomach such shaming had to then wait up to five years for a decision, which could just as easily be a no as a yes. Those lucky enough to marry the person they loved were then told they could have no more than two children.

Fire was another tool used to harm and control. With its roots in the colonial era, the Vacant, Fallow and Virgin Land Management Law stated that any building destroyed by fire defaulted to being government property. However the British intended the legislation to be used, its flaws were obvious, for it incentivised arson.

Unsurprisingly, the targets of the attacks were often Rohingya villages, which were routinely torched. When the inhabitants fled, the junta made little effort to lure them back. Quite the opposite: they offered subsidies and other lures to Buddhists in less wealthy areas, along with the promise of a better life. This was a version of ethnic cleansing – in fact, a mass relocation scheme – through legislative means.

The newcomers, once they arrived in these villages, were above the law. They stole equipment from their Rohingya neighbours and used it openly and without shame, knowing they'd never be questioned, let alone prosecuted. No longer at the bottom of the social strata, they enjoyed having someone even lower to look down upon. Keenly aware that the government wanted the Rohingyas to be intimidated and divided, their contempt for us grew. They even treated communal local roads as their own private property.

The relocation scheme had other effects. The new settlers crowded around and inside Rohingya wards and villages, cutting them off from each other, an isolation made worse by the establishment of military outposts at key junctures. It was not entirely unusual for a Buddhist to throw a Rohingya off a bridge if they happened to be crossing at the same time. As a result, frightened Rohingyas stopped raising animals that needed to go beyond their villages to roam and feed, putting an end to farming practices that had lasted for centuries.

Year by year it felt as if our prison got smaller and filled up with thousands of extra jailers. But life was far more dangerous on the other side of its invisible walls.

My first glimpse of the world beyond Maungdaw came in my teens, through a chance outing. My partner in this escapade was my cousin, Jonaid. Born just days apart, we'd been raised in the same neighbourhood with the same values, believing that if we studied and worked hard we'd be rewarded with a future of fulfilment and stability.

We also shared a sense of adventure. By the age of sixteen, we had graduated from high school and were eager to enjoy some freedom away from our parents. So when the offer arose to join a group from our mosque on an excursion, we were excited.

The group of about thirty people was permitted to travel to towns and villages in the nearby countryside and spend three days in each, offering religious outreach and general labour to help the locals. It was a rite of passage for boys who would soon become men – the Rohingya equivalent of spring break.

We'd be sleeping away from our own houses, which was officially forbidden, and required the assent of government authorities. Since the trip was a semi-regular occurrence, it was generally allowed to go ahead without too much hassle. But we were only authorised to visit certain places and our travel passes were only valid for forty days, by which time we had to be back in Maungdaw – or else.

It started out as a thrilling but physically exhausting trek. Although we travelled no more than fifty kilometres from Maungdaw, Jonaid and I felt like we'd entered another world. We took a boat up the River Naf, which defines the border with Bangladesh.

The countryside was breathtaking. At first glance it looked as though the Rohingya fishermen and farmers we saw along the way enjoyed a peaceful existence, growing rice and tending stock in lush fields. It didn't take long before we realised this rural idyll concealed something more sinister.

If Maungdaw was starved of essential services, the living conditions in the countryside were medieval. Farmers had no machinery or modern equipment whatsoever. They lacked fertiliser. They worked the land using hand-made wooden tools and their own sweat. Where Jonaid and I came from, if you needed to transfer water from one rice paddy to another, you used a diesel pump; in this area, farmers dug streams from plot to plot using their bare hands.

There was no electricity to speak of, so when the sun went down the only light flickered from fires and lanterns.

These rural Rohingyas were subjected to oppression harsher than any we'd seen. Every creek or river crossing – and there were many – was guarded by a Na-Sa-Ka checkpoint. Buddhists could freely pass through but the dirt-poor Rohingyas had to pay a toll, in the form of chickens, the best fish from their day's catch or cigarettes. People in the towns had to defer to the Na-Sa-Ka, but our cousins in the country were obliged to treat them like gods.

Na-Sa-Ka barracks were dotted throughout the region and Rohingyas who failed to pay the fee or follow orders were often called to the barracks, where they might be tortured for days. Some people crawled back to their homes after having been savagely beaten. Others never returned at all.

In one village that we visited, a man showed us an ugly scar across his back – a memento of the time the Na-Sa-Ka had branded him with a glowing-hot iron. Other villagers were battered and bruised where soldiers had beaten them with rifle butts, and some had boot marks permanently imprinted on their bodies where they'd been trodden on.

In another hamlet, the locals described how the Na-Sa-Ka would put a pot on the top of a steep rocky hill and force them to fill it by carrying water from the stream at the bottom of the cliff, one teaspoon at a time. In the next community, we learned the soldiers liked to bury villagers up to their necks in mud and watch leeches suck blood from their faces.

Jonaid and I had dreamed of spreading our wings and soaring away from the nest on a noble quest to help our fellow man. Instead we received an education about human cruelty that defied imagination. The further from our town we travelled, the more depraved the persecution became. It was clear that in these areas the Buddhist soldiers were both in and out of control – a battalion of demons in jungle boots and dark green uniforms.

Sundown provided no relief for the hunted villagers. When the junta moved divisions from one regional outpost to another, they usually did it in the dead of night. Dozens of marching troops could pass through towns at any time, accompanied by artillery and truck convoys in a show of dominance that struck dread into residents' hearts.

Whenever a convoy stopped in a village, devastation followed. Gang rapes and the looting of houses were common, and residents were often kidnapped to be used as forced labour and sex slaves when the military caravan rolled on.

I came to understand that Rohingyas weren't the only victims of Buddhist oppression. Other groups in different parts of the country, including some minority religious communities, were also abused. We heard stories about Christians being forced into minefields at gunpoint to step on bombs, sacrificing their lives for the safety of the soldiers.

Jonaid and I regretted ever leaving the relative safety of Maungdaw, and it wasn't long before we experienced trouble firsthand. Each time we travelled from one village to the next, our group leaders were required to inform the local border guards of our intentions. One day we were due to walk a short distance from one community to another, less than a kilometre away, and for whatever reason our leaders neglected to inform the Na-Sa-Ka.

We had travelled about 500 metres in a single file along a dirt road when we were stopped by a group of soldiers. They were armed and angry. As punishment for failing to report our movements, our leader was commanded to lie on the ground and perform 100 sit-ups in front of everyone. Then the soldiers moved along the line, one by one, and made us all follow suit. They laughed at us as we squirmed in the dirt, grunting and struggling to crunch our stomach muscles in the hot sun.

Compared to being buried alive or beaten with rifle butts, it was a light punishment. Yet the message was clear: they decided where we could go, and whether we lived or died.

At the time, I saw the arrogance and the abuse, without understanding why or how things had ended up that way. In the years to come, I learned more about the origins and organisation of the Burmese military, whose rallying cry was 'One blood, one voice, one command'. By that point, I knew enough of world history to consider the similarity of the slogan with the 'Blood and soil' chanted by the Nazis during the rise of the Third Reich.

Nativism and religious humiliation were the twin foundations of power in Burma. Before they were sent into the countryside to stalk the Rohingyas, soldiers underwent a program of brainwashing. They were drilled to believe that purity of race was the key to Burmese prosperity and sovereignty, and that they were the brave and pious instruments of the holy nationalistic vision.

When we returned to Maungdaw a month later, Jonaid and I were almost thankful we lived behind a ring of checkpoints. At least we could wake up each day with some assurance that physical torture or death were not around the corner. I didn't laugh or smile for the first few weeks back, knowing what people were enduring in the countryside.

Just a few years later, most of the villages Jonaid and I had visited on that trip were burnt to the ground. The inhabitants who fled the fire were shot in the back as they tried to escape.

However, by that point, when the wave of the genocide was starting to reach its diabolical peak, I had managed to escape the hoof print in Maungdaw – only to find myself in an even smaller jail, one with high walls and barbed wire, on a remote island half a world away.

TWO

'The tiger that wants to die leaves its own forest.'

Burmese proverb

A s I took the first steps into adulthood, I found myself at a cross-roads. Although Jonaid and I had earned high enough grades to qualify for Tier One university programs, our efforts were worthless. We would never have a chance of pursuing the dream of higher education in our home country.

It was a fact of life we were not ready to accept. As young men who had been raised to ask more of ourselves and our futures, we were unwilling to give up that easily, even if our confidence and ideals carried great risk. Each of us eyed a different path – one that meant we might never see our families again.

It was common for Rohingyas who aspired to better prospects to abandon the country and study abroad, usually in Bangladesh. This option had a sting in its tail. We would have to enrol at a Bangladeshi school under false names with false backgrounds. Ironically, we would have to assume the foreign 'Bengali' identity that had been wrongly foisted on us by the junta, and turn our backs on our people and culture.

It was a big sacrifice, but it paled alongside the long-term cost of leaving home. Once a Rohingya ran away from Burma, the regime never let them back in. Going to university, for us, meant going into exile.

Still, we both agreed we could never submit to the suffocation we knew in Maungdaw, so we planned a short trip to Bangladesh to investigate the schools there. Rohingyas were allowed to travel to Bangladesh but only for a short time. We each had to apply to immigration for a temporary travel permit. The permit was known among Rohingyas as a seven-day passport, but it was no passport – it was a leash around our necks. If we stayed away even one day longer, we could forget about ever returning home.

We'd be stateless and forced to survive in Bangladesh, a country that had its own appalling approach to the Rohingya refugee crisis, a stance that grew more merciless with each passing year.

Nervously, with our travel permits stamped, we once again travelled up the River Naf. This time we landed on the Bangladeshi bank in a fishing town. We had only been in there a few hours when Jonaid's phone rang. It was his father, my Uncle Fazal, asking us to return to Burma immediately. He may have found a way for us to get into university back home. It was a long shot, but it was worth a try, and we had to act quickly to make it happen.

Like my mother, Uncle Fazal had once been a full citizen. Unlike a lot of Rohingyas of that prior generation, though, Fazal and many of the other older members of our family had been careful to hold onto their original identity cards. It was a brave move, considering the authorities had demanded their surrender as part of the 1982 Citizenship Law.

More than that, my relatives kept track of their citizenship records and government-held files. They also tried to stay on top of the ins-and-outs of the regime's changing rules, in order to manoeuvre around them. They preserved for our family just enough ambiguity in terms of our status in the country to give me and Jonaid an opportunity to earn a proper education.

My parents' appetite for arcane details, their ability to study the system – turning it upside down to find its intricacies and flaws – would be passed down to the next generation. A family habit that would end up saving my life, more than once.

Using our parents' outdated ID cards, we applied for Tier One universities, as if we were proper citizens. It was an audacious approach but I liked it. I always had a strong sense of justice. After working hard to get high grades, why didn't I deserve the same opportunity that other boys in Burma took for granted? Why shouldn't I shoot for the moon?

Whatever doubts I had about our odds of succeeding vanished when we were both accepted. I was admitted into a degree program in industrial chemistry at Dagon University, 500 kilometres away in Burma's largest city, Rangoon. For his part, Jonaid would study medicine at a school in Magway in central Burma.

Consider this. A Rohingya friend of mine who had scored higher than me in his final grades applied to a raft of Tier One programs at the same time and was flatly refused. Not because he lacked merit, but because his parents had not managed to hold onto their old IDs. Multiply him by all the Rohingya graduates across the country, and you have a sense of the pure waste of human potential involved. A generation lost.

With our placements assured, the next hurdle was figuring out how to get away from Maungdaw and travel to the capital – something forbidden to Rohingyas for at least twenty years.

While we'd been plotting the trip to Bangladesh, Uncle Fazal had been pursuing a separate line of enquiry into how we might make the journey across the country to arrive at the Burmese universities where we had been accepted. He was hoping to draw upon an old practice that by our time was no longer allowed, whereby, under a bewildering set of pre-conditions, Rohingyas could apply for a forty-five day travel permit for reasons that included hospitalisation, pilgrimage and education.

It turned out Jonaid and I could also apply for these travel permits under our parents' names, as long as we were still minors. Uncle Fazal explained that these provisions had always existed, but you needed to speak and read Burmese in order to know about them. Even then, the decision as to whether we could travel was up to the discretion of a Buddhist immigration official and a positive outcome usually required an under-the-table payment.

My uncle's plan worked, and we became the first Rohingyas from our generation to enrol in a university interstate and actually manage to travel to our respective schools to pursue our studies. We were accidental trailblazers. It was all because our parents were savvy, resourceful and, above all, attuned to the byzantine and oppressive regulations of our country.

Although our 'racial' background, thanks to our assumed names, wasn't clear on our university paperwork, our typical Rohingya looks meant we were hardly going to pass through checkpoints easily. The uncertainty of the plan's success started to dawn on me and Junaid. So did the dangers. It felt implausible, a creaky contraption built of scraps of paper and thin air.

Although Uncle Fazal had arranged the travel permits, my first question was: 'What am I supposed to do when they expire after forty-five days?' After all, undergraduate degrees in Burma take three years to complete.

My uncle explained that, once I was safely out of Maungdaw, I could renew the permit at the immigration offices in Rangoon and keep applying for extensions. It sounded far-fetched but it was still a more attractive option than running away to Bangladesh, trying to master a new language and education system, and then never being allowed to go home again.

My parents worried about the proposal too. While they had done their best to position me for success, they were well aware of the hazards involved in the scheme, and the costs of failure. They needed to be, since both my mother and Uncle Fazal were required by regime officials to sign bond agreements, promising they'd go to jail if we didn't return. A single stumble could be the end of my family.

Maybe it was pride or optimism, or maybe they saw us, in grander terms, as a hope for our slowly suffocated generation. Whatever they believed, they did their best to help, selling their belongings to cover the cost of the travel and of the bribes that corrupt officials would demand along the way.

Since there was no airport in Maungdaw, the first destination was Sittwe (formerly known as Akyab and still referred to in that way by the

Rohingyas), the capital of Arakan. Jonaid set off first, accompanied for part of the trip by Fazal. Once Jonaid had made it safely to Rangoon, Fazal came back for me for a second run at the same journey.

The first checkpoint was on the outskirts of Maungdaw, about five kilometres from home. Although Akyab was just ninety kilometres away, Fazal and I had to stop at another three checkpoints as part of a nerve-racking, stop-start journey that involved a pick-up truck, a bus, a ferry and multiple humiliating interrogations.

While Buddhist travellers breezed past the Na-Sa-Ka outposts as if they didn't exist, we Rohingyas had to line up with precious documents in hand and submit ourselves to a fresh round of harassment. The soldiers stood on specially built platforms from which they could sneer down on us as we humbly shared our travel permits, passing them above our heads. Their body language was aggressive and their tone uniformly snide and suspicious. Seeing my uncle pass through these indignities was painful.

When we arrived in Akyab, a city of 180,000 people – mostly Rakhine Buddhists – by the Bay of Bengal, I experienced a new round of culture shock. It was the first time I'd ever seen a proper metropolis with a well-established infrastructure. The multi-laned roads were a complete revelation. All my life I had only ever seen pick-up trucks and jeeps plying shabby dirt roads in Maungdaw. In Akyab, cool-looking low-slung sedans glided along smooth asphalt arteries.

Even the coloured traffic lights blew my mind. There was no shortage of electricity either. Akyab was a lot to take in, both in its relative grandeur and in the way it threw into sharp relief the deliberately worn fibre of my hometown.

We booked into a hostel where I waited for three days while Uncle Fazal organised a permit that would allow me to board the plane and fly to Rangoon. When Jonaid had completed his journey a week earlier, he'd made it through without a problem, aside from the usual checkpoint harassment.

But in a country built on corruption, you can't predict the whims of the officials, who are deliberately difficult. For some reason the immigration officer we were dealing with in Akyab insisted that I needed a temporary ID card. These cards were not required of minors, as I was at the time, and they could only be issued in a person's hometown, which meant I had to make the perilous journey to Maungdaw and back again. And after all these efforts, the resulting ID would display my Rohingya name.

Just like that, I was back to square one. I felt vulnerable and scared, and even more so when Uncle Fazal decided, for financial reasons, to remain in Akyab while I travelled back to Maungdaw alone.

The return journey was as emotionally fraught as it was gruelling. The ferry trip ended up taking ten hours, after the boat became stranded on a sandbar at low tide. During the long wait, I curled up in a ball on a wooden bench beside a family of fellow travellers, feeling tired, frightened and hungry.

When the boat docked and let off the passengers, I meekly retraced my steps to my hometown. At each checkpoint my travel permit was stamped so I could present it to the local immigration offices in Maungdaw and prove I had returned through the same invisible gates from which I'd exited.

I arrived home around 2 am and banged on the door until my mother slowly opened it. Her bleary face fell as soon as she saw me.

'Are you okay?' she said, quickly pulling me inside and anxiously checking me for blood and bruises. 'Are you hurt?'

It was a terrible time of the night to wake a Rohingya mother. Her natural assumption was that I'd been beaten or tortured.

'I'm sorry, Mom. I had no choice but to come back.'

The next day I started the process of getting a temporary ID, which usually takes months. With Uncle Fazal waiting in Akyab and my university course now already underway in Rangoon, I somehow had to get it done in days. Once again the connections of my savvy family came in useful. One of our relatives had once worked in the local ward council where he still had loose connections. He was able to pay a bribe to expedite the process.

Meanwhile I had to fill out endless paperwork that proved my Rohingya heritage, extending backward to my grandparents on both sides. After I filed each form I was handed another to complete. It was a mind-numbing process that made me hope never to see another official document again, which was probably the point. With the ID application deadline looming, the waiting was hard to bear.

The immigration officer, despite now knowing all my family tree up to three generations, commanded me to repeat after him.

'So what is your race?' And then, to make sure I gave the right answer, he shouted, 'Bengali!'

'Bengali.' It was as much enthusiasm as I could muster.

'What is it?' His voice rose half an octave, to suggest he required a stronger delivery.

'Bengali!'

'What is your race?'

'Bengali!'

This was more than a provocation. Bengali was and is a derogatory term that the government used to label Rohingyas after 1982 to make it seem as if we were newcomers from Bangladesh, without roots in the country. All the fields on forms that had once been filled or labelled with 'Rohingya' were replaced with this term. If there were not so much at stake with my project to get into university, I would have gladly walked away.

When the paperwork was at last in order, my photograph was taken for my new temporary ID – on the last day I could apply for it. With my precious scrap of paper in hand, I set off from Maungdaw again and headed through the four checkpoints on my way back to Akyab.

This time the journey was even more trying. While my school acceptance letter carried my Burmese name, my new temporary ID showed my Rohingya name and stated that my nationality was Bengali, a clear mismatch. I had to produce a wad of other documents to show I was known by both names.

By the time I was allowed to board the plane in Akyab, nearly two months had elapsed. It had taken that long just to pull myself free of the bureaucratic spiderweb. It was all thanks to my family who had put their own safety and finances on the line to loosen the bonds of one of the most corrupt regimes on the planet.

Stepping onto the plane was strange enough for someone who'd never flown before, but I also felt a hundred eyes bore into me as I took my seat. I could almost hear the other passengers thinking, 'What on earth is a Rohingya doing on a plane?'

They might have felt they owned the skies as well as the land.

Rangoon is home to more than seven million people, hardly any of them Rohingya. In fact, the very word Rohingya is forbidden in Rangoon – you are not permitted to speak it out loud, and the Burmese media is prohibited from publishing it. As a result, Rohingyas who lived in the city did so in secret and in a state of constant fear, pretending to be some other kind of Muslim minority instead.

This was the case for my distant relatives on my father's side. They'd been part of a small group of Rohingyas who'd lived and worked in Rangoon prior to 1982. When the citizenship laws were introduced, they found themselves effectively marooned in a sea of Buddhists. Taking a risk, these same relatives agreed to let me stay with them while I attended university.

The first encounter was awkward. On the day I arrived in Rangoon, my cousins were too frightened to pick me up at the airport and instead suggested meeting at a nearby store. These people were strangers to me: they were names in stories my grandmother had told me over the years. In our conversation together, we revealed little about ourselves. Instead, in a weird moment of triangulation, I found myself fielding their heartfelt queries about members of my family that we had in common.

'How is your father? How is your grandmother doing? What ever happened to this uncle? Whatever became of that aunt?'

I felt like an alien bringing news from a far-off mother planet. It was obvious, not just that our sole point of commonality was these absent relatives, but that they were apprehensive about having me stay with them. After all, it was unheard of for a young Rohingya to suddenly walk off a plane in Rangoon and start studying at the famous Dagon University.

The Rohingya people flew so low under the radar in Rangoon that much of the wider population didn't even know they existed. Here in Burma's biggest city, the safety of these secret outsiders depended on avoiding any public and government attention. They were ghosts, hiding in plain sight, and their mantra was, 'Don't mess with the government and you'll be fine.'

If they ever showed their face, or poked their head above the horizon, Rohingyas could expect to be thrown into jail. People went to extraordinary lengths to remain invisible to the regime, even going so far as to pay Buddhist third parties to apply for a licence or simple jobs on their behalf. Anything to avoid having to show up in a government office.

If I had seen life as risky and circumscribed in my hometown, the situation for Rohingyas in Rangoon was eerie. As the truth began to sink in, I started to question my ability to pull off this harebrained scheme of earning a university education. I had put my fate in the hands of people I didn't really know, attempting to do something that possibly no-one had attempted in a generation.

At the same time, I was gradually learning something university couldn't teach. When you're backed into a corner, you have to take any way out you can. Conditions were deteriorating back home and I suspected they'd never improve. The only thing I had to lose now was the hope of a normal life. What a normal life was in Burma, I could only guess. I just hoped it meant a little less oppression, fear and racial hatred.

Because it had taken me so long to extract myself from Arakan, I arrived at Dagon halfway through the first semester, well after student orientation had finished. It was a huge school to navigate, both physically and mentally, and I had to work extra hard to catch up. Unusually, though, my ethnicity didn't pose a particular problem. I was enrolled under a Burmese name and, like me, most of the people there were not much more than kids. Thanks to the junta's efforts at ethnic erasure, I doubted if any of them even knew what a Rohingya was. I sat in the back row in classes and concentrated. Hard.

As much as I tried, I struggled terribly during the first semester. The teachers didn't understand me due to my thick accent. While I was fluent in Burmese, they spoke *Burmese* Burmese in Rangoon, which is different to the way we spoke it in Arakan. For all my pipe dreams about higher education, the truth was that my first months at university were a trial.

To complicate matters, just before the first round of exams began, I was told I'd have to move out of my relatives' house. It seemed they had offered me a place to stay out of politeness, thinking there was no way I'd be able to study at Dagon long term. When I stuck around, they realised they weren't so comfortable with the arrangement after all. I didn't blame them. the house wasn't that big and I didn't even have a room there, just a mattress laid on the living-room floor. I just wish they'd told me after exams. My grades were the only life insurance I had.

Fortunately, my mom had a stepsister who, like the other relatives, had been stranded in Rangoon after the 1982 crackdown. My mother asked if I could move in with her until I found a dormitory of my own. This aunt of mine picked me up that same night and I spent the second semester with her before finding my own small place. I paid the rent by working as a night receptionist in a hospital.

By second year of university, I found my footing. Academically, we were allowed a bit more liberty, exploring topics beyond the boundaries of our class lectures and even beyond our textbooks – an intellectual freedom I cherished. I grew used to physical freedom too. No longer confined to a glorified paddock back home, I was able to roam further afield. Because my student ID didn't mention my Rohingya name, I could travel anywhere in Burma, so long as I didn't go to Arakan.

During one break from university, a relatively well-off cousin of mine named Suu Myatt, who was close to my parents' age and lived in Rangoon, paid for Jonaid and me to visit a beach town in another state. For the first time in my life, I was able to tour the countryside easily. There were no curfews, no restrictions, no soldiers pounding down the door at nights, no forced exercises in the middle of the road – just freedom and free time to do whatever I wanted. It remains one of the best trips I've ever taken.

Still, there were moments when Burmese immigration reined me back in. I had to check in with them every forty-five days to have my permit renewed, and these visits felt like a recurring bad dream. The fear sharpened my focus and resolve to keep my grades up. If I fell out with the university – through a suspension or by flunking out of classes – the consequences would be dire. I'd have no valid reason to remain in Rangoon and I'd be deported to Arakan, where the troubles were deepening.

I never truly considered what the future might bring until my third year of university in 2012. Although I'd passed my exams and was on track to do well, my chances of being allowed to graduate were low. For it to happen, I'd need a national ID card. Although I had a patchwork of identifying documents, as a non-citizen I had no hope of getting the official ID required to have my degree conferred.

The gamble had worked to give me access to a Tier One education. Now I faced the realistic and fast-advancing prospect of leaving university without a degree, and having to find a place as a working professional in Rangoon, the city of the Buddhist overclass and a tiny minority of Rohingya ghosts.

By June 2012 sectarian violence had erupted back home. Rakhine Buddhists, backed by the regime, started attacking and burning Rohingya villages. Over the next few months things grew desperate. In the clashes between Rakhine and Rohingya, the former group had the government's full backing. Rakhine mobs attacked Muslim communities in nine towns and slaughtered hundreds of Rohingyas as the Na-Sa-Ka simply looked on. During increasingly depressing phone calls with my family, I was told to not even consider going home.

With the waters rising on every side, my best hopes lay in remaining a student at a government-approved college in Rangoon. That way I could buy time by rolling over my permit every forty-five days. To find a foothold in Rangoon I used my enrolment at Dagon University as a springboard to apply to a government-backed private IT firm that offered diplomas in information management. As a side benefit, the company operated in English, which would allow me to deepen my grasp of this global language.

A job in the IT world had long been my Plan B. With basic internet access I hoped to teach myself the skills I needed to get a foothold in the industry. Even in Burma, you could qualify as a Microsoft-certified technician by taking the company's qualifying exams. Unlike a career in chemistry, some IT jobs were almost blind to your creden tials, as long as you knew how to do the work.

Applying myself to the new challenge, I passed my exams with distinction. But interning at a government-run IT agency – the natural next step in a country that was entirely dominated by the ruling bureaucracy – was an impossibility to one who lacked citizenship. After all, as a Rohingya, I had no legal existence in the country. Meanwhile, the clock was running down on my latest permit.

Just two months after I finished the IT program, through a connection of Suu Myatt I learned of a pharmaceutical chain in Rangoon that was partly owned by Muslims. Desperate to keep my permit validated I convinced them to give me an internship, overcoming their strong misgivings. If the government discovered they'd taken on a Rohingya, there would be repercussions for them and for me.

By that time large parts of Arakan, including parts of my hometown and the surrounding villages, were being consumed by fire and terror. There were near-daily reports about communities being wiped from the face of the earth, tens of thousands of Rohingyas being forced to run for their lives.

Fortunately, for our family at least, my brother Shahed had been admitted to a business school in Rangoon before the worst of the violence erupted. He'd followed the same process I had taken in order to escape. His school was on the other side of the sprawling city-state, a trip of at least two bus rides and three or more hours of travel time. And because we were both staying in hostels, we couldn't sleep over once we arrived. As a result, we rarely saw each other. Still, I was happy to know he was relatively safe.

My parents were not so protected. As Maungdaw came under attack, they fled to a remote place in the wilderness and hid from the regime by living off the grid. They escaped just in time. Many of the educated aunts, uncles and other elders who had inspired the rest of us with their dignity and quiet intelligence were rounded up and imprisoned. From our discrete islands of safety, separated by the expanse of the city, my brother and I wondered if we would see them again.

As my internship as an industrial chemist came to an end, I found myself at a new crossroads. My reasons for renewing my passport had vanished. But returning to the killing fields of Arakan or trying to join my parents in their jungle hideout were clearly not viable options. Shahed had at least three years in which he could lie low and stay at school in Rangoon – but I'd run out of time. The safest thing for me was to try to leave our homeland altogether.

The thought of suddenly leaving Burma came with a shiver of confusion and fear. I'd been born and raised there, and for all its strife and despotism, it was my home. Running away to save my life had never figured in any of my career plans.

Although I didn't have a passport, I knew Burmese people could travel relatively easily to neighbouring Thailand and India – and also Indonesia – just with a visa. Nearly one million Burmese migrants were already living in Thailand. A Google search revealed the United Nations High Commissioner for Refugees (UNHCR) had a footprint in Indonesia, meaning they might consider me for resettlement in a third country. Other displaced Rohingyas were already in Jakarta awaiting UNHCR assistance.

Grasping at this discovery, I made urgent enquiries with family and acquaintances back in Maungdaw, and was given the phone number of a Rohingya man named Khaled. He'd fled to Jakarta with his family and was in the process of applying for refugee status.

It didn't matter that this man was a complete stranger. Rather than weaken our community ties, the shared experience of oppression helped forge a fast bond between us. After decades under the gun, it was second nature for Rohingyas to watch each other's backs.

When I phoned Khaled and explained my own hoped-for escape from Burma, he offered to help, saying I could essentially tailgate his family through the UNHCR process. 'I'll walk you through it and show you how to apply.' He even promised to pick me up from the airport. His kindness stayed with me, filling me with hope.

My ears rang with his promises. Below my feet, however, lay the abyss.

It was an immense and unfamiliar place. What did I understand about travelling the world? Thanks to the limits imposed by the ruling regime, I barely knew a thing about the countries on the other side of the border, let alone how to survive in them. While I'd taken some chances in the past, there had always been at least a wisp of safety that followed me in Burma, the promise of a family member stepping in when things went wrong to make them better.

Without their help, who could say? I was still in my early twenties, a thoughtful young man, a scholar at heart. My favourite home, my place of comfort, was in the middle of a book. Out there I'd be vulnerable, swimming in the open waters, easy prey to the creatures of the unknown seas.

The clock ticked down on my final travel permit, honing my courage, such as it was, to a fine edge. I had a friend in Indonesia, and that was the best I could hope for.

I took the first step. And just like that, I became a refugee.

THREE

A blast of hot air welcomed me at Soekarno-Hatta International Airport. It was a steamy afternoon in late May 2013 and the place was swarming with taxis, bicycles, buses, cars, and what seemed like every one of Jakarta's ten million residents. What I didn't see was a single Rohingya. Ghost or otherwise.

Khaled and I had no idea what each other looked like. I bought a local sim card at the airport, phoned him and eventually zeroed in on a neatly dressed man standing still in the swirl of the crowd. He struck me as a good man. He appeared to be about forty and was approachable, easy-going and oddly familiar. We didn't have to try too hard to get on with each other. Right away, I felt reassured.

As we drove away from the airport in a car he'd rented for the day, I had the strong sense of an invisible wall behind me, pushing me forward. Thanks to this unseen force, there was no turning back on a decision once it was made. I had to live with the outcome and keep moving. I'd first felt the presence of the invisible wall when I left Arakan for Rangoon three years earlier. Now it was close to my spine.

As we drove, Khaled told me some of his story. Scores of people in his family – including his brother – had been thrown into prison by order of the regime. One of his loved ones was sentenced to fourteen years because he'd been found in possession of a few coins of foreign currency. As violence tore through Rohingya villages near his home, Khaled managed to escape with his wife and two children, plus his sister-in-law and her young child.

They now lived in the slum outskirts of Jakarta, in a tiny apartment provided by the International Organisation for Migration (IOM), a UN-aligned organisation that assists displaced people, migrant workers and refugees. Khaled apologised and said I couldn't stay with his family until I'd registered with the UNHCR. If the immigration police of Indonesia discovered he was harbouring an undocumented migrant, he'd put his family in jeopardy. Having stayed before with a family who'd taken a great risk in housing me, I understood.

At the rundown dwelling that Khaled had found for me, he brought me some dinner – vegetables, rice and fried chicken, packed together in a single paper bag – and warned me not to go outside.

Next I contacted Shahed in Rangoon and told him I'd made it safely out of the country. A while later I was visited at my flat by some other Rohingya refugees who were living in IOM shelters and waiting to have their cases taken on by the UNHCR.

The first step in that process, I was informed, was to join a queue. The point of this queue was to get permission to join another queue. After a lifetime of being subjected to bureaucratic whims, the request struck me as normal enough, while also being annoying and dismally familiar.

After a few days lying low in the hotel, I was told by Khaled to be ready at four o'clock the next morning. We were to travel into the city so I could line up to get a token with a reference number that would let me meet with a UNHCR representative in a few months' time. Only then could I make my claim or submit paperwork to begin a lengthy wait to be resettled in a third country.

On the drive into central Jakarta, through a sea of scooters, I had a feeling it would be a long time before I saw Burma again. The finality and fragility of my situation stirred strong emotions: melancholy for

35

my lost home and for my scattered family, relief that I was safe for the time being, and guilt because I had escaped and survived while so many Rohingyas had died.

Arriving at the UNHCR offices I realised I was probably not alone. The sun was rising above the smoggy metropolis, and already hundreds stood in a queue that stretched more than two city blocks. Each person had his or her own story of displacement and loss, running from a horror that might never be addressed.

Welcome to the global refugee crisis. And now I was part of it.

I was dismayed to see so many women with young children in the crowd, many of them in floods of tears. I fell in at the back of the line, and within half an hour hundreds more people had queued behind me. For the first time since leaving Burma I realised how utterly exposed I was. A droplet in an ocean of lost souls.

Just weeks before, I had been a star student on track to an IT career. Now I found myself feeling small and defenceless. No home, no family and, worst of all, once again at the mercy of unseen bureaucrats, strangers behind the walls of a city office building.

This time there was no second path to take, or way to fix the situation. Without helpful relatives to guide me, my scope of decision making was reduced to a fine point, or rather a long line of other people in their own desperate need of help. And at the other end of the line lay a functionary who was empowered to decide my future.

After a wait of several hours, we learned that the office had reached capacity for the day, and that we'd have to return tomorrow. Khaled had heard that people often queued up overnight to ensure a place at the front of the line when the offices reopened.

That night we returned at 11 pm and slept on the cement. The following morning I was given a note to meet with a UN representative in two and a half months. The response gave me hope. I was on the books, which meant I'd be safe from the local authorities.

Now that I was on the waiting list to be registered with the UN, Khaled invited me to join him and his family in their tiny flat near the airport, which they shared with another Rohingya refugee named Shamsul. It was there, in a whirlwind of cooking and conversation, that I started to realise what I had gotten myself into by fleeing to Indonesia.

From the back and forth of chat and shared advice, it became clear that my view of the UNHCR as a paragon of justice and goodness needed an adjustment. Each new anecdote, relayed over coffee or a cup of tea, was like a thudding blow to the head, grapeshot aimed at a tilted balloon.

The UNHCR, founded to help the most vulnerable refugees around the world, came out sounding like just another broken bureaucracy. Despite its glorified history, which started in the world wars, it was compromised. In each country where it operated, it was essentially made to do a devil's bargain. The choice was to take direction from the national government and its immigration policies, or to take its people-saving business elsewhere.

In countries that treated refugees fairly, that demand was no problem at all. In countries like Indonesia, it created a big mess indeed. Having never signed the 1958 Geneva Convention, Indonesia had decided it could make the lives of its wards as uncomfortable as it liked. Refugees were forbidden from studying, working or even opening a bank account in Indonesia – on pain of imprisonment.

The fact that the UNHCR had an office and staff to hear refugee cases meant little. It could not offer help in the short term, or even in the medium to long term. People could expect to wait up to seven years to be accepted into a third country, sometimes longer. A few years after I left Indonesia, representatives from the UNHCR declared that refugees there, particularly single men, would be lucky to be resettled in two decades, if ever.

With no way to get things started in the present and few prospects for a better future, refugees were caught in a trap. They may have been safe, relative to horrors back home, but many questioned whether it was a life worth living. The suicides that regularly took place both inside and outside the detainment centres – and that continue to take place today – were a predictable result.

My first few nights in Jakarta, I caught a glimpse of what it would be like to be stuck in that limbo. Sitting in an apartment in an impoverished neighbourhood, staring at the walls as the best years of my life passed by.

With my usual optimism, a family habit, I hoped for better.

When I was at school we were led to believe America was Burma's number-one enemy, closely followed by Great Britain. These were amoral, corrupt, meddling bad actors that were not to be admired or trusted. It was classic grassroots propaganda – not to mention a textbook case of projection – on the part of one of the world's most despotic regimes.

These lessons in hatred, however, did not extend to Australia or New Zealand. Whenever those countries were discussed, which wasn't often, they were presented in a neutral light. I'd never given more than a passing thought to the Antipodes until I started hearing stories about the overall goodness of this large southern country, while staring at a bleak future from the apartment in Jakarta.

After a week or so of refugee limbo in Indonesia, I met two Rohingya guys who claimed to have found a boat that would take them to Australia – for a price. By then I'd heard stories about the compassion that Australians showed to refugees. One tale that caught my attention was about a woman who'd arrived in a part of Australia called Christmas Island with a severely ill baby. The child and mother were flown to the mainland where the baby received first-class medical care.

At first I thought these boat rides to Australia were the stuff of rumour – fairytales to give hope to the hopeless. Then the two Rohingya guys disappeared, just like they said they would. I wondered if maybe they had headed for the fabled Christmas Island. A few days later they phoned to let us know they'd made it:

they had lodged claims for asylum and the Australians were taking good care of them.

Meanwhile I was holding a token that would let me speak to someone in two months' time. Choosing between a life of seven years in a slum, or putting my fate in the hands of strangers, I decided to throw the dice again.

In daydreams about Christmas Island I pictured myself hopping into a small canoe paddled by a fisherman across a calm stretch of water under sunny skies. My imagination painted it as a remote, almost uninhabited paradise with a white lighthouse and a smattering of friendly Australian fishermen and immigration workers.

Today I'm embarrassed to admit I didn't even google the place. Had I done so – or had even the faintest clue how dangerous the journey could be – I doubt I'd have ever left Jakarta.

Island fantasies aside, open water had never been my friend. Just a few years before, I'd nearly drowned in a pool in Rangoon while learning to swim. So much fluid had poured into my lungs I couldn't walk, let alone breathe properly. My terror of dying in this way had a firm foundation. Water was strictly for bathing.

In the end naivety – even wilful ignorance – fed my decision to make a last-ditch run for Australia. Also urging me forward was the fact that Khaled had decided for his part that the costs of staying were too high. Life in a slum with no education was not a future he could tolerate for his children. Whatever the dangers that lay ahead, he would take his wife, his sister-in-law and the little ones across the sea to salvation. And if I shared his dreams of a better life, I could join them. It was more than just an idle prospect. Khaled had connected to a syndicate of people smugglers who had quoted a cost per person.

The cost was high, more than I could afford. With no ability to work, the only way I could finance the trip was with my family's help. I phoned Shahed and Suu Myatt in Burma: they managed to pull together the funds and wire them to me in Jakarta.

Doing business with people smugglers was an eye-opening experience. While refugees tended to have their shit together – because our lives depended on it – the smugglers did not. I quickly discovered there was no shape or definition to the process: no contracts, no guarantees, no paperwork and no planning. You paid the money and you took your chances.

The smugglers reminded me of people back home who fixed watches. If you gave them a timepiece they'd tell you it was only a small fix and very cheap. When you went to collect it, they'd spin a story about what a big job it turned out to be and how the cost was now three times higher. They were exploitative and shameless, preying on the desperation of the weak, and I hated them for it.

I'd also started hearing stories about smugglers collecting their fees and failing to deliver. Refugees who tried to get their money back were told, 'Oh, you'll be going on the boat tomorrow,' or 'You'll go next week,' or 'You're leaving next month.' False promises and equivocation. There were rumours, too, about syndicates taking money and simply disappearing.

Some choices are no choice at all. While the risks were significant, the alternative – a wasted life – didn't really bear thinking about. We paid the money.

Khaled dealt with the syndicate and discovered there were different routes we could take to Australia. One was a relatively short trip to Christmas Island; the other was a longer, more circuitous journey that led south-east along the Indonesian archipelago to Darwin, a city on the Australian mainland. For whatever reason, the syndicate we chose decided to aim for Darwin.

On a rainy day in early June, we took a three-hour flight to Kendari, the capital of Indonesia's South-East Sulawesi. We arrived in the evening and were taken to a building near the seashore where a large group of other refugees had already gathered.

We were rushed into the one-storey concrete bungalow – quickly, to avoid being spotted by the neighbours – to a room where the lights were kept low, and told to remain quiet: police had started cracking down on refugees moving through the area. The only sound was the rumble of a passing car, or the conversation of people walking by. I didn't really sleep. Nor did anyone else, judging by the barely audible outpouring of whispers in various languages from those gathered around me in the dark.

Around 5 am we were ushered to a beach and told to board a flotilla of narrow canoes. Each boat fit eight to ten people. In the pale pre-dawn light I could put faces to the furtive voices from the previous night. Some were from the Middle East, some looked like they might be Afghans, and others appeared to have come from different countries in Africa. Depressingly, there were children too – four, five and six-year-olds – and some women were carrying babies.

It was time to board the canoe. Pressed together on bench seats, our bags at our feet and our lives in our hands, we set out east on the choppy green waters of the Banda Sea. Because there were police patrolling the waters, a bright blue tarp was thrown over our heads, keeping us hidden, as if we were a cargo load of raw fish or other produce. The smoke of the diesel engine, which propelled the skiff forward, filled the gap under the canvas. The overloaded canoe was close to the surface of the water, so each time a wave hit, the water struck our extended faces as we gasped for oxygen.

Just after midday, under a tropical sun that brought out the foul, rotten seaweed smell of the sea, we landed on the beach of a tiny fishing island. The local village was so small and primitive, it was unlikely to feature on any map of the area. We waded onto shore, where I rejoined Khaled and his family.

Surprisingly, the locals almost fell over themselves to be as accommodating as possible, in a show of warmth and hospitality that seemed entirely genuine. After the ordeal of the last twenty-four hours, the night in the dark house and the perilous canoe trip across open water, it was a relief to feel welcomed and cared for.

Some people wanted to pray so the villagers cleared space and gave them mats, while others tended to the women and babies. While

I couldn't understand a word of what the villagers said, others in our group could communicate on a basic level. These refugees had spent time in Malaysia, where a similar dialect to Bahasa Indonesian – the language of the villagers – was spoken. Through these ad-hoc interpreters we learned the boat to take us to Darwin would probably arrive that night.

'Probably arrive tonight?' I said to myself. The uncertainty was starting to eat at me. Nothing felt organised or thought through: there was no proper time frame, no single person seemed to be in charge, there was no clarity and hardly any communication. We were relying on a trail of whispers being passed between one hundred desperate people and sifted through five or ten languages.

Around 10 pm the rumble of a diesel engine announced the next leg of our trip. As the fishing boat anchored offshore, we were ushered into knee-deep water and loaded into the canoes. It was a moonless night, with the only light coming from a torch and the screens of a few cell phones.

Once in the canoe, my anxiety turned to terror. As we pulled up to the large boat, the rolling swell caused our skiff to dance crazily alongside it. There was no ladder or rope to grab a hold of. We had to haul ourselves onto the deck using the strength of our arms alone. It was almost pitch black. Had I fallen, I most likely would have drowned.

The small vessel was already overcrowded when I made it onboard with Khaled and the family. Shortly afterwards people in the remaining canoes were told there was no more room and they'd have to return to shore. I couldn't see them in the dark but I could picture the looks on their faces when they realised they'd been tricked by the shifty watch-fixers of the sea.

There were now dozens of people on the overburdened boat, all anxious to get going. But the motor wouldn't start. Hours passed while the Indonesian crew banged away below deck to coax the tired machine to life.

At about one o'clock in the morning, the engine woke up and spewed out a cloud of acrid smoke. The anchor was drawn up and we lumbered forward. The relief of being on our way soon gave way to fear as the waves grew in size and the boat rolled from side to side. As someone who couldn't swim, who had never spent time near the sea, I found it a long and difficult night. I squatted on the outer edge of the main deck until my legs went numb.

First light revealed that we weren't on the open ocean but cutting a course that hugged the surrounding islands. As the sun rose, we were also able to get a good look at the boat. It was a weather-beaten wooden hulk that had seen too many days. It stank, was deafeningly loud and constantly blew smoke. Oil seemed to seep out of every crack.

We were permitted on the main deck and on the roof of the wheelhouse and cabin. While the engine room below decks was off limits, we were allowed to stow our bags down there to make room above. Even so, space was so tight we had to sit with our knees pulled up to our chests. Beyond the roar of the engine, there was a constant chorus of children crying.

After forcing down a packet of dry instant noodles, I decided to risk climbing onto the roof where there was a little more room to stretch out. While marginally more comfortable, the roof was a precarious place to be. There were no railings to stop a passenger from sliding straight over the side should the boat roll too far in the surge. It was nothing but a large, flat, painted wooden platform. By the time I realised how dangerous it was, I was trapped: a fellow traveller had climbed down and taken the spot I had just vacated.

Late in the afternoon some men placed a bamboo pole down the length of the middle of the roof. This at least gave us something to grab onto. As the sun began to sink I spotted another Rohingya on the roof. We talked for a while, each of us revelling in the chance to use our own native tongue. A well-built man in his mid-thirties, he told me his story. He was on the run from the carnage back home, having fled Arakan with his extended family, who were on the boat below. After comparing notes on our respective plights, we deduced that we were in fact distant cousins.

'What,' I thought to myself, 'are the odds of that?'

Night fell quickly that close to the equator. I took off my belt, looped it around the bamboo pole and joined arms with my new companion to make sure we didn't slide overboard. I wasn't looking to fall asleep but after two days and nights with barely any food or rest, it was easy to drift off.

I awoke in the darkness in a blind panic. I was soaked and shaking from the cold. Water poured onto my face and it seemed that my lifelong terror of drowning was about to come true.

FOUR

'They lose the day in expectation of the night,
and the night in fear of the dawn.'

Seneca

As the sky blazed with lightning, I realised the flood was coming from above, not below. We were caught in a merciless tropical storm.

The rain intensified and the wind drove the waves higher. Those of us caught on the roof were exposed and vulnerable. In the slick of the downpour, as the boat swayed violently, we could not risk climbing off the roof and into the hold below. Everyone on the roof was drenched but we were stuck.

In the space of a minute or two, I'd gone from thinking I was about to die to being relieved I wasn't, to fearing I was about to die again, from being tossed overboard or electrocuted. It was horror on top of horror.

The passengers below us were petrified too. Shreds of sound rose above the roaring wind and thump of the sea against the hull, the terrified chanting of dozens of passengers, crying out in different languages. The rhythm and the urgency of their voices told me they were praying for their lives.

The storm lasted for hours but it was still dark when the conditions eased, and the dawn seemed to never come. When the sun eventually arrived it brought little comfort. In the light of day I could see we had sailed into the huge expanse of the Banda Sea. There was no land in sight – just ash-grey water in every direction.

Exhaustion and two nights of exposure to the elements had started to take a toll on my body. I'd had precious little water, and only some dried noodles and pieces of biscuit to eat since we'd left Kendari. As the morning wore on I started vomiting. I figured it was probably dehydration: my lips had dried and shrivelled.

A chain of low-lying islands came into view late in the afternoon. I wondered what Australia would look like from the boat when we started closing in on Darwin. The boat slowed. Word was passed up from below that we'd entered waters scattered with coral reefs and careful navigation was paramount.

About 7 pm a violent shudder shook the boat. The engine was throttled back and people shouted that we'd hit a reef. Panic flared. The bamboo pole was untethered from the roof and passed down to crew members, who used it to try and lever the boat back into deeper water. When that failed they commanded those on the main deck to rock the boat. Soon it was clear we weren't going anywhere.

As the light in the sky faded, some passengers grew desperate. A group of men shimmied overboard and stood on the coral in chest-deep water, trying to shove us free. They were macho types with strong bodies and they called out for other men to join them, but not everyone was willing. We all knew, from when we'd first boarded in Kendari, that getting back on the boat from the sea would be no easy feat.

Before long the tone changed: the musclemen grew belligerent and shouted at the others in broken English to 'get in the fucking water and help'. Some guys started climbing down off the roof and those who didn't were insulted, called cowards and freeloaders unwilling to do their part in a crisis.

Then the threats began. 'If you don't get in the water right now and help, I'm going to beat your ass!' 'Get down here now or else!' 'We're in the middle of nowhere! If you don't help, we'll just run out of water and food and die here! Is that what you want?'

Men brandishing pieces of wood started physically shoving us towards the side of the boat. I had to speak up. 'Listen to me,' I said to a bearded man who was trying to force me into the water. 'I don't know how to swim, okay? I'll do anything else to help this situation from here on the boat. Anything! But I cannot go into the sea.'

He stared at me blankly. He didn't understand a word I'd said. A minute later I found myself climbing down the side of the slippery hull and dropping into the cold, dark water. Terror gripped me when my feet didn't touch the bottom. My legs swung about, searching for a foothold, until they took a bite from the sharp coral. When my feet skimmed the bottom I was up to my neck in water.

Others tried to push the boat off the reef while I clung to the hull for dear life. I didn't care that I wasn't helping, I just didn't want to sink or drift away. A sharp current tugged at my body as if the sea itself wanted me dead. It was pitch dark by now, too, save for a handful of flashlights and a kerosene lamp shining down from the deck.

After ten or fifteen minutes it was clear nothing was going to work. After all, the salvage operation had been a study in disorder. I don't even know if they'd coordinated themselves to work together or against each other. Everyone spoke different languages. When the strongmen accepted we were stuck fast, we were hauled back onboard – tired, freezing, terrified and hopeless.

Back up on the roof I began to wonder if we'd damaged the hull with all the rocking. The way forward was unclear and crowded with alarming possibilities. If we were lucky, the tide would rise and unmoor us from the reef. On the other hand, it might be high tide now, in which case we would be more trapped than ever.

If we didn't get out of there soon, we would be an easy target for the Indonesian Navy when the sun rose and revealed our location. The authorities of Indonesia were quick to detain refugees and keep them confined for years. It was probably out of fear of being discovered that the crew had switched the lights off.

About 3 am a commotion erupted on the deck below, followed by cheering and whistles. We'd drifted free. The tide had turned – literally and metaphorically – in our favour.

The engine took its customary time to start up again, but before too long we were moving. This time dawn broke on a clear sky, and we cruised on relatively calm waters, with no land in sight.

By mid-afternoon, there was another outburst from down below. This time the voices were laced with tension instead of joy. Until that point, no-one had realised we'd been taking on water, but when the bilge pump that had been draining the engine bay failed, we found out the hard way.

A short time later the engine stopped as the sea poured in through the cracked hull, swamping it. The gashed belly of the boat was filling up fast. Within a minute, everyone onboard knew we were sinking. Within five minutes every last bag had been dragged out of the hold and thrown into the open water.

Ours was a slow-motion demise. Bit by bit we inched a little lower in the water as the wind and waves picked up again. I had no idea if we were being blown north, south, east or west, whether a current was pulling us closer to land or pushing us further out to sea.

There was nothing we could do but bail water out of the hold. Hour after hour, the men worked in shifts. We used empty gallon containers that had held our fuel and drinking water, and passed them along a human conveyor belt to be tipped into the ocean. Up on deck terrified women wept and infants wailed.

No matter how fast we bailed, the water level in the boat's belly kept inching higher. By the end of my final shift around midnight, I had a good understanding of what would happen next.

'I'm going to die tonight,' I told myself with a strange sense of calm and clarity.

Since I first set foot on that boat I'd felt like death had been stalking me. Now that I was within its reach, I realised to my surprise I was actually okay with saying goodbye. Back on my rooftop perch, listening to the others praying, I did not bother to ask God to save me, only to bless me with a peaceful death.

I pulled my phone from my pocket and tapped out a farewell message to my family. Then I let myself sink into sleep.

This time, as the shouts broke out, pulling me to consciousness, the news was good. The men below cried with ragged voices that they'd spotted a lighthouse. I saw it too. At such a distance, it was hard to tell if it was flashing as it rotated or whether it was a fixed light that disappeared intermittently below the crests on the horizon.

It was the first time I'd understood the point of lighthouses. Back in my days of being a land dweller, I'd considered them outdated and redundant in the era of sat nav, smartphones and GPS. Now I realised the value they offered to those lost at sea. Even so, I didn't think the sighting would alter our fate. We had no propulsion, no steering and virtually no chance of being blown towards that welcoming beacon.

I was amazed to have woken up at all and even more to discover we were somehow still afloat when dawn arrived. While the daybreak brought partial comfort, it also washed out the flicker of the light-house. We were as lost as ever with no land and no boats in sight. I hadn't expected to make it to another day. I'd been resigned to never seeing the sun again. I didn't know if I should be relieved or disappointed to feel its rays on my back and have to face the anguish of my creeping death all over again.

The boat was half-sunk: saltwater lapped across the deck where the families were huddled. The more I thought about it, the more perplexed and even annoyed I felt still to be alive. I had wanted to get death over and done with in the night. In the light of day I got a better sense that everyone was thinking the same thing: 'What will I do when the boat sinks?'

There were a number of empty PVC containers onboard where fuel had been stored and people grabbed them to use as flotation devices. I made an agreement with the guy alongside me to share one with him when the ship went down. Since we didn't speak the same language we did this without exchanging a word. Our dire state required no explanation.

A pang of hope, unbidden and unwanted, struck me once again. Once we were in the vicinity of a lighthouse, the wind, waves and current might eventually carry the container ashore somewhere, and us along with it. After all, flotsam always seemed to wash up on beaches.

Around 8 am people began screaming 'Tolong! Tolong! Tolong!', which by this point I knew to be the Bahasa word for 'help'. Someone had spotted a lone fisherman in a canoe. Now everyone cried 'Tolong!' and waved their shirts over their heads.

I don't know if the fisherman saw us, heard us or both, but he came straight toward us. When he arrived at our boat, as far as I could catch on he claimed the land was not very far away and we just weren't seeing it because of the swells. He told the crew he was going to get help and went on his way, disappearing behind the green horizon.

Hours passed and the boat slid lower into the sea. Just in time, the fisherman returned around noon with a cavalry of wiry rescuers in canoes. He said we were close to the shore where the shallower water was dangerous. We should transfer people, beginning with the women and children, into the smaller boats before the hulk drifted into the path of the breakers.

With no training or safety equipment at hand, we began trying to transfer as many passengers as possible into the slender canoes bobbing alongside. Again, the tangle of languages threatened to derail the effort, which quickly descended into chaos. The pitch of water grew increasingly steep as the sea-floor rose toward the still unseen landmass nearby.

As the boat and canoes jerked about in the peaks and troughs, tragedy struck. A young mother passed her newborn to a fisherman in the very first canoe, but the infant was fumbled. Dropped into the sea, the child sank like a rock. Startled fishermen dived in but resurfaced empty-handed, I will never forget the screams of the mother.

With other lives at stake, the rescue continued until the remaining women and children had been safely ferried ashore. As I waited my turn I glimpsed the tops of what appeared to be buildings and knew that I was going to live. While I'd gone without water and food for two days and two nights, my overwhelming craving – stronger than hunger and thirst combined – was to feel my feet on solid ground.

Half an hour later, as my toes dug into the grit of pale sand, it was the most sublime feeling I could have imagined. For the first time I realised how much I missed solid land, the physical connection to it, and the safety it represented, after days on the treacherous swells.

Others shared my excitement and relief, and collapsed into prayers upon reaching the shore. Concerned villagers swarmed around us offering heartfelt support and care. Later on I heard it wasn't the first time they'd saved people from the sea, and local superstition had it that our salvation brought luck to the village.

As we shifted onshore, the facts of our voyage became clear. We'd drifted onto the leeward, less populated shore of Binongko Island, a densely vegetated outcrop 145 nautical miles from Kendari but a staggering 550 nautical miles from our destination in Darwin.

While the welcome party was a comfort after our hellish journey, not so encouraging was the sight of the authorities. Local law enforcement and immigration officials gathered alongside two trucks and a handful of police cars parked near the beach. Perhaps because we were clearly traumatised, the officers weren't pushy: they weren't even carrying weapons. Once the last of the men were brought ashore, everyone was told to climb into the back of the trucks.

A short time later we arrived at a large community centre on the middle of a wide lawn. Inside we were given hot tea, a powerful antidote to the chill of the ocean. Some doctors and nurses had been assembled and set about administering IV to those who'd become dehydrated. Others needed treatment for lacerations sustained while trying to wrestle the boat off the coral reef. Some children couldn't stop crying while others laughed and played on the lawn.

I kept thinking about the lost baby.

My grief was shaded with survivor's guilt. 'I could easily have died so many times. One slip and I'd have sunk to the bottom too.'

Roaming over the neatly cut grass, I relished the feeling of the soft blades on my soles. I stood next to a tree and caressed its leaves with my fingertips. Then I wrapped my arms around its trunk and hugged it.

I couldn't quite believe I'd survived. It was 15 June 2013, the day of my rebirth, and I have quietly celebrated it – more than my actual birthday – every year since.

The authorities left us alone and a contingent from the local mosque arrived in the afternoon. They offered to put the women and children up in the homes of locals for the night. The men were encouraged to sleep at the masjid. Until night fell, however, the islanders were happy to let us rest in their homes.

I was put in a group with four other guys and spent the afternoon with a family who lived close to the community centre. They gave us some soap and towels, and we used a well in the yard to wash away the filthy mixture of salt, diesel and engine oil that coated our bodies.

We'd arrived with nothing but the clothes we were wearing: in my case jeans, a t-shirt and underwear. I had my wallet and cell phone, too, but the thing had been fried by saltwater. We used the soap to wash our clothes. Despite the low-grade makeover we still looked like castaways. The villagers graciously served us up a feast of fish, vegetables and rice, but for me, no amount of hospitality and distraction could dull the fear of what was to come.

Although we were refugees, we'd broken Indonesian law. Our crime, ironically enough, was that we had tried to leave the country and, in that way, had violated its borders. While I was elated to be alive, I knew a jail sentence was almost guaranteed. We all did.

Over the next three days, consciously or not, a lot of the survivors sidelined these fears and celebrated their revival on a scenic tropical island. Kids played soccer, adults enjoyed food and deep conversations. People forced themselves to stay awake and savour the freedom, even when they were tired.

I took a long walk to a stone pier and looked at the sea, trying to fathom what I'd been through since fleeing Burma. Later I borrowed a cell phone from another survivor and tried to call Shahed, but it didn't connect. Before I left Kendari I'd promised to update him regularly on my progress. Now I could just picture him sitting in some classroom in Rangoon, certain his big brother was dead.

In the early evening of the third day immigration officers returned and asked us for identifying documents. Since most people's papers were now pulp in the Banda Sea, few of us could comply. The officers did not speak English and they never asked me for my name, age or nationality. They informed us, through impromptu translators, that a boat would arrive in the morning to take us back to Kendari. The thought filled me with a dread that kept me up most of the night.

Just after dawn a large wooden boat docked at the stone pier. Armed officials milled around a boarding plank, and directed us to get on the boat. Onboard, everyone was given a quick meal of rice and a piece of flavourless fish. As we sailed away from Binongko Island, I couldn't stop thinking about the baby somewhere in the deep below.

The way the food was distributed, plus all the guns on display, made it feel like a prison transport ship. The phalanx of armed police officers that met us on the concrete pier in Kendari confirmed this anxiety.

After we docked, we were ordered aboard a bus and driven to a nearby hotel that was guarded by armed officers. I'd arrived with Khaled and his family, but since I was a single male I was put in a room with six other guys. There was one bed for the lot of us, which made our later attempt to sleep that night an interesting challenge.

The next day some IOM representatives arrived and wrote down our names, ages and nationalities before taking our photos. It felt like a mug shot. I knew something bad was coming but the IOM workers refused to say what they had planned for us. We spent the following two days trapped inside the hotel room surviving on a thin ration of chicken-flavoured instant noodles.

On the third day we were permitted to visit a corner grocery shop a few doors away from the hotel to buy toiletries. We were told that this would normally be forbidden but since we'd been shipwrecked and left with nothing, the rules were slightly relaxed. Still, we could only go in pairs. I fished around in my wallet and found I had a few thousand Indonesian rupiah in cash. I was also pleased to find I had kept a library card from my days in Rangoon.

One of the guys in my room was a Rohingya named Abul. He'd been registered with the UNHCR but had wasted away in Indonesia for years waiting for a third-country placement.

Unwilling to settle for a life in limbo, he'd decided to board the same ill-fated boat as me. As we exchanged stories, the question arose as to whether we might be able to buy a new phone at the corner store, or at least get my broken one fixed. Through word of mouth we learned there was just one armed policeman guarding the main entrance of the hotel. Abul, who spoke basic Bahasa, asked him if we could go to the shop to get toiletries. The officer nodded and pointed to where it was located on the next corner.

The shopkeeper said he had no way of fixing my phone but mentioned he had cheap ones for sale. Abul didn't have any money, so I paid for a Nokia phone and a local sim card. I picked up a pair of flip-flops too, as well as toothbrushes, toothpaste and some toilet paper.

Back in the room I texted Shahed to let him know I was alive but in custody in Indonesia. Abul told me about a Rohingya friend of his named Zakaria who'd been jailed after he was caught by the Indonesian Navy a few years earlier while trying to make it to Australia. Apparently, Zakaria had been through a similar process to the one we were now in, and was even kept in the same hotel.

Abul had kept his phone number in a handwritten notebook that had been half destroyed in the sea. He typed in the numbers that were legible, and guessed at the rest, starting at zero and counting upward to nine. After twenty-six failed attempts, we got through to Zakaria at his IOM accommodation in Makassar.

'I did two years behind bars,' he clarified. 'We were picked up by the navy, we spent some time in a hotel and then we were locked away. I can almost guarantee you'll be put in prison too.'

'But we've just given our names and details to the IOM,' I explained.

'It doesn't matter. At the end of the day you violated Indonesian law and they will punish you with a jail sentence, probably two years. I would say your sentencing is imminent, within the next few days.'

I was lost for words as the nightmare scenario took shape. Zakaria broke the silence. 'You can always escape. After all, it's only a hotel.'

He said it was common for people to flee. 'If you understand the local language and you have some cash, then you should have no trouble getting away.'

I'd already noted how there was only one guard and I had cash in hand, but didn't speak a word of Bahasa. 'I don't know the language!' I told Zakaria. 'I can't read the street signs. And I don't have a smartphone, which means I don't have access to the internet. Navigation-wise, I'm blind. I couldn't even get in a taxi and tell the driver where to go.'

'It doesn't matter. Whatever happens, I'll help you figure it out. For now just leave the hotel. Otherwise you're looking at years in lock-up.'

Zakaria said he'd planned to escape from the hotel himself but left his run too late. Armed police had appeared at the door and that was that. He had, however, cased out an exit point.

'If you go to the second floor and enter the washroom second to the left, there's a window you can climb through,' he explained. 'There is a little shack below that window so you can drop down onto the roof, then lower yourself to the ground. You don't have to jump from two storeys up. Once you're on the ground there's a laneway. If you do it at two or three in the morning, you'll be miles away by daybreak.'

I was scared. On top of not knowing Bahasa or having any internet, I could be put on a watch list and hunted down.

That said, as much as I dreaded the thought of being chased across Indonesia by the police, I'd be damned if I'd endured so much already, only to be incarcerated for the high crime of trying to find a better life. As the water grew hotter, did I stay and hope for the best, or leap out of the pot?

One of my guilty pleasures while studying at university had been the American TV drama *Prison Break*. I was intrigued by the twists and turns in the plot, based around a man who has to figure out how to help his innocent brother escape from death row. Being a semi-fugitive myself during my days in Rangoon, I'd developed my own skill for reading a situation and knowing when it was the right time to make my move.

Zakaria had been right about the second-floor window: it would be easy to crawl through and drop into the rear laneway. I didn't, however, like his idea of breaking out at two in the morning. The streets would be empty, there'd be no taxis or buses running, and if the police saw us we'd stand out like a flashing light. It would be much better, I thought, to go when there was a crowd to melt into.

The following day, whenever anyone in the room wanted something from the corner store, I volunteered to go instead. With Abul at my side, I used the outings to get the lay of the land. I made mental notes about the surrounding buildings and businesses, the traffic flow and geography of the neighbourhood. On one trip around lunchtime I told Abul to keep an eye on the police guard at the hotel and let me know when he looked the other way. When he did, I darted around the corner and surveyed the laneway and connecting streets behind our two-star prison.

It was Friday afternoon and prayers were underway. As Abul and I prepared to return to the hotel, I noticed the guard was still gazing in the opposite direction. He seemed distracted and his body language suggested he might be totally uninterested in his job.

'Fuck escaping from the washroom!' I said, grabbing Abul by the arm. 'We're already out. *This* is escape!'

'What?' he said.

'Let's just go! We're out of sight, and with prayers going on and the police guard due to change, I bet we won't even be missed. That guy over there will forget and by the time anyone realises, we'll be long gone.'

Unfortunately, Abul wasn't exactly brimming with street smarts. He hesitated at the crucial moment. 'Ahh, but I have my clothing back at the hotel.'

'Fuck your clothing! We need to get out of here.'

I was in jeans, a t-shirt and my new flip-flops. Abul was unlikely to have more than a spare shirt or a hoodie back in the room. Everything we owned had been lost to the sea.

The stakes were high. If Abul decided to return I'd have no choice but to go with him because we had left the hotel as a pair. If he went back alone, even the most negligent guard would notice someone was missing.

As Abul stood there on the corner, umming and ahhing, I had my answer. I flagged down a taxi and dragged Abul in with me.

One silver lining to Abul's years languishing in Indonesia was the fact he'd picked up an awareness of local customs. When the driver asked, 'Where to?', Abul replied, 'Market.' It was a good answer, a place we could likely disappear into a crowd.

The taxi slid into a column of traffic and away from the hotel. I doubt our bumbling getaway would have made for a good episode of *Prison Break*, but it worked.

Just like that, we were on the run again.

FIVE

'Dive deep until you touch the pearl,
pull back until you reach the air.'

Burmese proverb

The taxi dropped us near the entrance of a sprawling market-
place about two kilometres from our hotel jail. Abul knew how
the local money worked so I gave him cash to pay the driver. We
climbed out and joined a throng of locals. With no idea where to go
next, I phoned Zakaria in Makassar. He was quickly proving to be a
valuable and kindly ally.

'We're out,' I told him as I pretended to check out some food stalls.
'We made it.'

'Oh my God! Good, good!' His relief was palpable. 'This is probably the best decision you've ever made. Trust me when I tell you the
last thing you want to do is go to jail in Indonesia.'

'Okay, okay, but what should we do now? Where can we go?'

Zakaria was silent.

'So,' I pressed, 'what is our next move?'

He admitted he didn't have a clue. 'I never got that far. I only knew
how to get out of the hotel. That's the main thing. You're free now,
while everybody else who was with you on that boat is going to jail.'

I thought about Khaled and his wife and sister-in-law, and the
three kids stuck in a room back at the hotel and felt a wrenching
guilt over leaving them behind. Our spontaneous escape had left no

time to see if they were even interested in climbing out a window and going on the run.

Abul said he knew some other people in Jakarta who'd be able to help us get back there.

'Things will work out,' he said casually as I handed him the phone.

He called his people and assured me they'd arranged someone to meet us at the market soon and walk us through how to get back to Jakarta. By 8 pm – seven hours after we'd escaped – there was still no sign of the rescue party.

We were hungry so I bought some food at one of the stalls. I was happy to cover Abul's meal. He was a Rohingya brother and we were in this together. Other matters, however, had begun to worry me. Abul was hamstrung by a complete lack of urgency. I don't know whether he was naïve to the danger we were in or just indifferent, but he seemed happy to cruise along and let things 'work out'.

The philosophy was at odds with mine. In my world, things didn't just work out. After a lifetime of struggle against a heartless regime, I was conditioned to engineer my fate with every ounce of my being.

By 9 pm I'd had enough of waiting around. 'Dude, we informed your friends at 1 pm. Now it's 9 pm and nothing has happened. It's dark and we just can't hang out on the street for someone who probably won't come. The police might be looking for us now and I don't want to go to jail.'

True to form, Abul just went with the flow and let me take control. 'Okay. Sure.'

I found a crumbling, out-of-the-way motel near the Kendari airport. We booked a room with a single bed and a couch. As soon as we got inside I checked to make sure the place had a rear exit if the police were to storm in during the night. Only after I'd thoroughly checked the place out did I lie on the couch, giving Abul the bed. I kept my flip-flops on in case I had to bolt for the back door.

The paper-thin walls made proper rest impossible. I heard every door open and close, every cough and every footstep in the neighbouring rooms, and each time I feared it was the police. Meanwhile, over on the mattress, Abul was snoring, happily dead to the world. He was coming across as more of a comic sidekick than a partner in crime.

In the morning Abul phoned his contact again and assured me someone would meet us at the motel soon.

'Are you sure? Because that's what they said yesterday. They know we are in danger – that we're escapees – and they didn't come! They didn't care even to call! Are you positive they'll make it happen today?'

'Yes, yes, it's fine,' he replied breezily. 'It's under control, it will happen. Let's go and eat.'

We waited and waited but no-one came. We'd been on the run for twenty-four hours and spent most of the time sitting around twiddling our thumbs. It definitely wasn't the stuff of *Prison Break*.

For my own safety I had to do something. I went for a walk in the local neighbourhood and came across a small travel agency. Thankfully the lady who ran it spoke English. She told me there was a daily flight to Jakarta and quoted me the cost of two fares. I had just enough money to cover the expense.

Back at the motel Abul wasn't convinced it was the way to go. 'My contact will arrange a safer passage,' he said. 'The airport isn't safe.'

He was right. The airport was unknown territory, packed with officials and police, and there was a strong chance we were on some kind of watch list. But we couldn't stay put indefinitely: while time wasn't necessarily running out, my money definitely was.

'We can't blow through this money just eating and sleeping in a hotel,' I pointed out. 'If we run out of cash, that's it – there's no way out.'

'I really trust my contact,' he replied. 'He'll arrange a safer passage. He said he'd definitely come today.'

The contact never turned up. I had to spend more funds on food and another night in Indonesia's saddest motel. I hardly slept again and Abul snored like a bear.

In the morning I made my case. 'Whether your contact is coming and getting you or not, I can't wait anymore. If you want to come with me, great. If not, you're on your own. I'll be broke soon. I can buy you the ticket back to Jakarta but you have to decide – now.'

After Abul finally agreed, we walked to the travel agency, where the woman at the desk informed us that all the fares to Jakarta were sold out. She suggested we try at the airport. 'They might have some last-minute cancellations.'

I ran out to the street and flagged a taxi. We reached the airport a mere twenty minutes before the flight for Jakarta was due to leave.

At the airline counter our initial relief in finding that tickets were available turned to anguish when we were told the price. Because it was a last-minute booking, the fares were more expensive, and I could only afford one. It was heartbreaking news.

'This is the situation,' I told Abul. 'If we spend one more day in Kendari – with food, accommodation and taxis – we won't have enough left in my wallet for even one of us to travel. So I'm going to Jakarta today, right now. When I get there I'll see if there's a way to help you get back too. I'm going to buy the ticket and give whatever cash is left to you.'

He sadly took in the news.

At the ticketing window the cashier smiled as she tapped away on her computer. 'Do you have your passport, sir?' she asked.

I knew I'd need an ID to buy a plane ticket, so I'd taken time over the past few days to fabricate a story that hopefully would sound plausible.

'Oh, look, my passport is in the embassy back in Jakarta.' I gave her a big smile. 'My tourist visa was due to expire so I applied for an extension and I have left it with them. Since I didn't need it for domestic travel I decided to come and check out Kendari while I waited for the extension. It was well worth it. What a lovely place.'

'Do you have another form of ID then?'

'Yes, of course.' I handed her the library card I'd unearthed from my wallet. This wasn't your average Burmese library card, it was member-ship to a library opened by the American embassy in Rangoon.

The information was in English and the American officials had made an effort to make it look as impressive as possible. It had sturdy plastic, a barcode, a high-resolution photo of me, and a large official seal featuring an American eagle. It looked nothing like a library card and everything like bona-fide credentials.

With the ticket in hand I turned to Abul and gave him the remaining money.

'Go find a place to stay and get some food and I'll see what I can do when I get back to Jakarta,' I told him.

It was hard to say goodbye. Even though he had not been much help, we had escaped detention together and I appreciated having him by my side. My hope was that he knew enough of the local language and customs to help keep us out of trouble. Still, my feet were heavy with guilt as I left Abul and headed upstairs to the departure lounge.

The plane was already boarding when I reached the gate. There were just six or seven people left in line when I jogged up, clutching my precious boarding pass. I had no bag and I was still wearing the same dirty clothes I'd been shipwrecked in, plus my $3 flip-flops – not exactly regular travel attire. I stood out like a homeless man who had wandered into a decent sit-down restaurant.

Two customs officers had been watching the gate and, sure enough, they zeroed in on me. They spoke in Bahasa but it was clear they wanted to see my passport.

'I'm caught!' I thought. 'I'm going to prison for a long time.' My heart pounding, I struggled to think on my feet. The lead officer looked young and possibly impressionable, so I decided to flood him in a nonstop torrent of English.

'Look, my passport is in the embassy in Jakarta because my tourist visa was due to expire, so I have applied for an extension to the visa but I was told the application would take about a week to process, so in the meantime because I don't need a passport to travel locally in Indonesia I decided to take a trip to Kendari because I heard it was a wonderful place to come and see and I certainly haven't been disappointed, and I have already explained this to the airline and they were happy to sell me the ticket without producing a passport which begs the question why do I need a passport to travel domestically when a passport is only necessary if a person is travelling internationally and *blah-blah-blah-English-English-English* . . .'

I was face-to-face with the officer throughout the verbal bombardment, while retreating backwards towards the boarding gate that the other passengers had almost all now disappeared through. I gesticulated, with what I hoped was the casual impatience of a veteran traveller, that the plane was about to leave.

Looking confused, the officer kept telling me I needed to produce a passport. I continued backpedalling towards the plane, spouting my English and pointing out that he was going to make me miss my flight. Feigning frustration I dug out my eagle-emblazoned library card and showed him. He didn't even look at it.

'Passport!'

I rolled my eyes, fixed him with an exasperated look and gestured impatiently at the waiting plane, trying to look as though I lived in the skies. 'I'm not going to miss my flight because of you!' I said, pointing at him and still pacing backwards. Suddenly, miraculously, I found myself through the gate. My bluff had succeeded.

A glance over my shoulder showed that the officer, judging from his expression, was dissatisfied but did not know what to do next. The door closed and fifteen minutes later I was in the air.

When I'd left more than a week earlier, I never thought I'd see Jakarta again, let alone wash up there so soon, traumatised and destitute. I didn't have a cent to my name. I didn't even have credit on my prepaid phone to call Shamsul, presumably still residing in the tiny apartment near the airport, where I'd stayed with Khaled and the family. Fortunately the phone carrier had an emergency feature that gave me the benefit of two texts in credit that would be debited the next time I put money on the phone.

I tapped out a desperate message to Shamsul begging him to call me on the new number. An hour later he picked me up at the airport. By the time we arrived back at the IOM apartment, I had told him about the saga at sea and the plight of Khaled's family in Kendari.

Back in the tiny apartment, my guilt about leaving them went through the roof. I had planned to talk to them about absconding, but when the chance to escape came up, I took it without thinking. On top of the guilt, I really missed them too.

I used Shamsul's phone to call Shahed in Rangoon. He listened quietly as I recounted my near-death experience at sea. 'It was a very, very, *very* narrow escape,' I told him. 'Razor thin, Shahed. To tell you the truth I'm traumatised. The sea terrifies me and I hope to never get on a boat like that again.'

As I gave voice to these feelings, their truth struck me, and I realised that I was backed into a corner, sentenced to a bleak and almost pointless future. Shahed had pointed out that the violence in Arakan had esca-lated, so there was no way I could safely go home. I had no passport so I could never fly back to Burma, or anywhere else for that matter, even if I somehow came up with a way to pay for a ticket out of Indonesia.

My only option was to wait for my scheduled appointment with the UNHCR to roll around in two weeks' time so I could begin the process of withering on the vine of life in a ghetto by the airport.

Once registered with the UNHCR I'd be prevented from earning a living in Indonesia. Working, like gaining a formal education and a hundred other natural ways to spend your time, was forbidden to refugees. That meant I'd have to rely on the charity of friends and family back home for years ahead – a prospect that filled me with embarrassment and dread. To use a Burmese expression, the sun was setting in every direction.

The hours passed slowly now that I had nothing to do and nowhere to go. I sat in the apartment talking with Shamsul, who'd been kind enough to give me some clean clothes. One distraction was the comings and goings of other refugees. Some said they were going to take a boat to Christmas Island and I wondered if they'd end up like Zakaria – caught by the navy and thrown into jail.

A few days later, I was surprised when they called to say they'd made it and were safe. Naturally it piqued my hardwired urge to find a better life, but when it came to the ocean I had learned my lesson. Getting on another boat now was out of the question.

I had long discussions with Shahed about what to do, but neither of us could plot a course away from that terrible setting sun. More concerning was that I started hearing news of people like me – as yet not UNHCR registered – being rounded up and jailed. After a week in this suffocating purgatory, I asked myself, 'What if I *could* get on a boat again?'

For all my tendencies towards caution and proper planning, I'd never actually done my research and looked at a map of the voyage. Maybe I'd been too scared to. I borrowed a smartphone, opened Google Maps and was stunned at how near Christmas Island was to Indonesia – only a fraction of the distance by sea from where I stood to Darwin. In fact, it wasn't much further than the distance I'd just sailed from Kendari to the shore of Binongko Island. Suddenly the accounts I'd heard from people arriving safely on Christmas Island made sense. A new design took shape.

A few days later I met a guy from my hometown named Halim, who'd organised a passage to Christmas Island with another syndicate. He offered to help me get a place on the same boat.

I thought about it seriously, but every time I imagined setting out to sea, I was reminded of the night I spent clinging to a broken hull and waiting to die. I remembered the storm and the pleas of the passengers for God to rescue them. I thought of the fumbling hands that dropped the infant into the water, and the heartbreaking sobs of his mother. These memories had to be given their due if they were to mean something, to do any justice to the hardship and loss that myself and others had endured.

So I turned down the offer, and inadvertently changed the course of my life.

*

Bang-bang-bang.

The late-night knock at the door was startling. It had to be the police. I shot Shamsul a panicked look. There was no escape route from the apartment. I was trapped. Once they found me inside with no passport and no ID, I might be placed under arrest. The invisible wall was at my back – and at my feet lay the edge of a cliff and a terrifying void, pulling me downward.

Bang-bang-bang-bang. Louder this time. Either we opened the door or the police would break it down. Shamsul slowly walked over and opened it just a crack. It was Khaled and the family. They looked scared and tired, particularly the little ones.

'Oh, thank God,' I said, sighing heavily, when it was my turn to greet them. 'I'm so happy to see you. How did you even get away from the police?'

Khaled confirmed all the survivors from our boat had indeed been incarcerated. The single men were transferred to a prison in Sulawesi while families like his were sent to a child-friendly detention centre in a neighbouring province. As he recounted their harrowing ordeal, Khaled and the women spoke over each other. From what I could understand they'd escaped from a transport van by bribing an officer at a rest stop.

In a few days, Khaled was already eager to get moving again. He told me he would make another run for Australia. 'I've seen enough. For people like us there is nothing in this country but hardship, poverty and jail. How can I keep the children in a place like this? Think of it this way, Jaivet, if you go on a boat and die, at least it will be quick – one moment of pain and then it's over. But if you stay here, the pain is bottomless.'

Khaled agreed the last attempt had been a shoddy and tragic failure, but stressed we had learned from the experience. 'We went the wrong way by trying for Darwin. The agents were untrustworthy, the boat was not seaworthy. This time we're taking the shorter journey straight to Christmas Island. People have been arriving there. I know dozens who've made it.'

He must have realised I was torn between fear and hope. 'Look, I'm not pressuring you to come,' he said. 'It's completely up to you, but just think, what is the alternative? There is nothing left to lose. You can't go back to Burma, you can't survive here. How are you planning to support yourself?'

I didn't have an answer. I knew Shahed could help me pull together enough money to pay the smugglers, but he couldn't support me while I squandered the prime years of my life in sadness and squalor.

'Okay,' I agreed. 'I'll make one last try and see how it goes. Surely nothing could be worse than where I am now.'

Somewhere out there, God, if He existed, laughed.

SIX

*'Only those who will risk going too far
can possibly find out how far one can go.'*

T. S. Eliot

Jumping into action, Khaled contacted a syndicate that ran boats directly to Christmas Island from a beach just a few hours' drive from Jakarta. 'The good thing about this is if you don't like the look of the boat or think it's not seaworthy, you still have the option of turning back,' he said. They were words of needed comfort.

In Rangoon, Shahed frantically called friends and family and managed to raise around US$1000 for the price of passage to Australia, a huge sum for them. My cousin, Suu Myatt, was as always a big source of help.

After paying the fees to the people smugglers, I had a few dollars left over. The day before we were due to leave, I went shopping for things essential for the trip: a large container for water, the inner tube of a truck tyre, and a hand-held inflater to fill it with air. Stuffing my DIY survival kit into a backpack with my Nokia phone, I told myself I was ready to face the ocean once again.

Although Khaled assured me things would run smoother this time, I still didn't trust the new syndicate we were dealing with. I didn't even fully expect to make it to Australia. At best I thought we had a 50/50 chance of sinking – hence the inner tube. I'd learned the hard way not to place my existence entirely in the hands of others.

Even after years of staring down risk, this latest adventure, coming so soon after one that had nearly taken my life, seemed particularly insane. 'Why are you doing this again?' I asked myself. 'After everything that happened before, why?'

In the end I concluded that if there had been the slightest chance of a life worth living in Jakarta, I would have stayed. But there wasn't. Shamsul knew it too and had considered coming with us, but decided to wait for his girlfriend to arrive from Burma. Later on he would consider that decision to be a win.

The night we left, the moon was barely visible, a fingernail clipping in the starless sky. By midnight, we had arrived at the rendezvous site, a parking lot next to a low-rise building on the outskirts of Jakarta. There were two trucks and dozens of fellow refugees waiting. As we boarded the transport, I was placed in a different truck from Khaled and his family. We were crammed in like livestock and covered with tarpaulins.

The darkness that night was unusually dense and oppressive, as were conditions in the back of the truck. You couldn't fit a needle between us. Just a few minutes under the tarps and the fifty or so mouths had sucked most of the oxygen out of the air. Taking a breath was like trying to inhale through a pinched straw. As the hours went by, the stink of stale air and human sweat was soured further by the reek of children who had pissed and shit themselves.

Whenever the truck stopped, communal panic swept the human cargo, a terror that the police had intercepted us. At one such stop I heard shouting before the truck was violently thrown into reverse. It spun around and the feeling of acceleration suggested we were headed back in the direction we'd just come from.

Later we discovered it *was* a police intercept, and the lead truck had been captured. Khaled and his family – on their last quest for freedom – were taken into custody. They spent the next six years in a state of limbo in Indonesia, until eventually being resettled in the Netherlands in 2019. My own fate was decided simply by virtue of being in a different truck.

As the sun rose, we rolled to a halt and the engine stopped. When the tailgate was opened we spilled out into a jungle clearing dotted with stands of tall coconut trees. There were no signs of civilisation. I felt very exposed. I'd heard credible stories about smugglers taking money before dropping their charges in the middle of nowhere and driving away. In another version, smugglers stopping halfway to the rendezvous point with a boat and extorting more funds from passengers to take them the rest of the way.

As we milled around the truck, I was amazed to come across the younger brother of a friend of mine from Maungdaw, who had come on another of the vehicles that had made it past the police.

He told me he was the only member of his family of seven to survive an attack on his neighbourhood. He didn't go into detail, only that some of them tried to escape but never made it out of the river they'd been forced to flee into. Only later, when I was able to view videos and reports on the genocide on the news and social media, was I able to get a glimpse into the sort of atrocities he must have survived.

As I listened to his dreadful story, my thoughts turned to the likelihood that we were about to be double-crossed by the syndicate. I decided to look around to get a sense of our location. The scent of salt in the air was a clue. It wasn't long before a glimpse of white beyond the edge of the jungle revealed we had stopped next to a beach.

It happened to be a glorious morning: the sun was bright and the sky a flawless, robin's-egg blue. When I pushed through the undergrowth I saw a large wooden boat in the bay, pulling against its anchor like a sea monster. A handful of canoes, skippered by boys no older than twelve, began ferrying people out to the boat.

As people rushed into the knee-deep water to climb into the canoes, I took my time, collecting my thoughts and savouring the feeling of the sand against my feet. Solid land was precious, and to be appreciated. I had left it behind before, and there was no saying how long I would have to wait before touching it again.

Slowly, and with a growing sense that I was making a lasting mistake, I boarded the canoe that ferried us to the boat. Others were giving cash tips to the young men for the short ride. Since I had no money, I unbuckled the watch my dad had given me and handed it to the smiling pre-adolescent ferryman.

We pulled up alongside the fishing boat. I was one of the last to get onboard. With its wood trim, painted turquoise and a rusty orange, the boat was in finer condition and better supplied than our sad fishing vessel, no doubt by now smashed into little pieces on the reefs around Binongko Island.

On this one, there were bottles of water and those ubiquitous packets of Indonesian instant noodles, in case we ever got stranded again. And space! While we were packed on the deck like fish in a net, we had just enough room to spread our legs. A tarp, spread across our seated bodies, provided cover from the splashing water and the roaring wind. A well-prepared group of men, hailing from Pakistan, had thought to bring a collection of orange life jackets, and used them as an extra layer of protection.

Keeping my survival kit close to me this time, rather than placing it below deck, I found an open space next to the wheelhouse and sat there. As before, my shipmates appeared to come from many different nations. There were children, families, women with babies, and an ancient-looking man from the Middle East. I was worried about the young guy from Maungdaw, now out of sight. My fears chased each other in a spinning wheel until I lost track of them and fell asleep.

When I awoke the next morning there was no land to speak of – just flat horizon in all directions. Having done my research this time, I knew we were heading south on the Indian Ocean. That second day at sea was fairly uneventful, save for the fact we saw the sun fully rise and fall again on the same wide horizon.

The crew only spoke Bahasa so I wasn't privy to their discussions. Once again, it seemed the skipper was navigating with nothing but the stars and a compass. Before we set out I'd calculated that if we were to go at the regular speed of an Indonesian fishing boat, we should reach Christmas Island in two days.

I was kept awake on the second night by the anticipation of seeing the lights of a new civilisation at any moment. Instead we sailed towards the dawn in darkness, apart from the still-thin moon and the dusty spangle of the Milky Way.

We should have seen Christmas Island by now, and I was not the only one to notice. A debate sprang up among the passengers, some of whom questioned whether we'd gotten lost. Others believed we were on course.

'Listen to me, these are good conditions,' said an older man. 'The sky is clear and the stars are visible. We're right on track. It's possible we're being slowed down by a strong current.'

The ocean sparkled in the darkness. At first I thought it was the reflection of stars until I realised the waters around us were lit up like a galaxy by the bioluminescence of tiny marine organisms. There were multitudes of them, just under the surface, as unknown to us as we were to them. Awesome to behold, but spooky too.

On day three I got sick. The guy sitting next to me gave me half a granola energy bar. Another passenger shared his dates. Out there, the swells grew larger, and more persistent. As the sea slapped hard against the hull, plumes of salt spray showered our burnt faces.

A pod of dolphins appeared near the boat, an inquisitive escort. The visit relieved some of the tension among the passengers, but the distraction was short lived. As people dashed to the port to enjoy the spectacle, the boat sloped to one side. The Indonesian crew shouted at everyone to return to their spots, or else we might capsize.

As a pink dusk lit up the third evening of our lonely voyage, I became intrigued by a group of young men and women standing in the stern, smoking cigarettes and chatting. They looked oddly relaxed, like they'd gathered for a casual catch-up at their favourite café. The sight of them was encouraging, and I felt a strong urge to join their circle, just to feel normal for a moment. I had been away from pretty much everyone I knew for months, and hadn't seen my family in years.

The smokers spoke in a foreign language, which seemed oddly fitting here in the alien landscape of the ocean, with its dolphins and glowing creatures. I felt a sense of kinship, without necessarily knowing how to share my thoughts with them. In the scenario that was playing out in my mind, they were my peers, or would be soon.

Gathering my courage, I readied myself to ask if anyone knew English – but when I stood up, the days of sunshine and saltwater took their toll. Feeling dizzy, I tilted sideways and lay still. Content to watch them from a distance, I imagined what new friends I might make in Australia, where my dreams of a brighter future were starting to migrate. Things would be better there.

A civilised country, with good people. What could go wrong?

SEVEN

'Full fathom five thy father lies; Of his bones are coral made;
Those are pearls that were his eyes . . .'

William Shakespeare, *The Tempest*, Act 1, Scene 2

That night I wound up next to a pipe that drew steaming water from the engine. It should have been pumped overboard, but spat the hot exhaust straight onto the deck where I lay. It was uncomfortable lying on top of a steady flow of moisture, which mixed with the ocean spray, disturbing my sleep. I knew I should move, but my head was too heavy to lift. I stopped caring and embraced the discomfort, a habit I would refine in the coming years.

The morning welcomed me with a migraine, as an invisible chain tightened around my skull. The slightest movement caused the bone in my forehead to splinter, and the rising sun threw bright grains of salt in the wound. I lay on my back, waiting for the pain to end.

We definitely should have arrived at the island by now. There was no land in sight and it seemed we were once again lost at sea.

I was too drained to care. Let us vanish beneath the shimmering plains of the Indian Ocean. Down there was a piece of coral or rock, an underwater gravestone, with my name on it. 'If I make it, I make it,' I reasoned. 'If I don't, then it was never meant for me.'

Hours dragged by as I drifted in and out of consciousness. It was mid-afternoon on the fourth day when the air vibrated with the rumble of an aeroplane. The guys around me shifted and strained with sudden urgency.

The metal shell of the aircraft appeared overhead. Flying at low altitude, it banked, revealing the word 'Customs', in a bold English script, on its side. The plane circled our boat a few times and left, heading east. On the final pass I noted a kangaroo painted on the fuselage. It was a joyful sight. In the Quran, Noah saw a dove, holding an olive leaf in its beak; we saw a painted kangaroo. I didn't know whether to laugh or cry with relief – in that moment I was probably physically incapable of either.

Back in Burma the sight of the military terrified me, but this time the appearance of the authorities was reassuring. They signified that we'd entered another country's territorial waters and were probably close to land. If an Australian plane was in the air, a customs boat was surely next, or a ship belonging to the Australian Navy – rescuing us, as others had been rescued who had been lucky enough to make it that far.

As another four or five hours passed with no further contact, this cheerful scenario faded. Maybe we had grazed an outer edge of Australia's territory and were now headed deeper into the Indian Ocean, fated to run out of fuel and eventually starve or drown. As the sun sank into the sea for a fourth time, it took our broken spirits with it.

Two hours of darkness, and the ever-present drone of the boat's engine. Then a great cheer went up. People on the roof of the wheel-house had spotted a blinking light straight ahead. As we thudded through the dark waves, a second light appeared. At first this second light wavered, as if reconsidering. It may have belonged to another superannuated lighthouse, stuck on the edge of a pitstop island.

Slowly the light grew calm and rose above the clear expanse. A few moments later somebody announced he had a signal on his phone. The steady light now blazed as a beacon of hope. It was a rainbow in the sky, promising the worst was over.

Two speedboats overtook our vessel. They appeared out of the darkness as marine spectres, a team of men in full commando gear. As they boarded, they stepped over my prostrate body to take hold of the boat and its exhausted passengers. There was an interpreter too, brought on deck to speak with the Indonesian skipper.

The newcomers were Australians, I assumed, because they were speaking English. I wanted to sit up and thank them for rescuing us, taking it all in, but I was still stuck to the wood floor.

With the interview with the skipper over, half the ghosts cleared the deck and rejoined the boats that flanked the side of ours. Around 2 am I rose from my side to catch my first glimpse of Christmas Island, a low-lying coral atoll. We had arrived. The sight of a line of mercury lamps flickering on a wharf represented the sum of my hopes.

We were not allowed to dock, not quite yet. New speedboats arrived, bringing commandos and immigration officials, offering bottles of water.

'Anyone speaks English?' asked a uniformed man. His heavy nasal accent, soon to become dreadfully familiar, was at that point hard for me to understand. 'Anyone sick? Who needs medical attention?'

When I tried to tell him I could use some Tylenol, no sound came out. Four days at sea had rendered me mute, immobilising my chafed and shrivelled lips. The man noticed I was unwell and gave me some water, and my voice slowly returned.

'I need . . .' I croaked. 'My head . . . hurts.'

The man gave me a quizzical look, perhaps out of surprise at hearing words in English come from this sun-blistered semi-cadaver. But then the Tylenol appeared.

We waited all night onboard, watched over by navy guards standing in our midst, and others on speedboats, filling the air with their never-ending walkie-talkie chatter.

At 8 am, we were offloaded in groups of four and transferred to a rusty tugboat, where we made the short journey to the dock, sandwiched between more men in uniform. When the tugboat reached the pier, it was attached to chains and lifted right out of the water, suspended from what looked like the top of an oil rig.

When it was time to get off, two commandos lifted me under the arms, recognising my weak condition. My shoes dropped off during the transfer, something I did not notice until my bare toes touched the wet floor.

Finally upright, I felt the blood circulating in my feet again, and I took my first wobbly steps. This was a serious, first-world jetty, with its overhead platform, solid metal handrails, and more steel underfoot.

Ahead lay the peaceful country that would grant me freedom, safety and a future. I had turned up on Australia's doorstep in a pathetic state and waited for the touch of a helping hand. All I had to my name were the clothes on my back – underwear, t-shirt and jeans, now with the button missing – and a dead cell phone. But I had never felt richer nor more fortunate.

The first formality was a strip search, carried out by latex-gloved officers from Australia's Department of Immigration and Citizenship. We were the saddest group of visitors imaginable – thin, sweaty and exhausted, dressed in sea-soaked beach clothes. As we submitted to the full weight of the Australian security apparatus, some locals appeared on the dock, a few older fishermen curious to see what the fuss was about. An alien invasion! It was a big news day on Christmas Island.

Next, someone fastened a green plastic band around my left wrist. On it was written 'EML 019' in black permanent marker. I assumed it was a clerical tag used to keep track of each new arrival. The officials took everything we had, even our medication, and placed it in bags, each with our identifying number.

The Australians didn't ask for our names or where we were from, or bother with any small talk. They were curt and businesslike, focused on the process at hand. The approach made sense to me. They had over 100 traumatised people to deal with. Their cold competence was a relief, after the past couple of weeks of shambolic treatment at the hands of the smugglers.

As we were directed towards some minibuses I noticed all of our wristbands bore the same letters 'EML', followed by different numbers. I found out later that EML referred to our boat, which someone (probably the Australians themselves) had named *Emelle*, the numbers denoting the sequence of our arrival on the dock. My wristband showed I was the nineteenth person taken off *Emelle*.

The minibuses were white, and marked with a lower-case 'serco' logo. Inside, the seats were double-layered with disposable plastic, to keep our salty clothes from causing damage. Someone had been planning ahead.

As the bus climbed the hill, a wide-angle panorama through the windows showed a richly jungled cliffside. The view filled me with the most amazing sensation, a hope I had not felt in days, or months, or even years. It was a defining moment. This was it. I had made it. At last, I could stop running.

Behind us, *Emelle* sat empty, tied to the dock. Abandoned, exhausted, her work done. The past four days did not seem real. Set against the expanse of the boundless ocean, *Emelle* was a speck of dust. Did we really survive on that tiny boat? We rounded a hill, and our valiant craft disappeared from sight.

The day represented the crisp first page in a beautiful new chapter of my life. It was 24 July 2013. The last few weeks of desperation, of grasping at this or that possibility – of what amounted to a lifetime on the run from trouble – had come to a definitive end. The terrors were fading, and it was clear, in my feverish state, that I had arrived.

From the top of the hill, I could see the curvature of the earth, the sea bending at the horizon. It was a lovely sunny morning, and the air shone with promise and possibility. This was a place where there was nothing to hide from, no despot breathing down my neck. The luxuries that lay ahead were those that other people were lucky enough to take for granted: a sense of security, the ability to go to sleep at night without feeling hunted, the gift of waking each morning with a ray of optimism. It was hard to believe these gleaming riches were now within reach.

We had come so far, with far to go. Despite being a protectorate of Australia, Christmas Island was a great distance from the mainland. When researching the journey, back in Jakarta, I'd been surprised to find the nearest part of the western Australian coastline was more than three times the span we'd just travelled: the closest capital, Perth, was 2600 kilometres away. To get to Darwin you'd have to sail 2700 kilometres to the east. By comparison, Indonesia was just 350 kilometres back across the northern horizon.

I figured when they took us to the Australian mainland it would be on a plane. Once they took our statements, filled out papers and forms, and . . .? Clearly I had not thought this one through. It was hard enough to plan one step ahead, let alone twenty. Since leaving Burma, the plan was to survive, to escape the killing fields of home, and the slow death of refugee limbo in Indonesia. The need to stay alive drove me forward, rather than a well-devised strategy. At that moment, I was just glad to be on solid land.

The bus slowed to reveal a high, grey fence, topped with barbed wire. A two-storey-high gate rattled open to allow the bus into a steel cage, a wire-mesh airlock to separate the outside from whatever lay within. A second gate clattered ajar and we were driven inside. A steel sign planted in the neatly cut lawn, next to a fenced enclosure, announced we had arrived at Christmas Island Immigration Detention Centre.

The facility was an estate of low, grey, steel-roofed buildings, covering an area bigger than twenty soccer fields. It was not, at first glance, a welcoming place, a low-lying compound with edges sharp enough to cut yourself. A summer camp as imagined by a machine with an unlimited bank account and little in the way of human compassion.

I felt very small. Since boarding the minibus, we had been under the control of security guards employed by Serco. As I was to learn, it was a British firm, contracted by the Australian government to staff and operate the facility. (The corporation's sunny tagline was 'Bringing service to life'.) While most Serco guards were Australian, there were also New Zealanders in the ranks, and it became a pastime to distinguish between the two accents.

The bus stopped and we were directed off. My legs worked again and the blood had returned to my hands, but I was not in a good state. After days on the sea my equilibrium was shot: I could only stand up for a moment before lurching sideways like a drunk. We all had balance disorders brought on by the voyage, but my case seemed more severe than most. Deepening my discomfort, the edges of my body had developed sea ulcers, painful weeping mementos of my time rolling in salt water on the hard deck.

Rather than to a doctor, though, I was directed to a shower block inside a nearby building and told to wash quickly. I rested my hands against the wall to keep from falling over as I drank water from the showerhead. A guard directed me to an adjacent room with three other men. We were given a neatly folded dark-blue towel and what appeared to be a bedsheet, cut from the same navy cloth. We were summoned by the codes that dangled around our wrists: 'EML 017, EML 018, EML 019 and EML 020 go into room four.'

The underwater lighting revealed a spartan room, with two steel bunk beds bolted to the wall and two military-style fold-up cots set up on the floor. 'We're over capacity so it's four to a room,' the guard explained. Crammed at the far end of the cell was a toilet, sink and shower. Every surface was hard and made of metal – even the toilet. The exception was the mattress, which had a firm, rubbery quality. There were no pillows.

The door was marked with a number and had a reinforced piece of glass to allow the guards to check on us at any time. If we wanted to speak to a guard, we had to use a buzzer and talk through an intercom. The door could only be locked from the outside. I had never been in a prison but this was what I imagined they were like.

It was past 1 pm and still we had only been given water. We were told food would be served in the evening, so I lay on a bunk and closed my eyes. When I opened them again I was lost in darkness. It was past 11 and the lights-out curfew, and I'd missed the evening food service. Hungry and disoriented, I pulled at the door handle. It was unlocked. I wandered into the common area.

After a few steps, a guard barked loudly at me. I couldn't understand what he was saying. He had a heavy accent – I later learned he was a Maori from New Zealand. He spoke again and jabbed a heavy finger in the direction of my cell.

I stood still. He talked faster but I had no hope of comprehending him. A chunky Australian guard with a ponytail made his way over.

'You can't be out here,' he said slowly and firmly. 'Y'got to go back to bed, mate.'

I did what I was told, but didn't sleep for a second.

The next morning, I ate for the first time in days. A small miracle: bread with jam, and coffee in a brown paper cup. To receive the meal I had to check in with a guard who was holding a clipboard. 'What's your number?' he asked flatly as I lined up at the cafeteria.

'What do you mean?' The request confused me.

'What's your *number*?' he repeated, impatiently raising his voice and nodding towards my wristband.

'Oh,' I said. 'EML 019.' I didn't know my wristband particularly mattered. It was made from that itchy fabric, something to cut off as soon as you got home from a live event. Now it was proving to be a durable irritant. The insistence on using letters and numbers instead of my name was a classic ploy I should have recognised by now. In Burma, I was forced to have my picture taken with a numbered plate, and to call myself 'Bengali'. Here I was EML 019.

By mid-morning we were hailed, by barcode again, back to the minibus with a group of others. We weren't told why. The guards shouted out our identifying codes and added a brief command:

'To the bus.' For those who didn't understand English, the tone of voice and body language of the guards conveyed the main message. 'You did something wrong, and you are here to pay.'

Our minibus convoy retraced the journey toward the more populated side of the island where *Emelle* still bobbed on the waters of the port, Flying Fish Cove. The lofty optimism that had filled my heart the previous day had faded. I was still grateful to have a new chance at life, but also had a dawning sense that everything I'd heard about Australia might not be true. It definitely didn't feel like a safe place yet.

We arrived at our next examination spot, a small hospital that was part of the sprawling camp, and were welcomed at the door by a series of body scans. The metal detector beeped several times as I crossed and recrossed the threshold, as if I were a passenger on a watchlist, rather than a barefoot and bedraggled former student.

The male nurse who checked me over was the first Australian to bother with my name. He asked for it with an odd tone, not necessarily in a getting-to-know-you way: 'How are you feeling? What is your name? What is your date of birth?'

As I answered, he scribbled down my name, without asking how to spell it. While it still seemed a stretch to compare a developed country like Australia to Burma, the carelessness was familiar. Back home, the disregard for details was intentional, a natural effect of the power imbalance. Making a proper note of your identity was low priority, because *you* were low priority. No wonder so many Rohingya carried around government IDs with incorrect birthdays and mangled names.

Next he did a vital-organ check, took my blood pressure, made an inventory of my vaccination history and sent me to another room for blood and urine tests. When that concluded I was handed an apple and told to wait in another room. A young boy seated nearby had finished his apple and absently dropped the core on the linoleum tiles.

'We don't throw it on the floor like that in Australia!' a raspy voice admonished him. It was an older hospital staffer with a pot belly and a goatee. 'Pick it up and put it in the garbage bin!'

It was the first mention by anyone that we were indeed in Australia. The day before I would have punched the air with joy at such a remark. Now I wasn't sure.

The blood test was followed by a full x-ray and the recording of my biometric data – eye colour, height, weight, skin colour, the fact I had braces on my teeth. I was then fingerprinted, photographed and asked to supply the names and details of my parents.

When I asked why my fingerprints were required, I was told, 'It's just for Australia.' Whether this meant it was for when I travelled to the mainland, or for some other reason, wasn't clear. Many things were unclear, and getting murkier by the moment.

A man entered the room and told me to follow him upstairs. He was an immigration worker of about fifty years, with a neatly trimmed grey moustache. He pulled a piece of paper from a table and handed it to me. The document had a logo on top, a kangaroo on one side and a large bird on the other. The crest of Australia.

'DETENTION OF UNLAWFUL NON CITIZENS WHO ARE IN AN EXCISED OFFSHORE PLACE,' announced the first line on the page. It felt like a misunderstanding. Using my best English, I explained that I was from Burma, fleeing an ongoing genocide, and I had come here to lodge an asylum claim.

The immigration officer leaned on the table and said he understood. It was simply not the time to lodge the claim.

'But why am I being detained?' I asked.

His response was measured, as if he had delivered the same answer to many others. 'I understand your concerns. This is just standard procedure for everyone who arrives at Christmas Island by boat.'

It seemed impossible that we would be served a detention order from a place where we'd arrived in search of safety. My mind shut down and I stared at him in disbelief.

'Immigration will contact you when the time comes,' he stated. 'For now, it's time for you to leave for the centre.'

He was eager to send me on my way. If I'd had a better sense of the trap being laid, I would have paused, and asked if I could write up my own statement. In the legal system, at least this particular legal system, only paper documents mattered. By merely stating my case verbally, I left no paper trail, which meant effectively that I had made no claim at all.

We returned to the detention centre where the scraping sound of the metal gates sounded more threatening than the day before. The slamming and clanging of metal doors was a regular feature of the place. Even the doors fitted with automatic hinges – devices usually designed to ensure a gentle closure – snapped shut with a kind of mechanical insolence. The cruel robot who had designed the compound cared little about softening the noise.

That evening we were told we could each make a ten-minute phone call. It had been seven days since I'd spoken to my brother, which meant my family had no idea whether I had made it to Australia or not.

Because there were only two phones between one hundred or so people, it wasn't long before tensions arose. Some people took longer than ten minutes on the phone, which was understandable. Many of those calls were once-in-a-lifetime exchanges, loaded with emotion. The people at the other end – well aware that boats could sink without a trace – only found out in that moment if their loved ones were dead or alive. Every caller had a story to tell and people further back in the line grew impatient.

I had never been one for lining up in long queues so I sat to the side and watched. 'Why don't the staff just organise it better?' I wondered. 'It's like the slamming doors. The fix is so obvious.'

So much of this place was planned and deliberate. Architects had drawn up the blueprints, engineers had built the buildings, consultants had determined the staffing levels, and hired the workers. First-world stuff.

Yet when it came to the basic task of allowing us to use the pay phone: chaos. The guards let the roiling phone scrum continue until lights out at 11 pm. Then they snatched the receivers off the people who were mid-call, dropped them and left them dangling on wire cords.

'Curfew. Lights out. Go to bed.'

This was a callous stupidity that almost felt deliberate.

The next day Serco guards removed our wristbands using scissors. At last I could say goodbye to EML 019. Next they handed us each a plastic ID card with a barcode on it. When I looked at mine I was dismayed to see EML 019 as the headline. Down near a barcode my name appeared, although it was printed in smaller letters and misspelled 'Javet'. Not that it mattered – they only ever called me by my number from then on.

That afternoon we were allowed into an outdoor yard, ringed by a high fence, for half an hour. Back inside, we were handed new clothes. Everyone got the same: white t-shirts, blue pants or shorts, and a pair of rubber flip-flops. At first I wondered if the bright white t-shirts had been chosen for some reason related to hygiene or sun protection, or just for the sake of flattening out our differences, in the manner of the boat IDs. Later I learned the bright shirts were intended to make it easier to hunt us down if we escaped. By the minute Christmas Island was feeling more and more like a jail, and I felt every bit an inmate.

That night I made it to the phone. Had I been able to call Shahed as soon as I'd arrived, I would have delighted in telling him I had made it safely to Australia, that they were looking after us and things were going to be alright. But now, three days later, I gave him something more akin to a logistical update.

'I'm alive, I made it,' I told him. 'Just pass the news to Mom and Dad whenever you have a chance to talk. Things are not so bad. I'm alive, that's what matters.'

I didn't tell him about my growing concerns: the metal fences, the dead-faced guards, the process of being fingerprinted and handed a barcode in place of a name. The complete loss of liberty. My family did not need more reasons to worry, while looking down the barrel of a genocide.

At that point I was still taking things in as an observer. Part of me took comfort in spotting the flaws, and seeing that things could be as ill-conceived as they were in my own homeland. The treatment of refugees on Christmas Island was a failed experiment by a rich country that should know better, but things would improve once we got to the mainland.

That night as I lay my head on a rolled-up towel, I developed a new theory that I hoped was not true. Maybe the Australians had delayed our first phone calls to give the reality of our situation a chance to sink in. It might work in their favour for the updates coming out of Christmas Island to consist of bad news. Perhaps they wanted the world to hear a not-so-happy story about the refugees who had arrived by sea.

I had no idea the Australian prime minister was already sharing that story quite publicly in the capital, Canberra, or that the political discourse in Australia about people like me was about to become far more ominous.

EIGHT

'Visibility is a trap.'

Michel Foucault, *Discipline and Punish: The Birth of the Prison*

The next day, our compound was visited by a cadre of Australian customs officials. Rather than introduce themselves or try to engage in conversation, they broke up into twos and threes and walked among us, peering at their subjects like we were exhibits in a zoo. This unnerving ordeal lasted for days.

Next, they announced they wished to meet us for a formal interview. The news circulated from cell to cell, passing like a flame on gasoline along the concrete walkways where we were allowed to get out and stretch our legs. One of my bunkmates, also from Burma, was the first to be summoned, and we were happy for him – and for ourselves. At last, it had begun. Our claims for asylum would be heard and we would start the process of being taken from this place and resettled on the mainland.

When my roommate returned an hour or so later, his face was a mask of affliction.

'What's wrong?' I asked. 'Is there something bad?'

'It has nothing to do with asylum or processing,' he mumbled. 'They didn't even ask my name, just my number, and all the questions were about the boat. "Who operated it? How did you meet them? Where did you find them? How much money did you pay them? Did you arrange for others?"'

The dismal pattern would be repeated as customs interrogated dozens of refugees, zeroing in on the boat that had carried us on our life-and-death trip from Indonesia. Missing from the discussion were the questions you might expect, like 'What are you running from?' or 'What made you want to take such a gamble with your life?' The aim was simply to identify those who'd orchestrated the voyage.

My number was never called. Maybe the officials had drawn a select sample of passengers and shut down the investigation when they got the information they wanted. Meanwhile, when we asked the guards when we could talk to someone from immigration, we were met with the same response: 'You'll see immigration when they want to see you.'

One afternoon we were rounded up and herded into the main yard, where we were faced by a row of officials, dressed in blue polo shirts marked with the Australian crest. They were flanked by security guards and a team of interpreters, distinguished by their striped yellow vests.

One of the men in polo shirts read aloud from a short statement and waited as it was translated into our various languages. He said there had been a change to Australian law on 19 July, five days before our arrival. Those entering Australian territory by boat and without a visa after that date would not be permitted to claim asylum in the country. They would instead be transported offshore and held in indefinite detention, either on Manus Island or Nauru, while their claims were processed.

It sounded like bad news and caused immediate confusion. No context was given and no questions were allowed. The man had just rattled off an update on Australian law as if we would follow what he was talking about. It was an execution sentence delivered with the tone of a dull announcement at a high-school assembly. As it filtered through a dozen or so interpreters, the statement left most people scratching their heads. I understood English and even I wasn't sure what was meant. It was also the first time I heard of Manus Island.

Over the next few days we pieced things together. The first clue was that Manus Island was part of Papua New Guinea (PNG), something the guys learned through phone calls to friends and family back home and in Australia. For me, the words 'Papua New Guinea' brought to mind the lessons of high school anthropology class, where I had been taught the progress of civilisation had happened unevenly in the country. There were still people who used spears to catch fish, or wore traditional clothing, or practised tribal warfare. While it was unfair to call it an undeveloped place, we had been taught it was definitely, by many measures, an unusual and sometimes dangerous place to live.

Others had heard of PNG through stories of civil unrest in the context of the West Papua uprising – the decades-long conflict in Western New Guinea between Indonesia and the Free Papua Movement – which summoned more images of violence. In the absence of the internet or other information sources, we imagined the worst.

Our only window into the outside world was a TV mounted in the mess area, tuned to the news on the ABC, Australia's national broadcaster. From time to time commentators discussed the new policy regarding offshore refugees. The focus of these reports was more on personalities and political niceties than what any of it meant. The main revelation seemed to be that, in June, Kevin Rudd had taken over as prime minister from Julia Gillard. Whoever they were.

Our worries grew as we began receiving our 'privileges', as they were coyly called. Each fortnight, detainees were allocated twenty-five points which we could use to make phone calls or buy toiletries or cigarettes from the detention centre canteen. It was a prison economy, disposing us to value the smallest favours we were granted by our keepers.

When our points were renewed two weeks after the announcement of Rudd's new rules, we might have been expected to celebrate. More cigarettes! More toiletries! Instead, people urgently called friends and family in Australia to get a sense of how long we were to be held, and what was coming next. Those phone calls triggered an avalanche of distressing rumours about the conditions on Manus Island and Nauru.

Manus, in particular, was portrayed as an alarming place indeed. People spoke in hushed tones about strange and violent rituals still being practised in remote parts of PNG. Only a month earlier I'd been euphoric about my future. Now I was petrified.

In early September, from outside the facility itself, ABC News reported on the dramatic scaling up of the Manus Island Regional Processing Centre. The journalist stood in front of row upon row of dingy green tents, set close together, with flaps of tarp to block the view from outside, and a further row of barbed-wire fence to keep out the surrounding world. The tents looked like they had been placed there recently, suggesting a combination of mobile army camp and a fixed development much newer than the prison.

Through TV news we'd also come to understand there was an election coming in Australia. Until that point there had been an understanding among most of us that Kevin Rudd was probably using threats against refugees to win votes. It was common, in my understanding, for politicians to say one thing before an election and do the opposite afterwards. But when those neat rows of tents flashed up on the TV, my hopes were dashed.

From that moment every one of us became transfixed by Manus Island. The news played on a loop and many guys hung around waiting for the footage to reappear so they could obsess about it – again. Each day, by the afternoon a crowd would gather in the mess hall to watch the grim-faced ABC reporter and the sinister tents arrayed in the equatorial jungle.

Manus Island became our sole topic of discussion. Some stuck to the view it was all about politics. After all, the election was only days away and TV commentators said the Liberal Party, led by a man named Tony Abbott, was ahead in the polls and Australia could be about to see a change of government.

It seems remarkable now but we were all rooting for Abbott to win. Although he pushed the hard line that he would 'stop the boats', the logic among detainees went: 'If Rudd was the one to open the Manus detention centre, then Abbott will be the one to close it.' That was how politicians worked: they cancelled each other's policies. And surely a party labelled as 'liberal' would take a gentler approach. We never could have guessed that both major parties in Australia had a history of deporting, imprisoning and traumatising refugees.

On 7 September we stood around the TV and cheered as Tony Abbott led his party to victory. The high-fiving didn't last long. Two weeks later, Abbott launched Operation Sovereign Borders, a newer, more aggressive policy toward the refugees arriving by boat. The policy had its own promotional graphic, a picture of a tiny vessel on a storm-tossed sea, and the tagline (in all caps, naturally): 'NO WAY: YOU WILL NOT MAKE AUSTRALIA HOME.' A map of Australia with a line through it, like a 'No Smoking' sign, underscored the point.

The irony of this approach, from a country that had been built on an invasion – a hostile takeover by sea, by white settlers forcing themselves on an unwilling Aboriginal population – was lost on the politicians.

Staking his claim on this policy of nativism, Abbott announced plans to intercept the refugee boats and turn them back to Indonesia. Christmas Island was to be emptied. The single men were to be sent to Manus Island, while women, children and families were to be dispatched to Nauru, a speck of a nation in the western Pacific.

By now, footage of the arrival of the first detainees on Manus Island had become a regular part of immigration policy coverage on ABC TV. The clip showed frightened men being herded off a plane under guard. Strangely they were wearing shorts and rubber thongs. 'Who travels like that?' I wondered.

Looking down at my own skinny self, dressed in shorts and flip-flops, I realised my life had reached a terrible turning point. This had stopped being a strange movie that I was watching from the back of the theatre. The project to deport us to Manus Island was more than a possibility, or a line of political rhetoric, or a story told by the fireside to scare children. It was my life and it was real.

The election was over and the plan was going ahead. Very likely it would sweep me up and take me with it.

NINE

The news clip of the first arrivals on Manus Island flipped a switch, draining the feeling from my face and the colour from my field of vision. Food lost its taste and sleep became impossible. Lying on the thin mattress, sweating despite the air conditioning, I lost track of day and night.

One fact tormented above all else. While the Manus Island detention centre looked like a military camp located inside a prison, it was in fact the reverse: a prison in a naval base. For those of us who had grown up under a military regime, this was a nightmare. The dark green of those Manus Island tents struck my eye as the same shade as the uniforms of Burmese soldiers. It was the colour of despotism the world over.

Knowing we were heading toward a place of confinement brought home the fact I was in one already. For two weeks I barely left my room, which I now accepted was a cell. I gave up my time in the yard to instead stare at the ceiling.

To say I spent my time thinking would be overstating things. It was worrying rather than reflecting, and it happened in a never-ending loop. For the first time in my life, I lost the capacity for progressive reasoning. There was no way to step outside the misery, even in sleep, to return with a fresh mind and puzzle through the problem. I was stuck inside an inward-spiralling circle of dread and could see no way out.

The physical constraints reinforced these mental binds. We were being held in a steel box inside a larger steel box, inside a steel building behind a high-voltage fence, on a small island in the middle of the ocean. We could not see outside, or even to the sub-compound on either side of us, where our fellow prisoners lived, since those compounds were surrounded by their own fences, and the windows between us were covered in metal blinds that never retracted. This kind of elaborate system of restraint, developed with great care and at great expense, put a straightjacket on the human mind.

Only the prison guards, in their reinforced glass booth between the compounds, had a view in every direction. It was the realisation of Jeremy Bentham's grim vision from centuries past: a panopticon where every prisoner was fully exposed to a controlling gaze, but saw little in return. The Christmas Island facility was a high-security prison. While the Australians preferred to play word games by calling it a detention centre and us detainees, we were held as securely as the most ruthless convicts.

Eventually I found the motivation to call Shahed and told him I might be going to Manus Island. At that time it was the peak of a third wave of genocide in Arakan, so Shahed agreed not to tell the family how much trouble I was in. There was nothing to be done. I had no choice but to submit to my Australia jailers.

After spending my formative years in an open-air prison, you might think I'd be prepared for this new coercive regime. We were subjected to a daily regimen of being told when to sleep, when to shower and when to eat. Three times a day we had to line up and tell the guard our numbers, so he could check them off.

Only then could we get food, which was just past – or well past – its expiry date. Meat was overcooked on the outside and raw inside; the bread was always stale and regularly mouldy. If you pointed it out, you were told, 'That's all we've got.'

The rotten meals, the over-boiled vegetables, under-boiled rice, mushy lentils and slivers of mystery meat, were served on flimsy paper plates. The knives and forks were made of a plastic that bent and twisted, and the cups were Styrofoam – all measures to prevent suicide attempts. Heaven forbid we might try to kill ourselves before they shipped us off to an even harsher island prison.

But first, they had more surprises in store. Guards started randomly waking people up in the middle of the night to tell them to pack their things – a sign they'd be moving cells or even be sent to the jungle on Manus Island. The never-ending terror of that sword hanging over my neck made it impossible to relax at night, and the daytime brought a cacophony of slamming doors and shouts from the walkway.

In this sleep-starved state I experienced weird episodes in which I'd be woken from a dream and fall back into unconsciousness, only to find my dream would resume precisely where I'd left it. They were surreal and disturbing, hallucinations that would switch off and on.

About three o'clock one morning a cellmate's coughing fit yanked me from rest. Because the toilet in our cell was broken, our cell door had been left unlocked so we could use the communal washroom on the other side of the sleeping quarters. I wandered out in the darkness, sat on a steel bench in the mess and stared up at the high perimeter fence. After a while the night-shift guard returned from his rounds and joined me.

He was a guard from New Zealand who I had met a few days earlier, by chance. There was a service counter out in the yard where we had to line up for water and for the pin code we needed to use the phone. With their usual spite, the Serco guards made us queue in single file under the scorching sun to receive these indulgences. Intense heat had always triggered me to have nosebleeds, and the nosebleed on that particular day was an epic one, causing me to pass out.

When I came to, a guard had slung me over his shoulders. He took me to a small medical facility on the other side of the prison, where a nurse helped stop the bleeding and checked me over. It was an act of humanity that distinguished the Kiwi guard from the easy sadism practised by the other Serco staff.

His kindness gave me the sense that I could trust him when we met again in the quiet mess hall.

'Hey, how are you?' His words came gently in the darkness. 'How is your nose? Are you feeling better?'

'Oh, I'm okay,' I said. 'Thanks for asking.'

'So, you're not sleeping?' he continued. 'Pretty soon everyone else will be up and you won't be able to rest at all.'

I told him how disrupted my sleep patterns had become and about the freaky mental editing of my stop-start dreams. He seemed fascinated and told me he was interested in all sorts of unusual phenomena, including those that involved the mysteries of the human brain.

'What have you been dreaming about?' he asked.

'It's hard to put into words,' I replied.

'You know what? I think you need to write it down.'

The next night he presented me with an exercise book and a ballpoint pen to chronicle my dreams. This was an exorbitant privilege. Because pens were potentially lethal in the hands of a traumatised or depressed person, they were forbidden inside the centre.

'Maybe there's a pattern in your dreams, something to learn from,' he said as he handed me the contraband writing kit. 'I'll be interested to hear what you find out.'

I was touched. While the pen and the book were useful, the most valuable thing the guard had given me was some dignity. He had dared to talk to me like a human being, and even went so far as to ask me my name and call me Jaivet.

Unfortunately I never saw him around after that, so I didn't get to share my nocturnal note-keeping. I found out later he'd resigned. Anyone with a heart did not stay employed for long in detention. Good luck to him, I thought, and wished I could have just quit and left too.

He was not the only one to make his departure. During the weekly yard time, when we had a chance to meet detainees from other sections, we learned of people who'd been moved but had never arrived at any other sections. They just vanished.

Their departures caused a constant, churning anxiety in those of us who were left behind. It was a practice of disruption that would bring a smile of recognition to the keepers of the Nazi camps.

The passage of time deepened the ties of trust and understanding between those of us who were detained. We were all in the same boat, so to speak, and our shared ordeal was an unspoken bond.

Recognising this, Serco moved us around the prison as randomly as shuffling a deck of cards, in case we ended up too friendly or united in a way that might allow us to play our own hand.

Twice I was moved in the first month and it definitely threw me. I'd just get to know my cellmates – often people with different languages and different cultures – when a guard would wake me at 5 am with a flashlight in my face. 'You've got fifteen minutes to grab your stuff,' I was told. 'Then come outside and follow me.'

Half an hour later I'd be in another cell in a completely different part of the prison with three new strangers to get used to. Despite Serco's efforts to sabotage relationships, I got to know a handful of people on Christmas Island and we compared notes.

One man I met, an Eritrean in his twenties, had landed a few days before my own arrival and was not affected by the new regulations. He was told he would be allowed to resettle in Australia and, indeed, was soon flown to the mainland. There were others who'd arrived on 19 July, and had their paperwork filled out as if they were going to Australia. But because of the overnight delay in bringing their boat to the pier, they were officially registered on 20 July. Later the authorities redid their paperwork to ensure they would never be allowed to set foot in Australia. The rules were capricious, changing on a dime, tossing lives in different – and irrevocable – directions.

While all of us had suffered before coming to this place, some stories were utterly heartbreaking. One man was from Iraq and was in his eighties. Everyone called him Ammu, an Arabic term of respect for a male elder, literally 'my uncle'. He'd arrived on the same boat as me. Ammu was stooped and frail, and had hardly enough teeth left to chew with. Everyone was protective of him and newcomers would always ask, 'Ammu, why are you in a place like this?'

He'd tried to make it to Australia because he had nothing left in Iraq and no chance of living out his final days in peace. At some point, every member of his family had been killed during bombings in his village. Ammu was the only one to survive the blast. He refused to stay in the place where the blood of his loved ones had seeped deep into the ground, and wait for another bomb, so he made a long shot for asylum. And now Australia, whose troops had helped stir a hornet's nest in his homeland, were fixing to send the old man to a jungle prison.

I also became acquainted with identical twin brothers who'd fled political and sectarian violence in Iran. They'd trained in graphic design and dreamt of a free life in the West where they could put their talents to use, pursue careers and raise families in safety. Sadly, their dreams were not to be realised. When I met them, they were at the start of a long refugee journey that would see them travel around the world only to end up back in Indonesia, where they gave in to a pathetic life in indefinite limbo.

With the exception of a few poor souls like our dear Ammu, most of those in immigration detention closely matched the profile of the twins, being young, educated, highly motivated, ambitious and hungry to succeed. There was a process of natural – or perhaps unnatural – selection that had ensured only the best of the best could make it this far.

By the time they'd arrived on Christmas Island, people had already been through so much. In almost all cases those who managed to escape from their bloody homelands were qualified and capable people within their community. In places like Burma and Iran, the government would try to hunt those people down *before* they had a chance to flee. The weak never made it: only the strongest, the most resilient, skilled and courageous ever got away.

That's stage one in the screening process that turned a person into an asylum seeker. There were other stages, other countries, other challenges, each more lethal than the last, before a person could arrive in the darkness of the Christmas Island detention centre.

If countries in the West, which often adhere to the Darwinian values of winner-takes-all capitalism, were true to their principles, they might have realised the incredible human talent they had at their disposal, if only they cared to discover it. These were smart, talented people, the most resourceful on earth: their survival and arrival on these foreign shores was proof of that. They were not the richest people in their home countries, or the most privileged – just the most capable. They had so much to offer the world. They only needed a chance.

They were not to get that opportunity, thanks to the poisonous discourse on refugees that seemed to be the norm in Australia, even leaving its stain on news broadcasts. It was on Christmas Island that I first heard the term 'Centrelink'. One television commentator said the refugees coming to Australia on boats were economic migrants, hoping to sign up for payments on Centrelink – Australia's welfare system – and never work again. Given the drive and sheer adaptability required just to make it to Australian shores, it was such an absurd and obnoxious statement, I could only shrug to keep from shuddering.

I had never met an economic migrant in immigration detention. Most detainees had abandoned careers and all their worldly possessions, and fled rather than face imprisonment or death. By trying to reach Australia they knew well they were looking at life on a much lower socio-economic level than they had once known. That's the opposite of an economic migrant.

Here, too, the mischaracterisation was the point. Language matters, a fact well known and understood by despotic regimes the world over. Words have material consequences: life-destroying consequences for many of us. While Australia's hater-in-chief kept repeating his mantra of 'Stop the Boats', his newly-appointed immigration minister, Scott

Morrison, instructed his department and detention centre staff to publicly refer to asylum seekers as 'illegal arrivals'.

And the spin worked on a depressingly large share of people, if the glowering, mean-spirited Serco guards were anything to go by. From the evidence of the news broadcasts, the rhetoric of diminishment and hatred had gone mainstream. We had been politicised, as a group, without being given a chance to present our cases to the Australian authorities let alone making an appeal to the decency of the wider public, which was being primed by the Liberal government to treat us with mistrust and revulsion.

Another trick of a despot is to keep its subjects, especially the ones it aims to bully into submission, constantly guessing. If you have no certainty as to what will happen to you from one day to the next, you are paralysed.

The shocks kept coming, as we headed toward the cruellest surprise of all, waiting for us in the warm seas to the north of Australia.

TEN

'The eyes of others our prisons; their thoughts our cages.'

Virginia Woolf

It was hard to fathom why our keepers would suddenly care about raising our spirits, but several months after locking us away they allowed us to sign up for the occasional excursion outside the wire. A mental-health break to provide relief, I suppose, from the emotional and psychological crisis that our ongoing incarceration had inflicted on us.

My first outing was to a mosque on the other side of the coast, under heavy guard of course. The bus trip across the lush green spine of the island was worth the price of admission, which included a strip search and a full scan with a metal detector.

Until that day I had never thought that looking into the distance was a privilege or something to value. In detention your vision is as circumscribed as your movements. In every direction there is a wall, a fence, a door or a guard standing between you and the wider world. Out of the bus window, however, my eyes thirstily took in the view.

The atmosphere was rich with unfamiliar scents and sounds. In the detention centre, there was a high pitch of sadness, anger and frustration that was as clear to the senses as it was to the mind, vibrating at a painful frequency. Fear hung in the air. But outside the barbed wire, the first gust of wind was a promise and a reminder of another life lying tantalisingly out of reach.

Other totems of civilised society drifted past our tightly guarded transport: a bus stop where a man sat beside a young girl; a group of people holding towels, and one with a surfboard, heading to the beach. These sights fired a pang of desire for an ordinary existence. I'd have given anything to be sitting at that bus stop on my way to work or walking to the beach at the end of a long day.

At the mosque, the guards stayed outside, keeping watch over the exits. An odd sensation occurred when I stepped onto carpet. My body – even the soles of my feet – had grown so accustomed to the hard slap of steel and cement that the touch of the worn rug felt like a caress.

The imam gave each of us a hug by way of a greeting. While it may have been a standard practice for him, for me it was the kindest benediction. The simple embrace from another human being caused every tense fibre in my body to release. It was a moment of letting go of something terrible that had been growing inside me, and of yielding to the comfort of our shared humanity. I could have melted onto the floor and stayed there forever.

As part of the welcome ritual, we were dabbed with the oil of agarwood from a tiny vial, cleansing us of the industrial smell of the hard white soap from the Serco storeroom. We joined together in prayer, and then stayed to chat with the imam and some regular members of his congregation, most of whom were originally from Malaysia.

Our conversation spilled onto the deck outside the mosque, where there was a table of dates and other snacks. A glance at the Serco guards, posted sentry on the yard just steps away, made clear we were not to touch the food.

Further in the distance was a beach where a group of locals wandered by. They, too, gazed at us, more in wonder than consternation. They must have known we were visiting from the detention centre.

'They are unhappy with the people from detention going out in general public,' a worshipper told me. 'They feel like the government of Australia is treating Christmas Island as a dumping ground for its problems. The only time this place gets any coverage on the news is in the context of detention, and the locals resent the association.'

That observation stayed with me during the drive back to the prison, and lingered through the strip search and my reluctant return to my holding cell. We were unwelcome guests. The locals wanted us here as much as we wanted to be here: that is, not at all.

The next and final excursion was to the Christmas Island National Park. We took a roundabout route to get there, since our visit coincided with the annual red crab migration, when more than 100 million crustaceans emerge from the forest and march *en masse* to the ocean to lay their eggs. The main road had been shut down to make way for crab traffic.

A park ranger, tasked with leading our unusual tour group of detainees, explained that Christmas Island was also home to the enormous coconut crab, the world's largest land crustacean. I always had a deep-seated fear of any living thing with multiple legs, but these particular critters, which resemble tarantulas but are larger than many dogs, are considered a delicacy in parts of the Pacific. They are protected on Christmas Island, where killing one carries a $5000 fine. It seemed both sad and strange that the same islanders who passed laws to protect these crawling eyesores recoiled at the presence of human migrants.

'They were the island's first inhabitants,' the guide suggested. Maybe that explained it. If you took the long view, the newcomers included the entire human race.

The road back took us past huge conveyor belts carrying phosphate from the island's mines to the port, to be loaded onto ships. Back in my cell that night I allowed myself to dream about living out my days as a free man on Christmas Island.

I'd been raised with the idea that if you worked hard for a good life, that was what you could hopefully expect. Now my dreams had been downsized. If I had a job in the phosphate mine or as a park ranger,

I'd quite happily forget about going to the Australian mainland, forget about further education, forget about science and all the promise that a young life had to offer. I'd trade it all to live a peaceful existence among the crabs.

It was now December. In my five months of detention I'd been moved to just about every subsection of the prison (and still had not been given a pillow). The stress of being continually relocated intensified as more and more people were hauled from their cells, only to disappear for good. We heard rumours that they'd ended up on Manus Island.

The timing of the transfers was designed to terrorise. A guard would appear at four or five in the morning with a list of numbers. Sometimes it was one detainee, other times the whole cell was emptied, the detainees ordered to collect their things within fifteen minutes and get out. No-one could tell if the bang on the door or a flashlight in the face meant you were going to another cell or to leave for good.

After two of my cellmates vanished, I came to think of each of the guards as personifications of the angel of death. In Islam, an angel named Azrael is responsible for collecting the souls of the departed, and taking them to the other side. Night after night, I would lie awake in a cold sweat, dreading that this spectre would come for me next.

The acceleration of the transfers to Manus was matched by the accumulation of dispatches coming from the government, as broadcast on the mess-room TV. Operation Sovereign Borders was in full swing, with Royal Australian Navy commandos turning boats like *Emelle* back to Indonesia. The immigration minister refused to answer questions about those events as they were 'operational' or 'on-water' matters.

He did, however, have a clear message for all refugees who arrived by boat, including those detained on Christmas Island, Manus and Nauru. 'You will *never* set foot in Australia.'

The atmosphere on Christmas Island had gone from despairing to almost panic-stricken. Every scary rumour about PNG that had ever done the rounds was resuscitated and amplified. 'There is cannibalism.' 'There is disease.' 'There are wild animals in the jungle.' 'The mosquitos and spiders are enormous.' 'We'll be there forever.'

The end of the year approached, and the shadow of Azrael drew closer. When you live in fear of something bad happening, and know it's coming your way, the wait is worse than the dreaded event itself. You start to hope for the end to come quickly.

On 18 December, the angel of death came for me in the guise of a Serco guard named Michael.

'EML 019. Wake up and pack all your stuff,' he said.

I was already awake and praying. 'Where am I going?' I asked.

'Just pack your stuff and follow me.'

Michael took me to a part of the prison I'd never been before. The new section was like a warehouse building, a giant steel shed plastered with threatening, security-related signs: 'Danger! Do Not Enter! Authorised Personnel Only!'

Things were not looking good.

I joined a crowd of other men who had just been plucked in terror from their own cells in the pre-dawn abduction. The guards ignored our pleas to know what was happening and silently took our numbered ID cards. Next we were strip searched and even had gloved fingers pushed into our private parts before being given a light blue disposable hospital gown to wear.

The meagre possessions I'd brought with me from my cell were confiscated. The grand sum of my belongings at that point included a towel I was rolling up to use as a pillow, a toothbrush, a few toiletries, medication I was taking for the ever-increasing pain in my braces, and the book I was given by the Kiwi guard, where I'd been jotting down my thoughts. I couldn't take the pen with me as it might set off alarm bells if discovered.

A team of medical staff swarmed around us and carried out a battery of procedures and vital-organ checks. A few hours later a guard approached me. 'The doctors have determined you are safe to fly,' he said.

'Am I getting on a plane?' I asked weakly, rattled by the revelation. 'Where are we going?'

He didn't answer.

Perhaps in a bid to cushion themselves from reality, many refugees on Christmas Island had allowed themselves to swallow a rumour that not all of us were necessarily being sent to Manus Island. There was a view that some were actually being settled in Australia, while others were detained in PNG, more than anything to show the world how tough the country was on refugees. According to our theory, the Manus relocations were an unevenly applied propaganda exercise, shared by the media, to maintain the government's posturing. Standing in the midst of that crowd of anxious, semi-naked prisoners, I reached for that feeble hope too.

After the medical probe we were handed a document to complete, including a page of ridiculous questions like: 'Are you carrying more than $10,000 in currency?'

I rolled my eyes. 'You just stripped me naked and stuck your finger in my ass,' I wanted to reply. 'Where do you suppose I'm hiding $10,000?'

With the paperwork completed, we were allowed to get dressed again in our flip-flops, t-shirts and shorts. We were given malaria tablets, another indication that we were unlikely to be travelling to Perth, Brisbane or Melbourne. Each of these procedures dragged out over several hours. We had arrived at 4.30 am and it wasn't until the afternoon that a phalanx of Australian immigration officers and interpreters entered the building to deliver an address. A line of muscled and tattooed Serco guards stood between us and the officers like a human shield. Deep down I knew what was coming.

'You are being taken to Manus Island and your claim for asylum will be processed there,' an official announced. 'If you are found to be a genuine refugee you will be resettled in Papua New Guinea. You will never set foot in Australia.'

In that split second the nightmare started in full Panavision horror. Although it had been a long time coming, the devastating reality caused my legs to weaken, and I struggled to remain upright.

'There are diseases on Manus Island, including malaria,' the official continued. 'There are mosquitos everywhere, which is why you have been given anti-malaria tablets. You are to take one every week if you wish to remain immune.'

A few men broke into tears but nobody struggled or protested. We were all so weak and mentally broken. They'd made us stand around all day without food or rest, so no-one had any inclination or energy to push against the strong arm of authority.

About 11 pm we were led outside, each accompanied by two guards who gripped our arms and marched us toward a waiting bus. At that point one detainee tried to resist, but was quickly overcome and handcuffed.

The guards assigned to me were brutes. My feet barely touched the ground as they loaded me onto a bus. Inside, the guards sat on either side of me as if we were starring in a classic prisoner transfer scene from a Hollywood movie.

After traversing Christmas Island one last time, two police cars, one at the front and one behind, led the bus onto the tarmac of the local airport, where a military jet was parked with its engines idling. We rolled to a stop in front of the aircraft and were escorted onboard. Inside we were each put in a window seat, our access to the aisle blocked by our two minders. We took off the moment the cabin door closed.

After a few hours, the jet made a refuelling stop in Darwin. When we took off again I craned my neck to catch a glimpse through the window of the fabled island continent I had risked my life to reach.

There was nothing to see. Australia was cloaked in darkness.

ELEVEN

*'Midway on our life's journey, I found myself in dark woods,
the right road lost.'*

Dante, *The Inferno*

A fter six hours of cold and gloom, morning broke. By noon our
flying fortress started to descend. The thick layers of white cloud
over the Bismarck Sea parted to reveal the outlines of an island cluster,
a smattering of tiny green patches in an expanse of indigo. As we
grew closer, the islands gained shape and definition, their dark green
ringed with sand that looked silver in the noonday sun. There was no
announcement from the pilot or the cabin crew as we flew low over
tall coconut trees and made contact with the tarmac.

The aerial prison touched down on Manus Island on the morning
of 19 December 2013: a lone aircraft on an empty airstrip in a far
corner of the world. I hadn't eaten for two days, but all I felt at that
moment was fear.

A squadron of armed men dressed in dark blue camouflage uniforms
approached the plane. They greeted what looked like another Serco
guard and exchanged paperwork, signing each other's dossiers.

The plane door opened and the air-conditioned cabin filled with the
hot breath of the equatorial jungle. Stepping onto the boarding stairs
in my flip-flops was like walking from a refrigerator onto a barbecue
grill. Although we'd arrived in another country, there were no customs
or evidence of immigration, just a platoon of heavily armed special

forces commandos, stretching from the foot of the stairs to two buses parked on the melting tarmac.

The Serco guards stayed in the cool of the plane. Our new keepers seized us by the arm and marched us forward. By the time I reached the bus, I was drenched in sweat.

The convoy of buses followed the dirt road into a thick jungle. Now and then, tents and bamboo huts appeared amid the broad leaves and thick vines. Some of these simple homes clung to the sides of hills, others were close to the roadside. The locals wore little more than rags. Some children waved at us; the adults stared.

The convoy was led by commandos in Land Rovers, with jeep-loads of soldiers bringing up the rear. The local residents must have thought we were criminals. Later on, I discovered that the residents of Manus had been taught to think of us as just that – as depraved and lawless miscreants. Like the people of Australia, they had been fed a steady diet of 'managed' news and slimy agitprop.

We rolled deeper into the steamy jungle, emerging into a wider expanse as the road skirted the dark blue ocean. We crossed a couple of old bridges that seemed indifferent to the messy green opulence of the natural world around them.

In a hacked-out clearing in the jungle, the sight of a huge anti-tank gun announced our arrival at a military installation. The bus stopped at a lowered gate, next to a steel sign that read 'Lombrum Naval Base'. A brawny soldier stepped aboard the bus and walked slowly and silently along the aisle, fixing each of us with a glare: a well-rehearsed pantomime that said, 'Now you belong to us.'

The convoy was waved inside the Lombrum Naval Base, past radio towers, water towers, military trucks and groups of commandos, before stopping at another high steel gate. This one was manned by Australians in dark sunglasses. We drove inside and stopped in a large quadrangle ringed by barbed wire. Here all evidence of the jungle had been removed, flattened and pounded to bare earth.

We were ordered to disembark and stand in the punishing

mid-afternoon heat. One by one we were addressed by our boat numbers, a roll call that felt dreadfully familiar from our last island stay. The new yellow IDs they gave us also followed the same format as the previous ones: in my case, with 'EML 019' in large type and my name much smaller underneath, once again spelled incorrectly.

What was new on the IDs was the name of the place: the Manus Island Regional Processing Centre. Processing, as in a package that was going down the assembly line. Or like a piece of processed meat.

We lined up at an army hut where there were new uniforms to behold: red and blue, with a badge identifying their wearers as members of the Salvation Army. The name of this organisation, which I had never heard of, suggested these officers had been sent by God himself, perhaps to hasten our entry into heaven. It was the angel Azrael in a new guise.

Despite their divine provenance, the soldiers of God posed the same dumb questions we'd been asked in the hangar before our flight. I wondered why they didn't just use the old paperwork. It was like Burma all over again. The process of documentation was an end in itself.

After a strip search by the Australian guards, we were given our belongings from Christmas Island. They were dumped on a table for a guard to go through piece by piece and then collected in plastic bags and handed back to us.

Next, a government official, dressed in a florid Hawaiian shirt and heavily escorted by commandos, strode into the yard. By this point, with all the colours on display – red, white and blue, and other shades in between – the gathered officials and military men resembled the members of a carnival or circus troupe, despite their attempts to look menacing.

'You are now under the jurisdiction of the government of Papua New Guinea,' the man in the tropical shirt read from a script, in heavily-accented English. 'You were transferred here to be processed under Papua New Guinea law, by Papua New Guinea officials to be resettled in Papua New Guinea. If your claim for asylum is judged to be valid.'

He stressed that we had no rights whatsoever and that PNG had complete control over our future. He ended his speech by declaring, 'You will *never* set foot in Australia.'

It was an incongruous phrase, given the pains he had just taken to establish the unique and inviolable laws of the nation of Papua New Guinea. At a stroke, he had given the game away. The line, if not the entire speech, had been scripted by someone in the Australian government. Just as the Australian government had devised – and funded, as it turned out – the entire system of detention and 'processing' that we were about to enter.

In fact, the utterance, which had been lifted from a talking point of the hater-in-chief or one of his deputies, would serve as an exclamation mark in every address to us in the future, whether it came from the PNG government, the Australian officials themselves, or the dark-blue uniformed security forces who now had us under their command.

As we waited to be introduced to our new home, a glance through the fence filled me with fear. Compared to the gates, guards, barriers and barbed infrastructure on Christmas Island, this appeared to be a fenced-in dumping ground. Hundreds of men roamed freely around a sad-looking settlement of huge canvas tents. It was a wild, lawless, chaotic human zoo.

We remained in the compound, named Charlie, for the rest of the afternoon. By 8 pm, with the heat of the day barely diminished, we were told we could make a five-minute phone call. The timing – after a day of letting us bake in the heat – was deliberate. We had seen this ploy before, after arriving on Christmas Island. In our broken state, we could be trusted to share the saddest news possible to our loved ones and the outside world. The schedule had been engineered to get the most from our suffering, and make sure we conveyed a message that would keep other potential asylum seekers from trying to follow in our path. Our detention on Manus Island was devised to turn us into death heads or living scarecrows, to keep the next wave of pests at a distance.

I half-heartedly called Shahed. 'It is much, much more terrible than the last place. I'm not even inside the main prison yet but it's already so bad, and only going to get worse.'

There was little I could do to help myself or alter the situation. 'Everything is out of my hands. I'll just have to see how things go.'

By that point, Shahed and I had an unspoken agreement: don't let our parents know anything. They had enough sorrow and anxiety to deal with.

Judging by the men crying all around me, my call had gone relatively well. I could only imagine the conversations they were having with mothers, fathers, wives or children back in their own strife-torn parts of the world. The sadness of it tore at the heart.

That evening, forty-eight hours after we had been pulled from our bunks on Christmas Island, we were given our first food, handed out in see-through disposable plastic containers. When I peeled the lid open, a dreadful odour of decay wafted out. The food – some kind of beans with rice – was rancid. Despite my hunger and weakness, I couldn't eat it. Hunger was better than getting sick.

Next, a dark-suited guard with a broad Australian accent briefed us on what to expect inside. The prison was divided into numerous compounds, each with a military name – Charlie, Bravo, Oscar and Foxtrot. We were to be put into Oscar.

'There are ten tents in Oscar,' he half-shouted, in the 'sir-yes-sir' style of a soldier. 'Oscar One, Oscar Two, Oscar Three and so on. There are fifty beds per tent. We're not here to find a bed for you – you'll have to find one yourself. Go in now and look for somewhere to sleep.'

We were each handed some sheets and a pillow – my first in six months – and herded through a high, iron mesh fence as heavy padlocks clicked into place behind us. Oscar was basically a rectangular patch of gravelly dirt, the colour of the nearby beach. Four massive floodlights – one mounted in each corner of the 2.4-metre-high barbed-wire-topped fence – shone onto the rows of tents. The glare of the floods, I soon discovered, lasted from dusk till dawn every night, irradiating the tent village and casting it into the spectral light of a perpetual day.

Weirdly, dozens of detainees were busily walking in all directions. I tried to imagine where they thought they were going. The feeling returned that we had found ourselves in a sci-fi horror movie, about an elaborate research centre where human experiments were carried out in secret.

Clutching my knapsack and bedding, I entered the first tent I saw, Oscar Ten. To my surprise, it was air-conditioned and quite cool. There was, however, no vacancy. Some men were asleep on bunks, others were awake, while the empty bunks were already taken. I went back out into the sweaty night in search of space in another tent, but without success. I stumbled exhausted back to Oscar Ten, scratched out a space to lie down on the dirty linoleum floor and passed out.

When I woke up, my bag was gone. Stolen.

It was a hard loss. When you've been stripped of almost everything – your dignity, your dreams, your future, your liberty, and just about every possession you've ever owned – little things count for a lot. My knapsack had contained a few changes of clothes from Christmas Island, napkins, a toothbrush and toothpaste. Now all I had were the clothes on my back, a blanket and a pillow.

I didn't really care about the stolen clothes, but I could not comprehend why anyone would want to make off with my toothbrush. 'It's a *used* toothbrush!' I thought, marvelling at the absurdity. 'What good is that to anyone? Who's going to put some stranger's toothbrush in their mouth?'

It was still early when I went outside but already the day was bright and aggressively hot. I needed to use the toilet, which I figured out was inside one of the shipping containers where ten to twenty men had formed a line. When my turn came, I discovered these weren't like the Spartan steel lavatories on Christmas Island – these were revolting. The broken, malfunctioning and sloppily plumbed toilets had left raw sewage on the floor.

It turned out the plumbing couldn't handle the harsh, low-grade toilet paper that the camp supplied. The pipes blocked and overflowed, but with no other way of disposing of toilet paper, we simply had to flush it in a reluctant act of disgusting self-sabotage. The floor, as a result, was always filled with flowing piss, or water from a leaking pipe, or a mix of both – the discharge reaching up to the ankles. The slurry on the floor formed a breeding ground for disease and infection, and created a stench that stung the nostrils.

Running the numbers, I realised the ratio in Oscar compound was one toilet per thirteen men. No matter how much of an emergency you were facing, you had to line up, often to discover the toilet paper had run out. Sometimes people in the queue would shout to those inside to hurry up. Other times, they would plead to those at the front to stand aside. With all this trouble to contend with, I would hold out until absolutely necessary.

There was only one shipping container that was outfitted with sinks, and it wasn't much better. There were just six basins for 500 men, so if you wanted to wash your face or brush your teeth, you had to share a tap and a sink with eighty other men. The showers were also built into shipping containers with feeble plumbing that offered a dribble of lukewarm water. There was no hot water, which didn't really matter in that climate, but there were no doors either, just thin plastic curtains between each grimy cubicle.

That initial trip to the toilet was my first taste of the dysfunction that lay at the dark heart of Manus prison. At first, I put it down to poor planning, poor funding or perhaps a general disinterest on the part of the Australians. Later on – after much needless hardship – I came to realise a more sinister psychology was at play.

When I returned to Oscar Ten, my sheet and pillow were gone.

*

Holding my last remaining possession – the ID card that reminded me that my name had been erased – I approached a guard to report my bag stolen and find out how I could get a replacement toothbrush.

'Look, mate, we don't handle that sort of thing,' he said, raising a hand to stop me speaking. 'The Salvation Army is in charge of your welfare, okay? Take it up with them. They start work at around 9 or 10 am.'

By 9 am the heat was already taking a toll: the threat of heatstroke was the price of eating in Manus prison. In order to get breakfast, we had to line up in the sun for about forty-five minutes. I eventually got some food – bread with jam – and waited for the Salvation Army to arrive. As I chewed drily on stale bread, I drew up a mental list of questions: 'If people keep stealing my stuff, do I have to carry it with me all the time?' 'If there is no bed, should I just keep sleeping on the floor?' 'How can I get a toothbrush?' 'Is it possible to see a dentist?'

This last point because my teeth, still ringed with metal, were constantly aching. I had got the orthodontic work done back in Rangoon, at a fraction of the usual cost, since my dentists were university students. The braces were to treat my molars, which had come in at odd angles and stopped me from biting down properly.

Here in detention, with no-one available to make the necessary adjustments, the metal on my teeth had aggravated my eating problems. My choice, at mealtimes, was to gulp down the already undercooked or semi-rancid food or endure the bleeding and pain that came from trying to chew. While most of the detainees on Manus developed digestive problems, mine were inflamed by the sorry state of my mouth.

When the Salvation Army workers arrived, I walked up to the first uniform that came through the gate and launched into my questions. He told me to back off.

'Whoa, whoa, listen, you can't talk to just anyone. You have to speak to the officer who is assigned to you.'

'I came yesterday,' I replied. 'Who am I assigned to?'

It took a while to get an answer. There were five Salvation Army officers assigned to Oscar compound and each was surrounded by prisoners desperate to get in their ears. I wasn't the only person on Manus Island who had problems. Everyone was suffering. After she'd dealt with the last of her wards, a young officer named Liz turned her attention to me.

'Hello, my bag has been stolen and I need to get a replacement toothbrush.' Before I could get another question in, Liz interjected.

'I'm sorry,' she said, 'I am going to help you but I have a thousand things to do right now. I promise I will try to see you this evening.'

With that, she turned and left Oscar. I was unsure if she was coming back, or how to reach her. Liz might have been my case-worker, but I shared her with one hundred other men. We were left to fend for ourselves.

The stolen bag was a sign of the social order of this place. Through negligence and poor planning, justice and mutual respect had been replaced with an ethos of every man for himself. If you didn't fight for water, you didn't get it. If you didn't tussle over food, you went to sleep hungry. If you didn't line up for a shower or the toilet, good luck to you.

The only thing the 500 men in Oscar shared was an obsession with their own survival. It was a brutish state of nature, but made to be that way through the most unnatural means. A grand human experiment, designed to crush the humanity of its subjects.

The language barrier made social cohesion more unlikely. With twenty-two nationalities locked away together, fights would erupt from simple misunderstandings.

Later that evening, Liz made good on her promise. She found me sitting outside Oscar Ten.

'Where are you from?' she asked. 'What language do you speak besides English?'

'I'm from Burma,' I replied. 'I speak Burmese and Rohingyan.'

'Okay. First things first. Follow me.'

Liz led me to Oscar Six where there were other men from Burma. It turned out, for obvious reasons, detainees tended to end up with those who shared their language. Oscar Six was home to around fifteen guys who spoke Burmese or Rohingya.

'I'm sorry,' Liz said. 'You'll have to manage without any pillow or blanket for now. I'll be able to get them for you tomorrow.'

As she left, a man approached with an extended hand. Before he could shake it, he wrapped me in a bear hug – as if he knew me. It turned out he did. This was Zakaria, the same man who had talked me through an earlier escape, when the hapless Abul and I had been detained in the hotel in Kendari.

There were other connections, so many they were almost uncanny. By this point, through our earlier phone conversations, I was aware that Zakaria knew my father, who was around the same age as him. He even knew my *grandparents*, who were neighbours of his own parents. In fact, my grandfather, who was a driver for British officials in Burma, used to have his truck fixed by Zakaria's father, who was a mechanic. (When Zakaria mentioned this, my memory flashed to an image of the Jeep his father used to own, the only one like it in the area.)

In some ways, our entwined family trees made sense. The Rohingya community was tight-knit, and in our culture it was normal to immediately ask new acquaintances about their grandparents, or their parents, for the sake of placing them in the network of kinship.

So while this was the first time I was meeting him in person, Zakaria felt close to me through my relatives, and these familial ties helped explain why he had been so eager to help me at every turn.

It had been months since we had last spoken. When I was on Kendari, Zakaria had been stuck for years in detention in Makassar. After that he'd escaped by boat and been detained on Christmas Island, arriving about six months after me. I had heard rumours he was on the island, but he was in a different compound and only stayed a few days before being shifted to PNG.

Having arrived on Manus before me, he was now the boss of this little piece of Rohingyaland: the other guys called him Uzee, which means 'the lead' in Burmese. He was ready to show me around, guiding me in person, as he had once done over the phone. Launching into a verbal tour of the detention centre, he laid out the unspoken rules I needed to learn if I wanted to survive.

'First of all, know about the guards,' he said. 'None of them care what problems you have. They couldn't care less who bullied you, who stole your things, who punched you. None of that stuff matters to them. They are only here to make sure you obey. And don't make a mess. That's one of the only things they actually do pay attention to.'

The bullies in the dark blue camouflage belonged to a multi-national security firm based in London, UK, called G4S. Most of the G4S employees on Manus were from Australia, and had worked in Australian prisons before. Many also had a military background and had 'seen action' (as in, 'probably killed people') in the wars in Iraq and Afghanistan. They carried with them an offhand attitude toward violence, especially violence inflicted on those of different cultures and skin colours than their own. The majority of them did not have to be trained to be racist thugs: they already were. That's how they got the job in the first place.

Also part of G4S was a substratum of employees drawn from the population of Manus Island. Referred to by the prisoners as 'Papus', because they originated from Papua New Guinea, they were assigned to manual roles as cleaners and helpers. In this national and racial hierarchy, there was no task they were allowed to carry out autono-mously. Their role was to take orders from the Australians.

The military-corporate culture of the security firm was an odd fit with the Papus, who had been drafted in large numbers when the Australian government had decided to carve out a piece of Manus for their island prison. Before the centre opened, the locals' lives were occupied with spear-fishing or picking tropical fruit from the jungle. And while they did their best to carry out orders, their relaxed attitude was clear to see.

'We get canteen every fortnight, like on Christmas Island,' Zakaria continued. 'You can use your points to access chips, crackers, a pin code for the phone – things like that. All I will say is use your points to get as many cigarettes as possible.'

'But I don't smoke.'

'It doesn't matter,' Zakaria insisted. 'Get as many cigarettes as you can, whenever you can. They are the prison's currency, and we are only allowed to get so many at a time, which makes them more valuable. If you run out of food, you can use cigarettes to buy something on the black market. You can even buy toiletries with cigarettes.'

Whether it was to pacify the detainees, or in the hope we'd all die from lung cancer, G4S deemed it necessary for big tobacco to have a slice of the action in jail. They must have ordered the burgundy-coloured packets of Pall Mall cigarettes by the truckload. When Pall Malls weren't available, Cambridge brand cigarettes were shipped in. The demand for Pall Mall was higher, though, because the Papu G4S workers preferred them, which greased the wheels of the black market. While I couldn't get a lousy toothbrush, I could smoke myself silly if I wanted to.

Stockpiling smokes was a good idea, since the canteen sometimes ran out of them, along with toilet paper and virtually everything else it kept in stock. 'Whoever has the most cigarettes is king,' said Zakaria.

His next suggestion was an eye-opener. 'Whenever you have extra points left over, use them to get any cold drink that you can,' Zakaria advised. 'If there's juice or a soft drink, just grab it and stow it away. We often run out of drinking water here, so it's good to have a back-up when that happens.'

Given the heat and the buckets of sweat it extracted from a person every day, I couldn't believe G4S would let the place run out of drinking water.

In addition to learning the rules, there was another benefit to being in Oscar Six: I had found safety in numbers. In a group, you can look out for each other's belongings. We never lined up for food at the same time: one of our tent-mates always remained behind to keep an eye on our things. We shared vital intel too: when there were cigarettes at the canteen, or which toilets were working and which queues were shortest.

Although I now had a bed, my sleep was still messed up. With no bottom bunks available, I was relegated to sleeping on top. There was a higher demand for the lower beds and that night I found out why. The tents contained twenty-five free-standing bunk beds crammed together so tightly there was no room to change your clothes. People got dressed while lying down. Since the metal bunks weren't bolted to the wall, as they had been on Christmas Island, the top section jolted and swayed like a treetop in the wind whenever the person below moved. I'd wake up every time.

Still, it was better than the hard floor. That night my new-found tent-mates even helped me fashion a pillow out of donated clothes wrapped in a towel.

In my prison journal, which I had started after losing the one from Christmas Island, I wrote the following on 25 December 2013.

> Wow . . . this place is on another level – a living hell. 50 people in a single tent and 500 in a single compound, served at one single kitchen . . . I wonder if things will ever get to a point where they at least function – like Christmas Island. Or I get to learn countless non-spoken prison rules and adapt to this shit hole.

When you're already suffering by simply being in detention, you have little extra capacity to take on more discomfort. The slightest thing can toast your nerves. In a normal life setting, a missing toothbrush doesn't feel like the end of the world; in the suffocating pressure-cooker of Manus prison, that loss took on epic proportions. It was bad enough that my braces pulled at my teeth more and more each day, causing my jaw to ache. The thought that I couldn't even keep them clean seemed catastrophic.

When I met with Liz the following day, she helped me fill out a form with my number – EML 019 – on the top, requesting a replacement for my stolen toothbrush and toothpaste. Three more days went by with no news on the brush. I was frustrated. At last, Liz delivered.

'Why would it take three days for a simple toothbrush and some toothpaste?' I asked.

'There's a process,' she replied.

If a prisoner needed an item, the first step was to speak to his Salvation Army caseworker. He was then given the proper request forms to fill out. The system of requiring a form for the simplest 'ask' was part of the prison's machinery to strip the dignity of its wards.

Once the paperwork was filled out, it had to be returned to the designated caseworker. Unfortunately, Salvation Army staff were only on duty nine-to-five and they had weekends off. On top of that, the Australians employed by the prison worked on a fly-in, fly-out rotation; three weeks on Manus Island and three weeks back in Australia. Three weeks at a time was the most they could stand.

Their comings and goings added a further wrinkle to the process. In the event that you had a problem to solve when your caseworker was away, your choice was to wait until he or she returned or place your papers in a wooden box. The request box was emptied at the whim of the guards, and its contents routinely ignored.

If you were lucky, on the other hand, and your appeal coincided with a time when your caseworker was on the island, there were more steps to the process. The sheet was passed from the caseworker to their supervisor for approval. It was then sent to Australian immigration, which kept a database of detainee pleas. Only then was it processed, and the item fetched from a storage facility, handled through G4S, and given to the caseworker to be delivered to the detainee.

The request forms, of course, could only be completed in English. People who didn't have a strong command of the language could forget about a quick reply, or often any reply at all. Their forms were often sent to Australia for translation, taking weeks to return to the island. A request for something as simple as Q-tips could take months.

Depressingly, when I received the toothbrush, it was too hard to use on my braces. I needed soft bristles, so I had to start the process all over again. This time the answer, when it came, was, 'We don't have any soft toothbrushes.'

The toothbrush fiasco dragged on until even Liz grew frustrated, but her hands were tied. When I saw her next, she told me the story of another Salvation Army worker who had been fired for smuggling in a toothbrush for a prisoner not long before I arrived. The message from the authorities was clear and firm: 'Don't mess with our efforts to mess with their heads.'

TWELVE

'No arts; no letters; no society; and which is worst of all, continual fear and danger of violent death; and the life of man solitary, poor, nasty, brutish, and short.'

Thomas Hobbes, *Leviathan*

It's common to hear people talk about a hot day as 'torture', particularly when the mercury climbs above 30 degrees Celsius. On Manus, it was over 30 degrees year round, with the humidity making it feel more like 50. Because the island sits just 2 degrees south of the equator, there were likely few prisons on earth that were closer to the sun, or subject to a more punishing swelter.

When the detention centre was built, the vegetation was bulldozed to make way for baking plains of dirt and gravel. Hardly a tree was left standing to cast a puddle of shade. For the detainees, sunburn was guaranteed, regardless of skin colour or complexion. Once in a while sunscreen would appear but, like everything else, it disappeared as soon as we started to depend on it.

This was a problem in a place where we were made to line up all day. We commenced the day with queues, first for the toilets, and then for breakfast, then for lunch, and then for dinner. It dawned on me why prisoners could be found moving around the floodlit compound at all hours of the night. They found it better to sleep away the day and spend their waking hours in the slightly cooler nights.

Those staying in the Foxtrot compound, where the wooden cell blocks lacked air conditioning, were given metal fans as loud as jet engines, but they often broke and replacing them could take weeks. Even when they worked, they were fairly helpless against the equatorial heat. Some people slept on the floor, rather than soak their mattresses with sweat. Another common trick was to splash your body with water and walk around the yard for the five minutes it took to evaporate, as a temporary reprieve before bedtime.

While there were reasons to stay up late, it wasn't easy to simply flip your sleeping patterns upside down and cheat the sun, since food was only available during the daytime. If you wanted to eat, you had to wake up and line up. Night owls missed out on other things as well. Between meals were other queues: for toiletries (once a week), laundry powder (every two weeks) and shaving razors (once a month).

The phone line did not have a regular schedule, or a start or finish time. That formation was a never-ending one. The phones were available on a staggered basis; for example, Monday to Wednesday was for prisoners in Foxtrot, Thursday and Friday was Oscar, and Saturday and Sunday was Delta. And just when you had the schedule clear in your mind, they'd change it.

Your slot might be in the middle of the night on Manus, or in the middle of the night where your friends or family were living. Or both! And there was no swapping of slots – it was not allowed.

If someone didn't show up for his own slot, that created what was called a 'chance'. When the guards were feeling playful, they would collect the IDs of those who were competing for the chance, shuffle them like cards, and declare the winner. When they were in a more vindictive state, they would let the prisoners fight over them. The result was gladiator games between combatants whose dearest wish was to speak to their loved ones.

If you were lucky enough to be selected, you lined up again, this time for the minibus that drove 400 to 500 metres to the east of Foxtrot compound, where about ten phones had been installed inside two makeshift wood containers. It was rare that all ten of them worked at the same time, so there was a regular tussle among the prisoners to get the seat on the bus nearest to the exit door.

To actually use the phone, you needed a pin code, which required its own line-up at the canteen. The codes gave unequal time, depending on the country you were calling. For example, a caller to Burma would get only ten minutes while a call to India would last twice that long.

It was never clear whether this had something to do with international calling rates, or if it was a way of randomly dishing out preferential treatment. The fact that all the pin codes were later adjusted to allow for the same talking time, regardless of the country we were calling, suggested the latter was the case.

Differentiation was a common practice on Manus, part of a strategy of divide and conquer. Rooms in Delta and Oscar were air-conditioned, for example, while those in Foxtrot were not. The water flowed at full pressure in some compounds, and slowed to a trickle in others. The same unevenness applied to the items that the various canteens had in stock, and to the meals served in the mess halls. The ability to jump the queue enraged those who were cheated from their place. The system was cleverly built to create hierarchies and keep us at each other's throats, instead of joining together against our common tormentor.

For all the time we spent lining up for meals, you might think the food was worth waiting for. As it was, the standard fare was a variation on semi-raw meat and unnamed vegetable matter in a stew concoction, served with undercooked rice. When it was meat, it was usually zebra chicken, as we called it, with scorch marks applied by scientific means, and barely edible.

These offerings were regularly alive with maggots, or seasoned with stones and bits of gravel. One poor man even found two human teeth in his dinner. The locals did not have much affection for their island guests.

Around one hundred people at a time had to consume these fine selections under heavy guard. Once we had finished, the next one hundred prisoners were served, and so on, until the job was done.

The rules were strict and the G4S stormtroopers made sure no-one was to take even one loaf of bread outside of the dining tent. Food was to be finished inside. Any violation or perceived violation led to a full body search at the exit, followed by confiscation – and shaming.

In this way, every aspect of our lives was regulated – how we ate, drank, slept, moved and used the toilet: our very biological rhythms. Domestication, in the sense of a cow destined for the slaughterhouse, was the price of staying alive.

Despite the planning and enforcement that went into this system of staggered meals, and despite the fact that our keepers knew exactly how many of us there were (1300 to be precise, growing to a population of 1600), they still managed to run out of food – all the time.

Conscious negligence or simply poor management: who could say? We just knew that the only thing more depressing than lining up in the sun for spoiled food was lining up in the sun for no food.

Now and then a rare treat arrived in the form of fresh fruit. Once every month or so, a guard or a catering worker would carry a box of apples, oranges or bananas into the yard at Mike, the newest compound, drop it on the ground and yell, 'Fruit!' The box never contained enough for even half of the detainees. As soon as it hit the ground, it caused a mad rush, as the gladiator games resumed.

The first time I witnessed the fruit drop, one hundred men in Mike launched themselves at a box of thirty apples. Some pushed others aside, some took more than one apple, and the shoving and shouting quickly led to physical fights.

Violence most typically erupted when just a few pieces of fruit were left in a box, and two or more people reached for them at the same time. If one man felt like he'd touched an apple first but another guy had snatched it from him, trouble would follow.

When things became really heated, the guards took charge and handed food out to the lucky few. Eventually, as the semi-regular fruit riots got out of hand, we were forced to line up while the meal staff passed out the produce individually. Yet unless you were among the first thirty or so people in when someone yelled 'Fruit!' you risked lining up in the burning sun for nothing. Again.

As long as I had been in the Oscar compound, contractors had been clearing the jungle on the other side of the steel fence. Bulldozers were brought in to obliterate any trees, vines and undergrowth, and replace them with a tarmac of gravel and compacted dirt. Cranes hoisted what appeared to be white shipping containers into the air and set them down in neat stacks on the construction site.

These capital works in the middle of nowhere were a clear sign that we were going to be locked up for a long time. Tents have a feeling of impermanence, but the appearance of shipping containers – stacked two high in DIY cell blocks less than 100 metres away – showed the Australians were digging in for a lengthy reign on Manus Island. The prison needed to grow to keep pace with the cancerous policies emanating from Canberra.

For weeks we'd looked on as the new jail materialised in front of our eyes, like dying men being forced to watch our own coffins being assembled, piece by piece. Every morning we awoke to the sound of heavy machinery as the shipping containers piled up.

Not long before the grand edifice was completed, Salvation Army officers carrying clipboards had asked the 500 or so men in Oscar compound if they wanted to transfer to one of the steel boxes.

I was alarmed, thinking, 'How could you even ask us that? Who asks another human being to choose between one lock-up and another?'

We'd soon learned the shipping containers in Mike didn't have air conditioning, just plastic fans. Still, quite a few men had signed up for the transfer to the new compound, where there was better access to the phones, shorter line-ups for the washrooms, and fewer people shared a room. G4S had come up with some kind of selection criteria so not all of the candidates were approved.

Watching the 'successful' applicants relocate to Mike reminded me of films showing the emptying of the walled ghettos in wartime Europe. Scared, defeated men carrying paltry possessions in twisted bedsheets were herded under guard toward a bus and a truck at Oscar's gate. Echo Block – the prison administration zone that stood between the two compounds – was off-limits to prisoners so they were driven around the perimeter fence to Mike, where they could resume their lives of pointless hardship.

More detainees were flown in from Christmas Island to take their places in Oscar, Foxtrot and Delta compounds, the site of the dreaded green military tents. Oscar remained at full capacity.

More details emerged. The 12-metre-long shipping containers in the new compound were divided into three cells, each housing four people. I figured it had to be quieter at night in one of those steel cages than in a tent with forty-nine other men. Since it had just been built, I also hoped Mike would have functioning toilets.

Motivated by a desire to get some proper sleep, I eventually applied to move to the new camp. My first application was arbitrarily refused but a few days later, in late January 2014, I was given the go-ahead.

It was a stormy day when Zakaria helped me pack my few belongings. I left Oscar Six for the main gate, and waited with him in the rain, dressed in a garbage bag that my tent-mate had fashioned into a raincoat. We waited over an hour in the downpour. Finally, my number was called, along with those of my cellmate and three Iranian guys – only to be told our transfer had been cancelled.

When we got back to Oscar, we saw our beds had been taken. My diary entry from 30 January, two days later, reads as follows: 'The last two days were long, really long. Found a bed. Maybe this is the old pattern, nothing will ever happen as planned or expected in my life. And be ready for the unexpected.'

By February I had arrived in Mike. My new home, named MA2-09 – code for Mike Alpha, Block 2, Room 9 – was located in the north-west corner of the prison, next to the perimeter fence.

The shipping container was one of four in our block, stacked on top of another and placed parallel to two more. The two upper containers were accessible by a steel staircase with a landing at the top. An open-ended corridor ran between them. From the elevated landing, I could see the tents and huts inhabited by the families who lived on Lombrum Naval Base. In the other direction was the ocean.

The conditions were as cramped as they'd been in Oscar. There were two sets of steel bunks and two tall metal lockers. If you wanted to change clothes, you had to step into the corridor: after all, our cells were designed to fit on the back of a truck. Each one had two 50-centimetre windows cut into the side, fitted with a steel mesh screen. It was definitely quieter with just four men per cell, but it was hotter too. Sleep was impossible with the door closed.

While Oscar had felt like an open-air madhouse, Mike more closely resembled a traditional prison. The interior of the shipping containers was coated in a thin plastic veneer. Everything else was made of iron. While the toilets were indeed new, they were the same design as in Oscar and connected to the same shoddy plumbing too. They didn't stay new for long.

Other parts of the infrastructure were in poorer shape. By the time I arrived in Mike, a limit was put on shower time. Every tap was replaced by a button that, when pressed, dispensed about thirty seconds of tepid water. When the water was running low or the generators broke down, which happened often, we could only press it three or four times.

The water at the Manus prison was syphoned from the sea just beyond the fence, put through a desalination process and pumped directly into the prison plumbing. As the population of detainees swelled, the desalination system struggled to keep up. The water supply grew steadily saltier until we were taking showers in seawater.

It was now six months since Kevin Rudd's government had revised its policy on refugees, four months since Tony Abbott's government had ramped up the transfers from Christmas Island, and three months since I'd been locked up on Manus.

Yet there was no sign our asylum claims were being processed. Thousands of us were suffering in a hot and squalid twilight zone and no-one would tell us when things would start shifting again.

Moving to the Mike compound had brought one unforeseen advantage. It was the only section of the prison where detainees were granted permission under the points system – to use a computer, parcelled out in forty-five-minute sessions once a fortnight. While our internet usage was heavily restricted, we had full access to Australian websites, where we could follow the news, public debate and opinion about the government's offshore processing policy. Far from keeping us in the dark, G4S wanted us to have a precise grasp of the political reality in Australia. So did the Australian government.

Three months before I'd even arrived on Manus, the newly-minted Minister for Immigration and Border Protection, Scott Morrison, visited the island to personally deliver a message to prisoners – 'transferees' as he liked to call them – on behalf of the Australian government. He made a hardline speech about his government's crackdown on 'illegal' arrivals in Australia. It was a one-way address, more in the style of a campaign dispatch, to a very dubious crowd – a captive audience, so to speak. There had been no Q&A, no opportunity for detainees to ask about process or timeframes. He just came in, hit his bitter talking points, and left.

The headline that day in the news was, as usual, 'You will never set foot in Australia.' At least he – like the Australian media, which seemed to consistently march with him in lockstep – could be credited with consistent messaging. Hopefully his communications director got a raise or promotion out of the staged event.

Now, months later, hundreds more prisoners were transferred to Manus. Rather than return for another performance, Morrison stood next to a flag in Australia and recorded what he described as an 'orientation video' to be shown to the transferees. G4S played it on a loop on the communal TV screens mounted around the detention centre.

'You have been brought to this place because you have sought to illegally enter Australia by boat. The new Australian government will not be putting up with those sorts of arrivals. You will never live in Australia. If you are found not to be a refugee, you will remain in this camp until you decide to go home.'

It was so bleak and demoralising, and a reminder of who was boss. We might have been under the legal jurisdiction of Papua New Guinea, according to the deal made by the previous administration in Australia, but, since coming to power, Morrison and others in the Abbott government had made it clear offshore processing was now *their* policy and they were pulling all the strings: 'If you choose not to go home, then you will spend a very, very long time here,' Morrison told us numerous times a day, with a face as impassive and inescapable as a modern-day Big Brother.

Each time there was a depressing update, the G4S staff made sure we saw it. If you paid enough attention to ABC TV news and Australia's online newspapers, you became well-versed in the local politics. The parliamentary debate and policy details were all there for us to take in. It was all negative. The bombast and posturing that accompanied these policies helped to drive the knife deeper.

One of the lines pushed by Morrison and others in government was that Operation Sovereign Borders was all about saving lives at sea. It was a diabolical spin. Turning boats around and indefinitely punishing those who had managed to survive that very sea was not really about saving lives. If people weren't drowning in the Indian Ocean, there were a thousand ways of dying a slow death in the ghettos of holding-cell countries like Indonesia and Malaysia, or faster ones in the strife-torn countries we once called home.

The Australian government just didn't want people collapsing on their doorstep. If they happened to lose their lives somewhere else in their journey, who was to notice, or care? Out of sight, out of mind, and all that – though there was no mention of saving lives at sea in Morrison's orientation video.

There was only so much of this we could tolerate. Morrison's threat that we would spend years in detention was like a nonstop finger in the eye. His incursions into our blighted world, made from the comfort of his office, heightened anxieties about when the claims process would begin.

With no hope or recourse, and desperate for our voice to be heard, detainees gathered in the main yard of Mike and other compounds from 5 pm every day. They waved handwritten placards and chanted, 'Freedom! Freedom! Freedom!' Each of these peaceful demonstrations lasted about an hour.

Many days I joined the protests. On other occasions, they became too much for me, and I tried to keep out of the churn. Those evenings I spent alone, sitting by the fence near my storage container home, in search of peace among the colours of the sky.

The sunsets on Manus were more dramatic than any I had seen, and the moon was different there – larger, closer, and often surrounded by a faint halo, like a fairy ring. It brought me comfort on those lonely, scary nights. I remember thinking that the moon was the only thing we shared with the rest of the world. Whether we were locked up behind a fence, or free to roam the earth, we had the same moon shining down on us, casting its cold, equitable light.

Like everyone else, I was angry, frustrated, frightened and despondent – but I also recognised our shouted demands were falling on deaf ears. We were locked inside a heavily restricted military zone that not only kept us in, but kept the rest of the world out. There were no reporters at the fence to record the rallies, no sympathetic activists to carry the news back to Australia. We might as well have shouted 'Freedom!' into our pillows.

I might have been at a loss as to where things were heading, but others had a better idea. One morning around 9 am, I was leaving the washroom block after taking a shower, when I saw a Papu cleaner picking up stones and placing them in a wheelbarrow. There was a line of gravel and the occasional larger rock, laid between the containers housing the shower and the washroom facilities. They had been placed there for a reason, to keep down the water that flowed from both blocks.

The cleaner was doing a thorough job, finding every stone, large or small, and when the wheelbarrow was full, he hauled them out of sight. The task and the effort involved struck me as odd. The rocks served a purpose, and if the man needed to clean up something, he could have started with the weeds, which grew in unsightly profusion in the same area.

At the time I did not think much of it, and soon forgot it entirely, until a few weeks later, when I saw a new way these stones could be used.

The protests began around 26 January, known Down Under as Australia Day – a time for national pride. For many Indigenous Australians, it is 'Invasion Day' that marks the beginning of British colonisation. The date, whether intentionally chosen or not, was one of the many historic echoes that helped make sense of our dire situation.

After all, the detainment centre on Manus had begun its days as a POW camp for Japanese prisoners. In a sign of what was to come, the wards were held by the Australians and their PNG proxies long after the Second World War had ended, without trial or due process.

Some of the old quonset huts once occupied by the Australian soldiers could still be seen on the island, tattered but still in use. One of the tents I shared on Manus was such a hut; others were used variously as mess halls, gyms, accommodations and storage depots.

Hatred, xenophobia, militarism and the spirit of conquest had deep roots on the island, and in Australian culture. Back in the days when the first white settlers cleared the territory for themselves, their efforts set off a long chain of events that resulted in some Aboriginals being sent to missions and other institutions to get them out of the way. All in the name of progress and civilisation, of course.

Those Aboriginals who resisted could be sent further abroad, including offshore prisons on places like Palm and Rottnest Islands. A strategy of containment and control familiar to those of us locked up in our own island jail.

Maybe these agents of colonisation were just following in the footsteps of history, carrying on the same tradition of 'throwing out the trash' that had seen the original settlers sent from England to Australia in the first place.

Taking cues from the authoritarian playbook, the Abbott government gradually militarised the name of its immigration wing. When I first arrived on Christmas Island it was called, rather blandly, the Department of Immigration and Citizenship. After the Coalition assumed power they named it the Department of Immigration and Border Protection. Perhaps not satisfied that this sounded aggressive enough, under Scott Morrison it was rebranded Australian Border Force (ABF).

On 16 February, the PNG immigration official, still draped in his lurid Hawaiian shirt, visited with a praetorian guard of Australian Border Force troops. His role, besides wearing tropical shirts, was to provide a Papu mouthpiece for statements of the Australian regime.

This time he appeared on the pretext of addressing the protests, and our concerns. Representatives of each community – who had been chosen to share news of the proceedings with the rest of us – were summoned from each of the compounds and assembled in the main yard of Mike.

First to speak were the representatives of PNG and ABF. Rather than answer our questions or pour oil on troubled waters, the men at the podium doubled down on Morrison's smug rhetoric. The message went something like: 'Australia didn't invite you to come to Australia by boat illegally. Nor did we send out open invitation letters. It's 99.9 per cent confirmed that everyone on Manus is to be resettled in PNG after a three-stage refugee status determination (RSD) process.'

The speech was delivered in a halting way that indicated the luridly dressed PNG official had never seen it before. Confirming this hypothesis, moments before he read the statement, the paper on which it was written had been handed to him by the female member of Australia Border Force standing at his back.

My friend Behnam, there on behalf of the Kurdish detainees, said the handover took place in plain sight. He caught the glance of those around him, confirming they had seen it too. Across the room, people were trying hard not to roll their eyes or laugh in disdain. So much for the integrity of the PNG government and its official messaging.

After the canned remarks came a tightly managed Q&A session. When questioned about how long the three RSD steps would take, and why those who'd already finished them were still locked up on Manus, the Border Force officer said there simply wasn't a timeframe: 'It can take anywhere from six months to ten years, depending on PNG immigration.'

And then a further clarification from another Australian military man. The refugees on Manus might soon be resettled elsewhere on the island or PNG by force, if necessary, and if they didn't like that, they could go back to where they came from.

When the meeting ended, the representatives left more dispirited than ever. They carried the news back to their various corners of the prison, where it was shared with others and grieved over.

Six months to ten years. I'd be in my *thirties*.

That night the peaceful demonstrations flared. The demands for 'Freedom!' were now screamed in unison, accompanied by the percussion of feet stamping and hands banging on walls. Some detainees in Foxtrot compound threw plastic stools into the walkway between the compounds, where only the guards were allowed. There were rumours that other protesters had escaped Oscar through a gate left open for a catering truck, only to be quickly rounded up by G4S guards. There were scuffles and some of the detainees were injured.

By 1 am, the mayhem had settled. My nerves hadn't, though. That night I hardly slept.

The next morning dawned dry and hot. Although communications were down – no phones and no internet – the drama of the previous night had given way to an uneasy feeling of business as usual.

When the internet was reconnected in the afternoon, detainees who had access to the news read reports that confirmed the rumours we'd heard about people escaping from Oscar the night before. Stories circulated that Papu villagers had caught the escapees and hurt them. Some were said to be in a critical condition, including one Iranian whose throat had been cut.

When the news reached his friends, they begged G4S guards to tell them where he was and if he was okay.

'What happened?' they asked, only to be shrugged off by a sentinel hiding behind sunglasses.

'What happened?!' they roared.

Instead of answering or taking steps to calm the situation, the G4S guards abandoned Mike compound altogether. This happened around 3 pm.

When they returned a couple of hours later, they came with muscle: a camouflaged contingent of the PNG mobile squad. It was members of the mobile squad that had brought us on the plane to Manus, and they could often be seen patrolling beyond the fence of the centre. Now they took up positions outside the front gates, holding guns and flanked by barking dogs.

With these well-armed paramilitary troops providing back-up, the regular guards came back into the compound and resumed their watch.

A few things happened which seemed minor, but took on significance in light of later events. Dinner, which normally was served as if by clockwork (to the point that, if you were late, you were not fed), was more than an hour overdue. While I was waiting with others for our food, I noticed that in addition to the usual pair of guards at the main gate, there were other men in uniform lurking around the perimeter fence, and some of them were holding what looked like metal rods, not a normal part of their kit.

About 10 pm, the generator was shut down. Mike was thrown into darkness. A moment later, someone downstairs shouted, 'The locals are here for us!'

A rock hit the outside of the shipping container – an opening salvo and declaration of what was coming.

Prisoners across the four compounds began to panic. Bed supports were pulled apart: their metal poles the only available instruments of self-defence. Some tore up clothing to cover their faces and hands to protect themselves from the baton blows. My own clothes were in the laundry, so I left the relative safety of the cell to grab them. As I crossed the yard, I saw that some detainees had managed to push over interior gates.

A crowd occupied the main yard and one man had climbed onto the roof of a building. Local civilians and G4S Papus were throwing rocks at the detainees, who used mattresses as shields from the incoming barrage. There was no point trying to fight back, since the only missiles were those being fired at us: thanks to the effort of the cleaning crew days earlier, the stones inside the detainment centre had all been removed. Mike soon became the focal point of the burgeoning uprising.

When I returned to my cell the other Burmese guys had left, to run away and hide. The only one who remained was Haroon, a gentle Burmese man in his seventies, terrified and cowering on his bed. I tried to assure him we were going to be okay.

Then the shooting started.

THIRTEEN

'A riot is the language of the unheard.'

Reverend Martin Luther King

M en scattered like a pack of cards. People ran for cover, threw themselves into the shower and toilet blocks, piled into washrooms or scrambled for the sanctuary of our stacked metal boxes – any shelter we could find.

Perhaps others had witnessed gunfire before in their violent homelands. For me, it was an appalling novelty. To borrow a Burmese expression, my blood cycled in reverse.

Outside the cell, the corridor was dimly lit by the pale red glow of an emergency exit sign. In the darkness below, Mike compound was a cacophony of screams, breaking glass, metallic clanging and more gunshots. I barricaded myself and Haroon inside. With no lock on our outward-opening door, I wrapped one end of a towel around the handle and tied the other to the frame of a bunk bed.

Footsteps thundered up the metal staircase and when I peered into the corridor a Manus local, a G4S cleaner still dressed in his uniform, appeared on the landing. He was followed by a posse of civilians from the local community. They were carrying rocks.

The men lunged for our door and pulled on it hard enough to drag the heavy metal bed frame across the floor. Somehow the barricade held. When they realised they couldn't get through the door, the cleaner moved to the window.

Our eyes met and, under the dim light of the exit sign, his eyes were as red as burning coal. He started hurling rocks at us. Thankfully he couldn't generate much damage through the small pane of glass, but a few rocks crashed into the cell and one connected with Haroon's mouth, knocking out two of his teeth. Partially thwarted, the posse left.

Although we'd avoided being stoned, a man across the corridor hadn't been so lucky. His eyeball had been dislodged from its socket and dangled on his cheek. He'd been struck in the face by a slingshot fired from beyond the fence.

As the cleaner and his posse turned their attention to other cells in MA2, a hailstorm of rocks and missiles fired from slingshots rattled the outside of the shipping container. Since our cell was closest to the perimeter fence, it was exposed if the shooting were to resume. I told Haroon that we'd be safer if we moved to a cell on the other side of the corridor. When I looked into the hall it appeared to be empty.

'Let me see if it's safe,' I whispered to the old man. 'If it's okay, then follow me.'

The poor fellow was rigid with fear. He was older, and less able to defend himself. When the rocks smashed into the cell and the locals kicked and pulled at our door, he surrendered to the onslaught. He didn't react at all, but sat on his bed and prayed.

Other Burmese and Rohingya men lived in a cell further up the corridor. 'If I can get them to open the door, then you should follow,' I told Haroon. 'It'll be safer if we're together.'

I took a few cautious steps into the darkened corridor. A mistake. Two more Papu G4S workers were waiting on the other side of the block. They spotted me as I ran into the nearest cell. It was empty. I shut the door behind me, but with no way to lock it I was trapped. They yanked the door ajar and in the unearthly red glow I saw one of them swing a metal rod. His accomplice was unarmed and used his fists instead.

The man with the metal pipe swung at me in a rage, but the real damage came from the bare knuckles of his friend. He smashed his fist into my mouth over and over. The sharp latticework of my braces ripped into my lips and cut the inside of my cheeks to ribbons. When I tried to cover my mouth, he pulled my hands away and his blows flew harder.

A moment later, the metal rod, swung by his accomplice, struck the back of my head, opening a gash in my skull. My vision grew black. As I fell to the floor, I heard an Australian accent say, 'Okay, that's enough.'

Before they left, my assailants pulled two metal lockers down on top of my battered body.

Darkness.

When I thought about it later, it was the ferocity of the attack by the Papus that most baffled me. We'd been staging peaceful protests for about two weeks and although they'd grown more intense as our pleas were ignored, we posed no threat at all to the locals.

It wasn't until years later that I learned of the fire that had been stoked in advance of our arrival – that the locals had been told we were hardened criminals, sent into local detention because we were too dangerous to be controlled inside Australia.

Evidence of this disinformation effort was easy to spot; if hard, at first, to understand. You just had to look outside the fence to see a Papu signalling, with a swipe of fingers against the throat, what would happen if we were to try to escape. It made sense. They were afraid of an incursion of fugitives taking over their tight-knit community. And we were even more terrified of them.

The campaign of deception had taken in the members of the PNG police force, who were the ones to fire their guns. The shooting was indiscriminate. One bullet tore through a detainee's backside while other rounds were sprayed into the compound, randomly striking their victims.

When the shooting started, mobs of local G4S staff, accompanied by hastily-armed civilians from surrounding villages, pushed over the perimeter fence and stormed the compound. They'd been lying in wait. The mobs rampaged through the prison in droves, hunting us down and beating anyone they could find.

Mike was transformed into a blood-spattered arena of violence. Detainees were picked up and thrown off first-floor landings, hurled out of windows and slammed in the head with rocks and clubs. Men were kicked, punched, stomped on and flung against the hard edges of beds. Some fled through the downed perimeter fence and into the night, to be tracked down later.

In a way, I was lucky to be knocked out so early in the melee, since it put me out of reach of the later, more vicious offences. When I woke up, I was surrounded by three Burmese friends, who had found me in the empty cell and carried me to another cell in MA2. But the rampage continued.

Using towels to jam the door shut, we waited. One of the guys tried to peek through the outer window to see what was going on beyond the perimeter, and a single gunshot rang out. The bullet grazed his shoulder and struck the metal locker I was sitting against. If I'd been standing, it would have put a hole in my chest.

When I had first heard the gunshots splitting the air, I'd assumed they were warning shots or rubber bullets. It seemed inconceivable that anyone would be firing live ammunition – let alone from automatic rifles.

As relative quiet descended, we could hear people all over the compound shouting for help. It was the only word we heard for hours – until news spread that someone might have been killed.

Reza Barati was a young man, full of promise. He had studied architecture in Iran but was unable to finish his degree. As a member of the persecuted Kurdish minority, he found life had grown too dangerous for him. He fled in 2013 and arrived on Christmas Island soon after me.

He'd hoped to resume studying architecture in Australia. Instead, he ended up on Manus Island in the prison block that stood next to ours. He was a tall man, physically robust, with an easy-going nature that made him a popular figure.

Reza was among a group who, instead of sheltering in the shipping containers, ran to the phone room, maybe to seek shelter or call for help. When the barrage occurred, Reza had tried to return to his cell to seek safety. Seeing this large man running past, one of the Papus hit him hard. He collapsed in the darkness of the upper corridor of MA6, and the marauders kept striking him, each passerby taking his turn at hastening the end of this amiable young man.

A coroner's report later clarified that he was killed on the spot when the back of his head was crushed by a rock. He was just twenty-three years old.

As the night wore on, new troops appeared on the scene. Belonging to a squad called the Incident Response Team (IRT), they came to retake control of the prison. I'd first heard about the IRT a week earlier from a Burmese man who worked for the Salvation Army. As a heads-up to his countrymen, he'd let slip that a special force was being trained within G4S ranks, to deal with any uprising in the detention centre. Recognisable by their all-black uniforms and riot gear, including oversized transparent shields, they now fanned out and searched the prison, moving cell by cell.

They were not a calming presence. Far from being our rescuers, the IRT punched and kicked us, as they herded us into the main yard of Mike. By then the electricity had been restored. I was alarmed to see how much blood I'd lost: my white t-shirt had been dyed a dark and sticky red. The IRT stormtroopers were undeterred by the bleeding, and kicked me in the back a few times to keep me moving. My pain receptors were so overloaded I was numb to their blows.

The IRT then encircled us. There was no attempt to give us medical attention. If you begged for some water, the reply was a fist or a boot. If you asked for a napkin or toilet paper to stem your bleeding, you were struck with a baton or a shield.

More than sixty detainees sprawled in the dirt, reeling from injuries that ranged from cuts, bruises and broken teeth to multiple fractures, head trauma and major lacerations. One man's throat was an open wound. Some of these men took years to recover, if they ever did.

We were forced to cower on the ground until dawn. At first light, we were marched under guard to a nearby football field on the navy base and again told to sit. Terrifyingly we were left under the watch of local G4S guards – the very Papu men who had bashed us senseless and murdered Reza Barati hours earlier. When we were rounded up and ordered to the ground, it seemed reasonable that we might be next.

The fear hung over us as the sun rose and the heat kicked in. We tried to sleep in shifts in the 40 degree swelter in case the guards launched another attack.

As the adrenaline subsided and the astonishment wore off, the pain set in. Hundreds of the injured lay on the ground and moaned in agony. My swollen face throbbed with every heartbeat, and all I could smell and taste was my own blood. The blow to the back of my skull had triggered a headache that was bottomless. Each time I moved I was reminded of the man with the steel bar. There was not a nurse or a medic in sight.

That evening, the guards ordered us to stand and march back to our compounds, but we weren't allowed into our cells. The accommodation in Mike was now a crime scene, strung with ribbons of black and yellow police tape. We were corralled into a cement-tiled square that had a metal roof but no walls. As it was night again, we were expected to sleep. There was just enough room for most of us to crouch, and wait for the morning.

The locals had looted the detention facility over the course of the night, taking food, cigarettes, mattresses, pretty much everything that was not nailed down. Infrastructure had been damaged or destroyed, including the mess area. As a result, we were served our usual slop on pieces of paper, and forced to eat it on the ground using our hands, with no water to wash ourselves.

We lived like this for weeks. Mosquitos preyed on us, day and night, in the open air. Other flies came to feast on the wounds of the injured, and on the decaying food that filled the cracks between the concrete tiles where we ate and slept.

The roof wasn't wide enough to cover us, so the rain would soak us while we slept. With all of us huddled together, lashed by the wind and by our fear of dying, it was like being back on the hard deck of the boat on the dangerous swells of the Banda Sea, the most unforgiving of water bodies. It was not just me that felt this way. We had all made that boat journey, and talked about it often. Mostly when it rained, or at night, when there was nothing else to do. It was a distraction from the pain and unease.

We slept in shifts, and even then we were packed tight, each of us getting kicked in the head or doing the same to the next guy.

As I fell asleep, I felt the gentle return of the rolling waves. It was a perverse form of nostalgia, this yearning to return to our ocean journey. While that trip had been full of its own mortal dangers, it also carried in it a spark of optimism that lit up those moments of deprivation. There was a feeling of movement toward something better, and that hope had been extinguished.

Some nights I even yearned to be back on Christmas Island. Back there, we had been stigmatised, terrorised and robbed of our dignity.

Here we were just animals.

FOURTEEN

*'Power is in tearing human minds to pieces and putting them
together again in new shapes of your own choosing.'*

George Orwell

In the wake of the attack, G4S staff were forbidden from entering
the prison. Even with that threat removed, the mood upon returning to our own compound and storage container homes was one of
apprehension and dismay. The memories were too fresh, and we were
as trapped as ever.

The physical hardship continued, unaddressed. The injured
were not offered a single painkiller. Those who had been launched
off balconies had suffered multiple fractures. One had two broken
legs, another had a large shard of glass embedded in his side. He was
advised not to remove it for fear of major blood loss. An old Iraqi man
lost his eye to an untreated blood clot.

Medics flew in a few days later and set up a makeshift clinic out
in a football field, which was soon blanketed in injured men lying in
military cots and attached to IV drips. The open-air clinic was barely
able to handle a simple sprained wrist, let alone dozens of cases of
major trauma. Some of the most critical – including the shooting
victim and my neighbour, who, like the older Iraqi man, had also lost
his eye – were medevaced to Port Moresby.

Since mine were mostly soft tissue injuries, especially inside
my mouth, I was left to heal on my own. Each time I tried to eat

my food, my mouth filled with blood, a condition that lasted for weeks. Yet at least I had my life. And there were others, still living, who had suffered much worse.

During the long wait for care, I had time to reflect on the events of the past few days. When my mind cleared of the worst images, it was the incidental details that took the stage. The Papu cleaner, clearing the rocks. The delayed dinner. The extra guards, with their metal rods. The shutdown of the generator. Any one of these things would not be peculiar in itself, but taken together – in the context of the violence – they suggested that a more deliberate pattern was possibly at play.

The giveaway to me was the appearance of the IRT troops. As I had learned from the Salvation Army worker who had first discussed them with us, they consisted of G4S guards who had received special training to overcome an emergency situation by force. That training, as well as their special outfits and riot gear, would require a great deal of advance planning.

Every action taken by the prison authorities that night required a decision, carried up the chain of command, and, in the case of the IRT troops, a special budget to cover it. While the recent violence would later be described as a riot, it was no such thing. A riot implied chaos, and that we were the cause of it. This was the opposite. It was an attack on us, from without and within, and in my view a deliberate one.

The attack triggered a series of changes at the detention centre. We were told that local officials, and even a judge from Australia, would investigate the events of the night. Eventually, anyway. And of course, the comfort we drew from this news was offset by the track record of both countries and their legal systems when it came to protecting vulnerable people like ourselves.

Reza, who was killed in the attack, would have to wait for justice. One of the key witnesses, a roommate who was with him during the attack, identified the assailants in court. The attackers included both Manus residents and expat G4S guards.

Yet only two names remained on the list when it came time to press charges, and they both belonged to Papus: a G4S and Salvation Army employee. The Australians were nowhere to be found on the island. And while there were calls from local PNG civilians and officials for the accused Aussies to be brought back for their day in court, their demands fell on deaf ears.

The guards' convenient departure might seem an effect of the normal revolving door of staffing on Manus, until placed in the context of later incidents. Fast forward to August 2015, a year and a half after the attack on the detention centre, when three prison guards would be hurriedly flown out of the country after being accused of sexual assault by a Papu co-worker. A regular critic of the island's detention system, Manus Island MP Ronny Knight, described the disappearance of the guards as just another example of Australians escaping the PNG justice system.

The pattern of evasion and secrecy continued in January 2016, when an Australian guard left the island while being investigated for an attempted robbery. This time, Knight was scathing in his response: 'The locals don't matter, and the expats get off, they can do what they like.'

In a similar manner, the attack on the prison also fell under a legal and legislative process that went nowhere. An inquiry into 'alleged human rights violations', led by a PNG judge, came to a premature but predictable end in March 2014, when it was shut down under accusations of judicial bias. Lawyers for PNG's chief immigration officer filed for the judge to be disqualified in part due to his role in a previous legal challenge to the centre.

In December 2014, the Australian Senate launched its own investigation into the attack, and found it to be 'eminently foreseeable'. In the same manner, perhaps, that applying a lit match to a pile of wood, which someone has taken the time to pile together and then soak in kerosene, might have a foreseeable result.

While these developments lay some way off in the future, those of us in detention saw some immediate changes. In another example of bait and switch (and dodging responsibility), a new corporation took over from G4S in running the centre. The Australian company, Transfield, had already won the $1.2 billion contract: the handover was merely expedited after the riot. When the Salvation Army's $74-million contract ended in early 2014, Transfield took on responsibility for prisoner welfare too. Capitalism, like playing poker, is all about turning risk into opportunity, and when it came to the assault on the offshore detainees, there was plenty of money to be made by those who knew how to play the cards well.

The prison's security services, meanwhile, were contracted to another Australian company, Wilson Security. As a result, the prison was now staffed and run entirely by Australians. Many of those employed by the new regime were Aussie G4S guards who'd taken part in the riot, just in different uniforms. They had been gone long enough to change their clothes, like snakes that had shed their skins. Within a few months, the Papus were back too.

Like their British predecessors, the new Australian firms favoured staffers with a military background. Many were ex-soldiers who had served in Muslim-majority countries. So it might be expected that some of them had developed a habit of stepping on the necks of people, much like the prisoners for whom they were now responsible.

Because I spoke English I sometimes talked to the guards out of boredom. They usually spoke of their time in military service, with explanations of how they were just following orders, and sticking to their lawful duties. They had a part to play and were not there to ask the big questions.

When they were relaxed enough to open up, however, their take on the big questions was put on display. It was an alarming Pandora's box of rumours and speculation about the Illuminati and the meddling of the Rothschilds and other prominent families (read: Jews) who secretly controlled the world economy.

I also heard and understood their spiteful banter when they mocked the detainees. They'd learn curse words in people's native languages and seemed to think that using these slurs to abuse and humiliate made them appear worldly.

Their disdain was as casual as it could be lethal. One day we were subjected to a loud conversation between two Wilson guards watching us on the concrete. Having seen us eating and sleeping on the ground like dogs for weeks, one decided it was a good time to regale his colleague with a story of how he'd bought his son a hoverboard for his birthday. The guard was at pains to emphasise how he'd spent the best part of two weeks' pay on it.

In normal circumstances, there'd be nothing wrong with such a chat. Who would begrudge a man spoiling his kid on his birthday? But there is a time and a place, and this was not a quiet aside to his co-worker: it was a loud brag for everyone to hear. It was a case study in the banality of evil, in which the excitement of buying a crappy toy could blind a person to the suffering bodies lying at his feet.

In some ways, the callousness and emotional disconnect on display were predictable. The guards, like pretty much all Aussies who worked on Manus, did not actually stay on the island. Rather they lodged at a 300-room floating hotel named, strangely enough, 'Bibby'. Owned by a British company and retrofitted in Singapore, this 'coastel' was outfitted with a large bar, restaurant, gym and roof terrace, when tanning was popular. The cost to Australian taxpayers: $73,400 a night.

The staff attracted to a working vacation on Bibby, we had heard, were drawn from the castoffs of the Australian workforce, whose need for a fun sunshine excursion verged on desperate, given the nature of the work they had agreed to take on. I understood all that. Still, this man's gross insensitivity made me see red. I walked over and confronted him.

'Did you tell your son how you earned the money for his toy?' I asked bluntly.

'What about it?'

'I'm just wondering. Did you mention the money has our blood on it? Does your son know you have our blood on your hands?'

The Australian flushed with either embarrassment or anger. 'Here's a question for you,' he said. 'Do you have a preference for which solitary confinement you want to go to?'

'If you promise to tell your son you paid for his hoverboard with blood money, then I'm happy to go to a solitary of your choosing, not mine.'

'Listen,' he shot back angrily, 'you're now stopping me from executing my duties.'

'I thought your duty was to watch out for the security and welfare of these people,' I said, gesturing to the damaged men sprawled on the cement. 'I didn't know it was your job to brag about what's happening at your home.'

I expected the guard to grab me but he radioed for back-up, not what I expected. The guy was a lot bigger than me, and he had the training and the authority to crush my slight frame under his army boots. Yet he felt threatened enough – by my studious young self, just out of my teens, dangerously malnourished and exhausted – to call for assistance.

The supervisor came, accompanied by another G4S, and Mr Hoverboard released me into their custody, his face still lit with anger. Maybe I was right about the blood money: the words had stung.

At any rate, by daring to ask a guard a question about ethics, I was on my way to my first stint in solitary confinement.

The chauka bird is only found on Manus and it plays a big role in local customs and folklore. So revered is this white breasted honey-eater, it appears on the flag of Manus. It's best known as a kind of living timekeeper. Villagers interpret its piping calls as alarm bells that mark life's daily intervals. Its song, and that of other native birds, was the only music we heard on the island.

Chauka also happened to be the name of a solitary confinement block. Separated from the main jail by several hundred metres, Chauka consisted of three 20-foot shipping containers arranged in a triangle.

Each one was empty, save for a green military-style canvas cot and a blanket. No pillow. There were no windows either; just a vent that pushed the hot, stale air in circles, and a lightbulb in a cage, with no light switch to turn it on. When the guards shut me in, it was pitch black and silent, except for the birdsong.

Strangely, for an area dedicated to punishment, Chauka wasn't as sweltering as the cells in the main prison. The containers had been placed beneath trees and I was spared the additional body heat of my usual companions. An average visitor might expect to be carried out of Chauka on a stretcher after a short stay, but after months of 40 degree heat, I found the 35 degrees of solitary a small reprieve.

Time slowed down in regular detention. In my shipping container cell in Mike, an hour felt like it might last a day. In Chauka, the passage of time went into freefall. Separated from day and night, circadian rhythms were scrambled. There was little to listen to, except the birds and the gloomy scraping of the tree branches against the metal sides of the container. Without the senses to grasp onto, my mind entered a sunless place of its own making, a jungle of shapeless forms and eerie impressions. Nightmares, memories, fears, despair, yearning for family, anger, resentment, frustration, sadness: each took its turn at the front of the pack, and then fell back to let the next tormentor take the lead.

Although I felt remote from humanity, the Wilson guards were never far away. When I wanted to use the toilet they'd let me out, which brought a new kind of pain. In the five metre walk to the filthy lavatory, the sunlight was incandescent and disorienting, requiring me to cover my eyes until I made it inside the stall. At night the walk to the lavatory was marked by the bright fluorescent flares that pricked the eyes and left me with an instant migraine.

Then it would be back to my cell and my lonely cot, hanging from an invisible chain above the void. I was told I spent three days and three nights in Chauka but the time seemed to stretch on too long to measure.

Just as my eyes grew painfully sensitive in my period of isolation, so did my perception change when I returned to my old life in the detention centre. It was with a new x-ray vision that I took in the high fences and the decaying prisoners they held in check. The guards, too, seemed to be peeled back and exposed, revealed as more fleshy automatons than human beings. They could walk and talk, but their brain function was at a minimum, as it would have to be, to keep them going through the paces of their grotesque duties.

Each of us, jailer or prisoner, was trapped in our own way in that abject place, with no purpose or direction, no past or future. Our living, changing and hopeful selves had been stripped. Where once vibrant personalities had brought energy and light to the world, now we were robots, reacting to remote-control inputs of the prison machine. The policy makers twiddled with their procedural buttons, thousands of kilometres away, and we complied.

When we could eat, when to sleep, where to stand and where to take a shit: these decisions were for others to make. We had to be careful not to shout out in unison for our own freedom, or question the ethics of our keepers, lest we cause offence. Any expression of free will was taken as a flaw in the source code, causing us to be extricated from the system and thrown into solitary, to limit the potential for the damage to spread.

The view gave me hope, since recent events had surely changed things. The prison had been overrun and looted: someone had been shot, someone else been killed, still two others had lost an eye; people had been hacked with machetes and beaten with clubs. If that wasn't evidence the place was unsafe and the policy a disaster, then nothing was. It was hard to imagine that a rational decision maker would think it wise to return to business as usual. The system had failed, and was due for a massive reboot.

The hope lasted for a few weeks, which was precisely how long we were cut off from the internet after the attack and looting. When communications were restored, I was stunned at how the recent events on Manus were being characterised in the Australian media. I should have known better.

By this point, I also should have anticipated how the politicians would invert reality to keep themselves on top. In his initial public comments, Scott Morrison, the faux-pious immigration minister, stated that Reza Barati had been fatally injured *outside* the detention centre, as if he were part of a marauding group of jail breakers who had jumped the fence to fan out and terrorise the locals.

The truth – later ratified by official investigations – was that the attack had come from outside the fence, causing the detainees to flee for their lives. But by then it was too late, as the narrative of the rampaging prisoners had already taken hold. And the minister's evasions took a more subtle and characteristic turn, with terms like 'riot', 'escape', 'violent' and 'illegal' joining in the effort to reverse the flow of blame.

'I can guarantee their safety when they remain in the centre and act co-operatively with those who are trying to provide them with support and accommodation,' Morrison stated to the media after the attack. A pronouncement that deftly omitted the fact that those who were caring for us were also the ones who were killing us.

Injustice had always galled me, but since my first taste of it back in Burma, it had seemed wiser to me to direct my anger at the system as a whole. Most of the time, from what I had witnessed, people and the way they behaved were products of the power structures in which they operated.

For the first time, it seemed that an individual shared a unique portion of the blame. Scott Morrison appeared to relish the task of delivering his harsh and punishing policies. You could hear it in his speech, read it in his words and see it in his body language. He delighted in playing the tough guy – the bureaucratic fist deployed to bash us as a warning to others. And, as it turned out, to grasp at his own political ambitions. In the nativist culture of Australia, where anti-immigrant sentiment was fairly mainstream, getting tough on refugees could put the highest levels of power within reach.

The gears continued to turn as the system moved to restore itself. While we were still sleeping outside, the detainment centre was regularly visited by officers from the Australian Federal Police. They busied themselves in documentation, taking photos of every bullet hole and broken lamp. They were too focused on the property damage to take notice of the nearby encampment of prone bodies, where people were begging for blankets and medical help.

With the damage fully annotated, we were briefly allowed back into our cabins. Soon after my arrival from confinement, the crime-scene tape was taken down and we went to our rooms to gather towels and clothing.

It was a return trip to a nightmare. We had to step around shattered glass and dried patches of blood, and pass cell doors smeared with crimson handprints where people had tried to barricade themselves. The place was littered with signs of mayhem: broken light fittings dangled from the ceiling, torn clothes and towels were scattered about, and shoes lay in the hallways where people had run for cover.

In my room, rocks were still scattered across the floor but I couldn't find any trace of the teeth that had been knocked out of Haroun's mouth. I hurriedly grabbed a change of clothes and a towel and returned to the concrete slab.

A few days later, after all the blood and glass had been cleaned up, we returned to our cells for good. While I still felt uneasy back at the scene of the crime, it was a relief to sleep on a bed again, after a month on the concrete tiles.

For the Australian government, the riots were taken as proof that, rather than needing a rethink, the system was due for reinforcement. The new double-down approach included the installation of higher, stronger double fences topped with razor wire and CCTV cameras. It was an imposing, robust new cage befitting a facility that was transforming from an ad hoc jungle camp to a high-security prison.

Once again the bulldozers were brought in and a new site adjacent to the old prison was levelled. Each pass of the bulldozer's blade pushed me further and further down a dark tunnel, away from my eventual release.

'For a very, very long time,' said Scott Morrison's voice, which had taken up residence in my head.

The jail was now referred to as the Detention Centre 1, while the new section was dubbed the Detention Centre 2. The first thing to be constructed on the site was a metal frame, which grew to become a cell phone or radio tower. This time there were no shipping containers: the new prison had proper buildings, erected on poured concrete foundations.

Each new wall boxed us in further. And because we still had not heard from the officials about the immigration process they had promised, we only had the noisy voice of the construction site to tell us the truth of our new condition. We were trapped, worse than ever.

Once the new fence was finished, the local guards who weeks earlier had attacked us in a frenzy of hatred were welcomed back to their old jobs.

FIFTEEN

'Perfer et obdura, dolor hic tibi proderit olim.'
(Be patient and tough; someday this pain will be useful to you.)

Ovid

One of my happiest memories of life in Burma revolved around Eid. The annual holiday heralds the end of Ramadan, the month-long period of fasting, and ushers in the turning of the year for Rohingyas. Marked by the first appearance of the crescent moon, Eid is a celebration of renewal. When Shahed and I were little boys, Eid was a festive time, much like Christmas is to many people in the West.

In the morning, we'd dress in fresh new outfits, and accompany our family to prayers at the open square that was only used for Eid celebrations. As soon as the new moon appeared in the sky, we would go to this square to look at the decorations, and chant, 'Tomorrow is for new year, and tonight is for the music.' The magical note of anticipation that hung in the air was deeply felt, and stayed with me until adulthood.

But the real fun began when we returned home. Our older relatives – especially our grandparents – made a great fuss and presented us with crisp, brand new banknotes that had been carefully pressed between the pages of books. Shahed and I would eat sweet confections and play all day, proud of our new clothes, excited by our new-found riches and glad to be safe in the loving embrace of our family.

Those days – and those feelings – were now a lifetime ago.

Back in the detention centre, Eid was marked by a new development, causing both hope and disquiet. Six months after I'd arrived on the island, PNG immigration had finally begun interviewing the detainees to officially determine, based on our life stories, whether we could be classified as refugees.

We were asked at the outset to declare whether or not we were 'participating under duress', though it wasn't clear whether 'fleeing to save my life' qualified. When it came my turn to tell my story, I explained that my physical discomfort had become too acute to allow me to maintain the focus needed for such a crucial testimony.

It may seem odd, at first consideration, that I would make the choice to delay the process of being declared a refugee. In most places, gaining official refugee status brings certain protections.

This was not one of those places, however. Quite the opposite. By taking part in the process, we were effectively declaring our wish to be resettled permanently in PNG, a country where we had been brought against our will, and whose citizens posed a daily threat to our existence. The fences that surrounded Manus were as much to keep them out as to keep us inside.

The view of many of our lawyers and advocates was that we should treat the process with great caution. We still had some hope of reprieve. The legality of the detention centre was a topic of active debate in the Supreme Court of PNG. If the centre was itself unconstitutional, so was any legal process that took place inside its fence.

There were other concerns. Our fate was being decided by an immigration ministry that was in thrall to that of a foreign government and its spiteful policies, and on its orders acting as both judge and prosecutor.

While most countries decided for themselves whether someone qualified as a refugee or not, the process only worked properly when handled by an independent tribunal of some sort, free of government interference, which was certainly not the case in PNG – or in Australia, for that matter. Otherwise such important matters were better handled by (somewhat) less compromised organisations like the UNHCR.

Still, with the weight of the legal and detainment system pushing us to take part in the process, it took courage to resist. There were those who didn't participate from the beginning, and those who stopped halfway through as they realised its true aims. By April 2016, there would be about 200 'negatives', and we'd develop a closeness that was based on having chosen this lonelier, riskier path.

One of these was my neighbour, Amir, whose room was next to mine in the converted shipping container: I was MA2-09 and he was MA2-11. He was one of the youngest guys on Manus, having been detained while still a teenager, and he looked more youthful than his years would suggest.

Back in Iran he had been a soccer player, playing on his country's national team, and a coach as well, before catching the attention of that country's notorious regime, whose sense of right and wrong was often the inverse of what might be expected.

In Mike he was a source of light and levity, and I was a regular object of his gentle teasing. As friends we were an odd couple, with his rambunctious energy set against my own reflective nature. But there was more to him than the joking athlete. He had a sharp intelligence when it came to people and their motivations, and an iron will that spoke to his achievements as a competitor. Like me, he had come to see the refugee process as a travesty and a dangerous one, and he wanted nothing to do with it.

Another dissenter was Behrouz Boochani, from the Kurdish region of Iran. He had been a journalist, with a professional background that taught him to see through official cant to what was happening underneath, the machinations and power moves. And despite his wiry frame, he was tough as nails, with a 'fuck you' stubbornness that may have been an Iranian trait, or, more specifically, a Kurdish one.

He kept himself out of the asylum-seeking process, but they declared him a 'positive' anyway, without a shred of testimony or evidence relating to his case. This confirmed an observation of ours, that the refugee process was a roll of the dice: your status could be reversed on the whim of the authorities.

The fickleness of the system struck most of us as darkly ironic, if not actually funny, until the joke ended and those same authorities made moves to separate us into different parts of the detainment centre. Suddenly our official status, randomly applied, had real and material consequences.

Many of the negatives were scared about being isolated. As non-refugees, they were in this country (where again, they had never chosen to come) illegally, and could be treated as criminals, or, worse, deported back to their home countries. The positives were anxious about being sent out of the detainment centre, into the wider community of locals, who had been taught for years to fear and hate us. And all of us were reluctant to be separated from the friends we had made, the people we had come to know and trust.

Behrouz, for one, was not going to give in so easily. On an early morning in April 2016, he would climb a tree to protest against being thrust into the refugee process of PNG against his will. He stayed there all day and into the evening, with a group of other detainees sitting around the base of the trunk to show their support. Because the tree was the highest point around, I could see him above the fence on Mike, shouting for justice.

It made the news back in Australia, and by the time he climbed down from the branches, his voice had been heard around the world.

Things were changing too fast to commit to a single course of action that might determine the course of the rest of your life. And every option seemed more damaging than the next.

In any case, immigration interviews had serious consequences, and you had to get them right. I asked that mine be postponed until after my injured mouth had healed.

Five months had passed since my braces had been bent and broken in the beating I sustained during the attack, and the pain in my mouth had become an equal partner to the mental anguish of daily life.

Mealtimes were agony. If the food was hard – which it often was – I just couldn't eat at all. Chewing caused my gums to bleed profusely. When I asked for softer food, I was given the standard response: 'What you see is what you get.'

Although I tried to stop myself, I couldn't help darting my tongue around in my mouth, tentatively probing where broken wires had sliced into my inflamed gums and torn holes on the inside of my cheeks. The requests I made for dental help were ignored.

Eventually, someone in the shadow bureaucracy saw my pleas, uncovering doctors' notes dating back to my Christmas Island days, and decided I had suffered enough. Not only would I have my braces seen to and my mouth fixed, it would be done by an orthodontist in Darwin.

In late July 2014, I left the detention centre for the first time in eight months for the drive to Manus Island's Momote Airport. While the road was as potholed and treacherous as ever, there were enormous new construction sites cut into the jungle. We passed block after block of concrete structures, with workers and machines swarming over them like mound-building termites.

This was a rare glimpse beyond the limits of detention, and it showed, with stark clarity, that our freedom was not coming any time soon: a statement in concrete and rebar that spoke more plainly than any amount of government hot air. Rather than processing and releasing their current crop of prisoners, the government was spending millions to accommodate a swelling population of new captives.

Momote Airport, on the other hand, was its old humble self, a single airstrip with a single-storey steel-roofed shed serving as a terminal. I bypassed the building and was marched onto a midsize jet, flanked by Wilson guards as if I were a criminal. The cabin was full of Transfield staff and other Wilson guards, no doubt looking forward to rotating back to Australia to enjoy a three-week break from the horror show.

When we landed in Port Moresby ninety minutes later, my security detail was beefed up with the addition of armed officers from a company called Tactical Solutions International. Their guns made me nervous. Did they think I might escape? If I tried to run away, would they shoot me dead in the street? Or was Port Moresby so dangerous you needed to carry a weapon? Any way I looked at it, the armed security seemed like overkill.

I was escorted through the terminal and bundled into the back of a van that had dark tinted windows. Ten minutes later, I was led inside a kind of hostel fairly close to the airport. This was the Granville Hotel, later to be converted into a prison for refugees, and to become a hot spot for clashes between the newcomers and the locals – there was even a hostage taking in its future. The red-roofed accommodation was simple and at that point served as a way station for detainees en route to Australia for medical purposes. I was told we'd be staying overnight and travelling to Darwin the following morning.

While the room was small, with a basic en suite, it was a vast improvement on what I'd grown used to on Manus; but not for one second was I allowed to forget I'd lost my freedom. The windows were covered by reinforced metal screens, and there was the constant scrutiny of the armed guards. When I wanted to use the bathroom, I had to leave the door open. Apparently one of the guys who'd been medevaced before me had managed to slice open his veins on a visit to the toilet. A dead prisoner was of no use to anyone.

A nearly sleepless night followed, and a day of sitting around the stuffy room, as I waited to be taken to the airport. Around 4 pm, one of the guards came in and announced in a broad Australian accent, 'Hey, mate! Your flight to Australia got cancelled!'

He didn't offer details or say what would happen next. I assumed there had been a problem with the plane and the flight would be rescheduled soon enough. I spent the next three days sitting in that room, watching the Australian news on television, and going to the toilet with the door open. On the third night, a nurse from International Health and

Medical Services, an Australian company contracted to run the medical services for the offshore detention centres, arrived with bad news.

'You won't be going to Darwin,' she said bluntly.

'What? Why not?' I asked.

'Policy changes,' she replied.

'Policy changes? But you're a healthcare worker,' I said. 'You can see my mouth is a mess.'

'That's out of my hands,' she dismissed me. 'The best I can do is try to get you an appointment to see an orthodontist here in Port Moresby.'

At that point, any help was welcome: I just wanted relief for my deteriorating mouth. Since I wasn't a PNG citizen, though, we had to climb through a series of administrative hoops to get an appointment. The IHMS nurse could not find an orthodontist who'd see me, but she eventually arranged an appointment with a local Papua New Guinean dentist.

His advice? 'You really need to see an orthodontist.' When the nurse explained that wasn't possible, he referred me to see another dentist two days later. Although not an orthodontist either, the new guy was said to have some expertise with braces.

I woke particularly early the next day to see a clear blue sky through the security mesh on the window. It was 29 July and I was overcome by a wave of anticipation and yearning, mixed with bittersweet memories of the past. I wrote about it in my journal.

'After breakfast, through the window between the blinds, the way the sun's rays penetrate is mesmerising. I know from my instinct that today is going to be Eid. How amazing is it that this sun ray could still look and feel exactly the same as when we were young, when we were free outside?'

I doodled a picture of Shahed and me standing in the bright daylight. Still, it was only a hunch because Eid is determined not by the sun but the sighting of the moon. I spent the rest of that day cooped up in the little room longing for some kind of rebirth. What

I wouldn't have given to take a long shower and put on an outfit that had at least been washed, and be with my brother again.

With more hope than good sense, I asked the guard if I could have something sweet that day, instead of the ordinary bland noodles.

'Sorry, mate, we don't have anything like that,' he said.

Around four in the afternoon, I caught an ABC TV news bulletin from Australia that showed Muslims celebrating Eid in Sydney. Swept by a wave of sadness, I asked the same guard if I could make a call to my family. He stated that while I was permitted to use the phone, there was a process. I'd have to fill in a written request on the proper form and approval would likely take a week. Meanwhile, the well-fed guards used their cell phones to chat happily with their loved ones about any old thing whenever they liked.

The next day I was escorted into the office of the second dentist in Port Moresby. He was an Australian and he refused to let my platoon of minders into his waiting room. After they were hustled outside to wait, I took a seat in the neat lobby and, for the first time in over a year, experienced something close to normal life. I was unrestrained, unattended and unmonitored; just a regular person waiting to see the dentist. I usually hated waiting in line, but that occasion was something to savour. I could have happily stayed there forever.

When my name was called, the guards again tried to enter the treatment room, but the dentist would have none of it. They had to go. It was another feel-good moment: to be treated like a patient, not a prisoner. The soft-spoken Australian examined my battered mouth and reported that I had lost four metal brackets from my teeth. Broken wire was cutting into my jaw, which had become infected. On top of that, as a dentist he had to duly report that I had developed gingivitis in my gums.

He said he could make some rudimentary repairs that would allow my wounds to heal, but they would require me to stay in Port Moresby for six to nine weeks of regular treatment. Needless to say, the Australian Border Force rejected the idea out of hand, and I was put on the next flight back to Manus Island.

Even from 3000 feet above, I could feel the waves of desperation and sorrow rising from the detention centre. Coming back to land was in some ways more dispiriting than my first arrival. I may have been fearful of the unknown back then, but now I knew exactly what awaited, a place of regimented torment that the Australian expats had fittingly named 'the arsehole of the world'.

One month later, Scott Morrison flew to Cambodia to sign a $40 million deal to resettle refugees from Manus and Nauru. He was photographed in Phnom Penh raising a glass of champagne to toast the new agreement with local officials. The policy was a clear threat to any detainee who happened to be listening in from afar: 'If you don't go home, we'll send you somewhere worse.'

The minister for immigration was tireless when it came to pushing pawns around his regional chessboard of prison camps.

I started to wonder if we would ever be free.

SIXTEEN

'My God, my God, why hast thou forsaken me?'

Psalm 22, The Torah / Old Testament

Countless prayers were recited inside our metal boxes, despite the lack of a place to worship, and the constant meddling of the guards. The majority of detainees were practising believers, from different faiths and manifesting varying degrees of piety. In a typical impromptu religious gathering, you might see Christians from Iran, or Hindus from Sri Lanka, or Muslims from many places.

Some prisoners bowed to Mecca five times a day. Some prayed in groups, others joined in now and then, and still others weren't religious at all.

In the early months I was one of the now-and-then guys. After about a year, though, I stopped bothering with outward displays of religious devotion. I internalised my faith and narrowed my focus onto that one nightly prayer: 'Please, God, let me die before I wake up.'

Returning from Port Moresby was to descend further into the depths of adversity on Manus Island. When I followed up with PNG immigration about when my asylum interview might take place, I was told it had not been rescheduled and it never would. According to the official line, I'd 'refused' to take part in the process – a complete misconstrual of events – and that was the end of that.

Still nervous about being declared a negative, which left me vulnerable to being deported back to Burma, I persisted in pushing for a new date. But after going through all the proper legal channels I only ran into brick walls. The system was designed not to work, only to punish and demoralise.

It succeeded brilliantly. When I looked around the compound, I saw hundreds of intelligent men in the prime of their lives being deliberately trampled. Like me, a lot of guys were in their twenties – a time when we should have been setting the foundations for our later years.

Instead, our futures were being systematically dismantled on the say-so of an Australian political party. I worried that if my twenties were lost in offshore detention, I would become permanently isolated from the world. It would take a heroic effort – maybe an impossible one – to become 'normal' again.

Some people thought suicide was a better option. Although it was a challenge in a place that was under constant surveillance, I saw many detainees try to take their lives. I could relate to their efforts.

My old prayer from the boat came to me more urgently than ever, and with greater regularity. Surely that wasn't asking too much of God? All I wanted was to fade away, to evaporate into the air without drama or consequence.

I'd been a good believer all my life and I'd tried hard to keep the holy laws. Now I was in immense pain and there was no escape. Why did I have to wake up again and again just to suffer for another day? If ever there was a time for God's mercy, it was upon hearing my nightly plea. But every day I'd open my eyes again to face the heat, filth and protracted sorrow of Manus Island.

At first I was disappointed my prayers went unanswered. Then gutted. As the months dragged into a second year I grew frustrated with God. 'Why do you want me to suffer?' I asked. 'Why won't you let me die?' In the face of his silence and insouciance, I began to wonder whether God himself was dead. Eventually, I questioned whether he'd ever existed at all.

Still, I maintained an admiration of those for whom the terrors of this place had brought on a stronger religious conviction. Paradoxically, my esteem for them grew as my own faith faded. They had it good, in my eyes, a holy justification and rationale for their pain. They prayed often, and drew comfort from their sense of communion, from the shared experience of sorrow, and hope of redemption. Their torture at the hands of the Australians was part of God's plan, and the harder they had it, the more devout they became. They were able to retreat from the pain to a quiet and blessed place.

Others, like me, who were too soft or thoughtful, felt that spiritual certainty erode as the dark days wore on. We may have suffered the most from the exquisite torments of Manus.

I didn't expect to lose my religion. But looking back it seems inevitable: a progression from doubt to doubt, until I went full circle and arrived at a place of certainty, and realised no higher power was looking out for me. I was alone.

Arriving at that conclusion took time, as religion was one of the only consolations I had left in that desolate place. When there was no source of beauty or mercy visible to my eyes, I had to find these things inside or beyond myself. Where else could I turn for comfort if not to the promise of judgement day, when justice would be served and a new life would begin, free of pain?

There were compelling reasons for and against an interventionist deity, and I moved between them, from one side to the other, like someone playing a game of chess against himself (something I actually did, out of boredom, from time to time).

'I must be part of a bigger plan. This is a temporary ordeal,' I'd think one minute. Then the next moment I'd be forced to admit, 'If there's no God, there's no judgement, and if there's no judgement I'm suffering for nothing.'

There were other forces in this exchange that lay deeper than the intellect. Islam was a common faith. It was the religion of my parents, and of those with whom I shared my accommodation and my daily life – men who might be offended by my change of heart, if they were to learn of it. It was a source of strength and contentment for most of the people I had ever known, loved and held dear.

Moving past it was like learning a new language, at the cost of having to forget the old one. From then on, I would be able to understand my parents, but not reply to them, not convincingly. And not just my parents. It was a reluctant letting go of my childhood, of how I understood the world until that point. That world vanished into a terrifying vacuum. An appalling loss, not to be lightly risked.

In the end, I based my view solely on the available facts. All I knew for sure were the things I could see, hear, taste, smell and feel – the tangibles of my wretched existence in detention. There was not a thread of evidence for God among them. If there had been, I'd have grabbed it with both hands. Instead, all I had was the life I was living. It was awful and it was not going to get any better.

Suicide was prohibited in Islam, and my dwindling faith had been the only reason I hadn't tried to kill myself already. Now that I'd thrown off the fear of God and the threat of damnation, I was free to seek my own way. I had lost all authority over my own life: that claim had been assumed by the Australian government and sold to corporations who destroyed us to reward shareholders. There was no glint of hope in the darkness. To wake up in the morning was to sign up for another day of anguish.

As calamitous as that loss was, losing God had a bright side. With him out of the picture, I had regained autonomy over my own soul. I had the power to make the biggest decision out there, whether to live or to die. I could choose to stay, or I could attempt to escape.

I chose escape.

The relief of this moment of clarity was instant and powerful, to the point of euphoria. Living was the hard part. Suicide was relatively easy. Death was the welcome remedy to the agony of existence. I was overwhelmed with a supercharged sense of freedom – inner freedom – and self-determination. After that moment, there was no turning back.

I wondered whether I should call my mother and Shahed one last time, just to hear their voices, but I decided against it. The situation had deteriorated to a point where there was no hope of pasting over the horrors of the end with touching words of goodbye. Besides, I had lost the will to make peace with anyone. All I cared about was the promise of my own coming mortality.

Others had begun their own love affair with easeful death, and our keepers knew it. The elaborate measures put in place to prevent suicide at the detention centre were evidence of that. Security cameras covered almost every angle, sharp implements were contraband, and hanging points were sealed behind metal screens. Hoffman knives, effective at cutting the noose of someone attempting to hang himself, had become a standard part of the guards' kit. Then there were the natural impediments: with a population of over 1300 crammed into one small area, you were never truly alone.

Still, we tried. Apart from attempting to smash in your own skull, the most obvious option was to climb to the highest place you could find and throw yourself off. Even then there were preventative measures in place. Mattresses were positioned on the ground next to the shipping containers where others had jumped.

I was determined not to make that mistake: the last place on earth you wanted to be badly injured was in the detention centre. From what I could tell, from the roof of MA2 – a good five metres off the ground – I could dive head first into a square cement base that supported an adjacent steel lighting tower. From the point of view of basic physics, it gave me the best chance of a broken neck and fatal head injury.

It was dark when I climbed up onto the corrugated steel roof of MA2. From this vantage point, the night walkers of the detention centre looked even more like automatons, crossing back and forth and in every direction under the white floodlights.

On the other side was the beach and the sea, remarkably close: the ocean rolled right up to the perimeter fence. A wide open expanse, as grand as any vista, and yet our eyes were trained inward, on the next danger, the next indignity.

The air was fresh, touched by the saltwater and the jungle, and free of the noxious scents and sadness that we breathed like oxygen in the depths of the detention centre. The vast darkness of the sky was pressing down on my head and slight frame, and yet for the first time in many months I felt larger than myself, connected to the larger world, at least in spirit. Hope returned, and the optimism that was once such an unquestioned part of who I was. It was a sweet, warm breeze that may have come straight from childhood.

Peering over the edge, I found my target in the concrete cube below. I took a few deep breaths and leapt out into the soft Manus air.

Except I hadn't considered the physical mechanics involved. To reach the concrete light support, I had to jump forward, without enough of a runway to properly send myself aloft. And I didn't realise leaping in such a manner – straight ahead – causes you to fall on your legs, no matter how hard you try to pivot in the air to land on your head.

As it happened, my left side smashed into the concrete box at the same time as my skull slammed onto the metal light pole. The terrible noise of the impact brought guys running outside from the lower container of MA1. They found me – somehow still conscious – in a heap on the ground.

'Fuck!' I berated myself as pain raced across my body. 'You didn't even succeed in knocking yourself out!'

Each beat of my heart inflated my head with unbearable pressure. My ears boomed with the sound of an echoing bell that thankfully receded as my vision went black.

When I came to, I was in a bed in the little clinic inside the detention centre. It could have been the same day as my failed suicidal plunge, or a month later – I had no idea how long I was out for.

The doctor surveyed the damage. I'd shattered my left rib cage, suffered a major concussion and had multiple sprains and abrasions. For me, the worst news of all was that I was still alive.

The next two weeks saw me shuttled between nearby 'assisted accommodation' – i.e. lock-up – and medical appointments at the clinic. After an initial crop of powerful painkillers, doctors prescribed the antidepressant Escitalopram, and demanded that I see a therapist.

The first psychiatrist I met was a bookish Australian woman who worked for the International Health and Medical Services. She opened the conversation with: 'So, what was going through your mind?'

This was a line of questioning more appropriate for a psychiatrist's office than where we were now. There was no couch or neatly framed ink blots on the wall. We were in a bare room, sitting on metal chairs, next to a metal table that was bolted to the wall.

'Hmmmm . . . that's a tough one,' I wanted to reply. 'Perhaps I was hoping for a spot on the national gymnastics team.'

'Everything you tell me here stays in this room,' she continued.

'Yeah, right,' I thought, looking at her white nurse's uniform, with its IHMS logo. I would have had more respect for a person in her position if I had not seen the capricious ways such honours and status could be granted in the detention system. There was one guy working in the centre, a Papu, who during my time there had been promoted from janitor to Wilson guard, and finally an IHMS nurse, presumably as qualified as the one interviewing me now.

'So, would you like to tell me what led you to do this to yourself?'

It was like asking someone who'd had a hand cut off, 'Is there a problem? Why are you screaming?'

On Manus Island I developed a preference for physical pain over the mental kind. I would happily accept punches to the mouth rather than sit through the abuse of heart and soul that was doled out in the centre. Bodily hurt lasted only so long but the mental laceration never stopped. The ache was there when I tried to sleep and there again when I opened my eyes to endure another day in hell.

Many nights, I skipped the break in the middle and wept for eight hours instead.

And it was all by intent. Whether the offshore policy had been cribbed from a torturer's how-to guide, or conjured out of a spirit of original evil, the place had been designed to crush us, and was as cleverly engineered to rob us of our spirits as it was to prevent us from disposing of our own physical bodies.

'Why did you jump off the roof?'

The question was so daft it hardly deserved an answer. After a few more rounds of my answering her script with silence, we both gave up. When I refused to attend any more sessions with my inquisitor, she cut off my medication, giving the lie to the notion that she was there to heal, and not deepen the harm.

Like many others in the detention centre, I had been prescribed sleeping pills. Some people became dependent on sedatives and would do anything to get their hands on them. Unlike cigarettes, guards kept the downers under lock and key.

If you'd been prescribed medication you had to line up daily, wait for your number to be called, and swallow your tablets in front of the guards. They even checked inside our mouths to make sure we'd taken them. I'd become reliant on the Escitalopram and sleeping pills to sleep, so I had no choice but to resume the sessions with the shrink.

My suicidal thoughts continued for a while. The urge would arise involuntarily and remain, mocking me from a distance. The certainty that it was time for me to die was now as much a part of how my mind functioned as the sleeping pills.

Despite the rocky start, I did pick up some helpful tips from the counselling sessions. After the assault on the prison I had started experiencing panic attacks. I'd be randomly struck by terror so intense that I'd choke up and struggle to breathe.

The psychiatrist walked me through how to deal with the episodes by convincing myself the danger wasn't real, but merely a projection of my own fears that triggered a fight-or-flight response.

Once I learned to manage the anxiety, I felt slightly more in control, at least until Manus dealt its next sordid surprise. With my heart and mind still set on dying, I lived in a no man's land between life and death for months.

In the end my release from the twilight world of suicidal intent had little to do with medication and psychiatric intervention – and everything to do with a book.

SEVENTEEN

'Freedom is what you do with what's been done to you.'

Jean-Paul Sartre

I had always loved reading, but there were no books in the detention centre. If you wanted a literary experience you could log onto the internet for half an hour twice a month – hardly enough time to scour a few newspaper articles, let alone lose yourself in a novel.

Detainees were permitted to print five A4 pages every fortnight – nominally for asylum claims and legal proceedings. When the old black-and-white printer was replaced by a colour model, a craze swept the prison that had nothing to do with reading. I couldn't decide whether it was funny or heartbreaking, but people started printing mouth-watering photos of food and sticking them to their walls.

It was common to dream about food in the detention centre. Hours could be spent discussing your favourite dishes in minute detail. 'The first thing I'll eat when I get out . . .' was a fairly normal way to start a chat. While I often thought along these lines, I didn't see the point in adding to my troubles by staring at photos of fine cuisine all day.

Instead, I printed out a grid so I could tick off the days since the start of my incarceration, like an old-time prisoner, and stuck the calendar on the wall next to a poem that I looked to for inspiration. I'd vaguely remembered a few lines from a documentary I'd once seen and looked it up online. 'Invictus' was written by the English poet William Ernest Henley in 1875.

Henley's defiant poem – penned in a moment that should have silenced him with despair – shed its light on me, from afar:

Out of the night that covers me,
Black as the pit from pole to pole,
I thank whatever gods may be
For my unconquerable soul.

In the fell clutch of circumstance
I have not winced nor cried aloud.
Under the bludgeonings of chance
My head is bloody, but unbowed.

Beyond this place of wrath and tears
Looms but the Horror of the shade,
And yet the menace of the years
Finds, and shall find, me unafraid.

It matters not how strait the gate,
How charged with punishments the scroll,
I am the master of my fate:
I am the captain of my soul.

Every line opened up a new path of possibility and understanding. The only area Henley and I diverged was on the matter of tears: he might not have cried aloud but there were times I could hardly stop.

I found myself discussing 'Invictus' with a former Salvation Army worker who'd stayed on after Transfield took over prisoner welfare. We were in fairly deep conversation about the ordeals of being detained when she made a suggestion. 'I've read something you might like. It's called *Man's Search for Meaning*. It's about what you're going through.'

The caseworker couldn't just walk through the gate and hand me a copy. Like sharpened toothbrushes and cell phones, books were contraband at the detention centre. Since she had access to the same computer as me, however, she left an electronic version of the text discreetly on the desktop. I was able to print it off – five pages at a time, twice a month.

To begin with I read each little bundle straight away, but quickly grew frustrated at having to wait two weeks to print off another five pages. I decided to be disciplined and hold out until I'd printed the entire book before I resumed my reading. After all, it wasn't as if I was going anywhere. It took me many months, but I eventually ended up with a large ream of A4 paper containing *Man's Search for Meaning*.

There was an occasional sewing class in the detention centre where we could repair tears in our clothing. I took the loose pages along one day and neatly sewed them into a basic book, using a needle and thread. It may have been the first-ever copy of *Man's Search for Meaning* hand-bound inside a prison.

If so, it would be fitting. Written by the Austrian psychiatrist Viktor Frankl, the book is an account of his experiences as a prisoner in Nazi concentration camps. Frankl managed to survive the Holocaust with his body and spirit intact. Even as he faced cruelty and depravity on a scale that was unprecedented in history, he realised he was ultimately the one in control of his humanity. Not even the Third Reich could take that away.

'When we are no longer able to change a situation,' Frankl wrote, 'we are challenged to change ourselves. Everything can be taken from a man but one thing: the last of the human freedoms – to choose one's attitude in any given set of circumstances, to choose one's own way.'

Reading those words was a revelation. Until that moment, I felt like I had lost control, and that ending my life was the only way to take it back. Writing as a fellow prisoner, the survivor of a genocidal effort that took the lives of millions, Frankl was in a unique position to show me the terrible flaw of this stance.

'It did not really matter what we expected from life,' Frankl observed, 'but rather what life expected from us.'

It was a turning point. While I may not have had agency over the conditions in which I was held, my inner life was still my own. Suffering was ultimately external. Whatever constraints imposed by the guards or the governments of PNG and Australia, they could never touch my soul. The choice of how I responded, or who I wished to be, was still my own to make.

There was no higher power or guide to what it all meant. Meaning itself lay in the hands of the individual. The insight was both strange and powerful, especially coming at a time when I was just losing my faith. With no afterlife awaiting me, and the clock ticking on the current one, I realised that the present – and what I did with it – was all I had left.

Meanwhile, the prison expansion continued. By this point there were penal colonies on Port Moresby and Nauru, with a plan to ship other arrivals to the latter island. As early as 2015, Australia had built a 'transit centre' in Lorengau, for those who succeeded in qualifying as refugees after going through a hearing with PNG immigration – a group that included a number of my fellow detainees.

The only town to speak of on Manus Island, Lorengau was a humble community of just 6000 people – and we lived in fear of every one of them. And now the Australians wanted to push us into their arms.

As work progressed on the lock-up in Lorengau and the upgrading of fortifications on our own nearby detainment centre, the mood among detainees sank further. We had been kept in our tropical cage for more than a year. We had been beaten, shot at, stabbed, maimed, humiliated and degraded to the point of suicide – with no public recognition of our ordeal, or of the conscious efforts to intensify it.

For many, the threat of forced relocations to Lorengau was the last straw. Since vocal demonstrations and even a riot had proved to be of no use, people stopped eating. The hunger strike started small. Guards put the strikers in solitary and refused to let them use the washroom or sleep until they caved and agreed to eat. In response to that tactic, some guys used a needle and thread to sew their lips together.

Before long it became almost morally impossible for the rest of us to line up for meals. By the time I joined the hunger strike in solidarity, three Burmese guys in my inner circle had stitched their lips closed.

A hunger strike has to be the saddest form of protest. You sacrifice your own flesh, blood and bones on the altar of your cause until your body starts to feed on itself. Men were falling like flies. I lasted four days before I collapsed and blacked out, waking upon an army cot on the local football oval, an IV drip inserted into my arm.

'If you don't have something to eat, you are going to have irreversible organ damage,' a nurse from the IHMS warned. 'This is no way to fight for a cause. You're not getting any response from anyone. Nobody is hearing you.'

It was not a very nurse-like thing to say, but it was the truth. Hunger strikes, suicide attempts, a self-harm epidemic – none of these mattered to our tormentors, for whom this nurse was a representative, willing or not.

Recalling Viktor Frankl's time as a living skeleton in Auschwitz, I ate the apple she handed me and was sent back to Mike the next morning.

EIGHTEEN

'One great use of words is to hide our thoughts.'

Voltaire

Discovering the facts was one thing. Doing something about them was another. Any satisfaction we might gain from knowing and uncovering the truth of our condition was poor consolation for the fact that we might end up taking our insights and experiences with us to the grave, as we waited for a fair process, or divine intervention that was never to materialise.

The reality of our condition needed to be shared. But there was much standing in the way of that taking place: a double ring of high fences, a wide-open sea, and a media and government spin machine that filled the atmosphere with its chilling distortions.

This effort to shroud reality in a giant invisibility cloak was familiar to me. Back in Burma, the truth was considered the private domain of the ruling regime. Even the language we used was carefully managed by the junta, who at one point banned the word 'poverty' from the media and official discourse, as it had done with the word 'Rohingya' – and had removed us from the list of ethnic groups acknowledged by the notorious 1982 Citizenship Law.

(The Burmese, and not just the Rohingyas, got around these strictures through a clever linguistic strategy that included using metaphors and reverse talk – using a term to convey its opposite – to make our criticisms known.)

In the Burmese education system, subjects that encouraged any sort of critical thought – like politics, history and the rest of the humanities – simply weren't offered. Instead, the curriculum favoured the sciences, mathematics and technology: practical topics that were governed by clear rules and required logical thinking.

The aim was to keep the population compliant, and it largely worked. There was little liberal-minded resistance to government policies, no matter how wicked or corrupt they happened to be, because our ability to question the status quo had been schooled out of existence. The regime didn't bother with spin. It did not need to sugar-coat the truth, or twist its words to trick the public or control how people thought, because it controlled the words themselves.

It was an approach quite unlike that of the double-dealing Australian politicians, who dressed up the most appalling policies in a lot of virtuous talk of moral and legal principles. 'This democratically elected government' was a phrase often repeated on the news, to defend its latest shady manoeuvre. Whereas any look back at history – at South Africa under apartheid, the US under Jim Crow laws, or Nazi Germany – would show that 'democratically elected' and 'legal' in no way equalled 'right' or 'fair'.

There had been a time when I had considered Australia, as much as I thought about it at all, as a civilised country, with egalitarian principles that gave me hope for the future. Now I knew the Antipodean utopia was a myth. From where I stood, this first-world democracy served up the same shit as back home, just in different colours.

The government spent billions – *billions* – refining its merciless tactics, which were then repackaged and sold to the Australian taxpayer as plain common sense, packaged with a layer of false advertising about the urgent need to secure the borders and save theoretical lives at sea.

Meanwhile, real lives were being destroyed. Refugees were locked up without charge, rebranded as transferees, their names swapped for numbers, as they were dumped in a third country to be terrorised indefinitely. How was that different from what was taking place under other dictatorial regimes?

One difference was capitalism. The press in Australia was dominated by a businessman named Rupert Murdoch who owned more newspapers in the country than anyone else. During my period in detainment, Australia was ranked third in the world for media concentration, behind only China and Egypt.

The xenophobic views of Murdoch, who was a stalwart backer of conservative politics, had a monopoly on the country's airwaves. And the country repaid him generously for his efforts of mass persuasion. Because so many Australians already skewed toward nativism, his monopoly was tolerated. His media empire, built on foundations of hostility and fear, was a money maker for Mr Murdoch and his family.

His power in Australia, as I later learned, surpassed that of the country's leaders, according to those leaders themselves. In a Senate inquiry into media diversity, Kevin Rudd, who was prime minister when I landed on Christmas Island, said even when he was in power he was 'fearful of the Murdoch media beast'. In the same hearing, Malcolm Turnbull, who later succeeded Rudd in the PM's chair, said, 'The most powerful political actor in Australia is not the Liberal Party or the National Party or the Labor Party. It is [Murdoch's] News Corporation.'

The politics of Australia and PNG became a regular topic of my online research. The writing in the news stories was subtle, camouflaged to look like fair and balanced reporting. If you were not on Manus, you would have no idea of its festering inaccuracy.

This was more than a matter of intellectual curiosity. The longer we waited on Manus, the more likely people would die, and the facts of our deaths would be omitted from the public record, as those of the riot had. The erasures would continue in the years to come, as the compounds on Manus would be razed to the ground, for the sake of optics. Gone, as if they had never existed: even as new prisons were being built down the road on East Lorengau, and across the sea in Port Moresby.

Before that could happen, I needed a way to get our stories out there, in the hope that someone might be listening. A cell phone was a good tool both for recording and sharing the evidence, but finding one was not easy. The only possible source was someone outside the detention centre – which would require a bribe. It was pointless talking to any of the Australian guards, who were likely to throw me back into Chauka. Better to try with the Papus. They were markedly poorer than the expats and had more to gain.

My first attempt at breaking into the contraband economy was a comic disappointment. I befriended a cleaner who worked the 3 am shift. It was my habit of going to the washroom at that unholy hour, when the first janitorial rounds had left the facilities a little less disgusting than usual. The toilets, used by hundreds of men, were cleaned only once a day.

This man had a good grasp of English, and I tried to build a rapport across a series of casual early morning encounters. When I eventually pitched him the deal – cigarettes for a cell phone – I was worried he might balk or, worse, report me.

Instead, he reluctantly agreed to the deal, with the proviso that I give him the cigarettes upfront since he did not have enough cash at home to buy a phone outright. This sounded reasonable enough, and I spent the next two months building up a bankroll of tobacco at the canteen.

Once I had handed him the contraband, however, the cleaner stopped showing up for work. He had tricked me at my own game, just when I was starting to think of myself as a smooth operator.

And who could blame him? In the casual economy of Manus Island, cigarettes were a cheap and dirty shadow currency. There wasn't much of a culture or tradition of saving money, of keeping bank accounts or making personal loans. The real wealth was found under the ocean surface. The locals got by on seafood, available on their doorstep every day, all year. As long as they had enough to eat and a place to sleep, that was usually enough.

My next move into the black market ended just as badly. My target this time was a local guard, a position that was a step up from the level of cleaner in the Papu hierarchy of workers. He accepted the offer immediately, asking for twenty-five packets, as if the terms of the deal were clear and well established.

Over the next few months, I hoarded every cigarette I could get my hands on until it was time to do the exchange. When he delivered the phone to my cell block, my hope grew, and it seemed like I could finally forgive myself for my first rookie mistake.

But I'd been so focused on receiving the cell phone, I neglected to specify what kind of device was needed. As it turned out, the one he delivered was a Nokia touch-tone 'dumb phone'. No camera, no data, just the ability to text – slowly and painfully, in the manner of using a rotary dial to spell out a friend's address. I could hardly believe people still used them, let alone sold them new on Manus Island.

The deal was a disaster. Hundreds of cigarettes and months of effort wasted on a gadget that brought me no closer to the outside world. This old brick could not take usable pictures, and offered no internet access or data plan to make international calls. I should have tossed it over the fence during one of my 3 am washroom excursions.

Instead, despite myself, I began to worry about it being discovered. Phones were strictly prohibited in the detention centre. While I considered how to conceal my unwanted treasure, the men around me were gathering their own tools. Terrified of a repeat attack, some men shaped toothbrush handles into shivs, while others had armed themselves with pieces of glass and debris left from the attack. Those discovered with weapons were sent to solitary confinement. I was unlikely to be able to stab anyone with my crappy Nokia. But in this Orwellian experiment, banned technology fell into the same category as deadly weapons.

When I steeled myself to try again, I clarified to the guard that I needed an Android with a good working camera. The problem was

Androids cost a lot more than the primitive Nokias. With no other option, I asked my bunkmate, a Burmese guy named Mohammed, if he wanted to share the cost.

'The only way we can afford an Android is if we combine our cigarette rations,' I explained. 'If we're able to get one, we can share it. You can have it one day and I'll use it the next.'

Mohammed had a wife and daughter back in Burma. 'You wouldn't have to wait two weeks every time you wanted to speak to them,' I urged him. 'You could call your daughter whenever you liked.'

This time our efforts paid off, and we became the owners of a bright blue Alcatel Pixi, an Android phone, complete with a charger. We had to keep the cigarettes coming, however, if we wanted to top up the prepaid sim card.

The Android worked well – but my brain didn't. After more than a year of lockdown trauma and incarceration, I'd forgotten how to operate a smartphone of any kind.

Mohammed remembered. He made his first call home, and when that worked, lent it to another of the Burmese guys to do the same. During these calls, one of us would wait at the door and watch the corridor. When a guard appeared, we would bang on the wall or shout 'bull' in Burmese, a slang term for people with plenty of muscles but little in the way of brains.

After a few close calls, I decided the bright blue cover had to go. A black phone would be hard enough to conceal, but keeping one with such a lurid case was asking for trouble. I managed to remove the plastic shell – a tricky manoeuvre without any tools – but Mohammed was displeased by the partial destruction of our shared property.

I hadn't told him the reason I wanted a cell phone was to secretly record the conditions inside the detention centre. Having a contraband device to make calls to family was one thing; using one to document human rights abuses was a risk on another level altogether.

When it was my turn with the phone, I'd wrap it in a cloth and hide it inside my shirt with the tiny camera lens exposed. Over the course of a few days, I roamed around Mike – my hands shaking with adrenaline – as I tried to document the living conditions, the tainted food, the open sewers that served as toilets, and the daily abuse.

Unfortunately, the phone would automatically shut down after about five minutes. Each time I stuffed it in my shirt, a proximity sensor was triggered, telling my phone it was actually in my pocket, and putting the device to sleep. If I wanted to take a picture or video, I had to fidget around inside my shirt to bring it to life again: a quick way to get caught. It was soon clear the thing was less than stellar as a surveillance device.

My calls to my family had slowed down lately. All my mother knew was that I had made it to Australia and was waiting for my claim to be processed. This was a lie I'd told her when I was on Christmas Island, and now that I was on Manus it was too late and too damaging to share the truth.

This was a common tragedy on the island. Many detainees were leading imaginary lives in Australia, for the benefit and comfort of their families back home. They took pictures that were carefully framed and cropped to avoid the fencing and prison tents in the background, or the hundreds of others sharing their space. We all had loved ones who needed to be shielded from further pain.

Even with a phone of my own, I was reluctant to speak to anyone from home. Rather than let the device go to waste, I used it to tap into Facebook Messenger. That way, I was able to connect with Abul, my old partner in crime during the escape from the hotel prison in Kendari.

He'd eventually made it to Christmas Island. But because Abul was married to a woman who was already being held in the immigration system in Darwin, he was spared the depredations of Manus. He was instead permitted to join his wife in detention on the Australian mainland.

Inmates in Darwin had less restricted access to computers than we did on Manus. Through Messenger, we compared notes on our condition, the parallel universes that Australia had placed us in, each with its unique afflictions. Abul said he knew conditions were many times more oppressive on Manus than in Darwin, and he'd heard about the attack and the death of Reza Barati, which had been big news in Australia, even if the facts had been reversed in a smear campaign of blame the victim.

Unexpectedly, perhaps, sharing his experience of internment with someone – in his case, his wife – made things harder for him.

'If you're a single person, you can suck it up and get on with it,' he said. 'But being in jail with family, with a person you love, you are a constant reminder to one another of how much you're hurting.'

In other ways, he had it better than me. Being on Australian soil, he had access to advocates and others who helped manage the legal affairs and claims for asylum of refugees.

'We have an excellent woman helping us,' Abul said. 'She lives here in Darwin. Her name is Tessa.'

Hearing the name Tessa, I just as quickly forgot it and returned to the misfortune of life in Mike compound, unaware of the transformative role this woman would play in the next chapter of my life.

Mohammed and I weren't the only ones who'd managed to get their hands on a cell phone. I heard rumours that there were four or five contraband handsets stuffed into hiding spots around the detention centre. I had also learned that the guards had caught on and wanted to confiscate them.

We had to act quickly. Keeping the phone in our rooms was not an option, as they were checked constantly. We scrutinised the toilets for possibilities, and then the sinks and garbage bins, as if we were connoisseurs of dreck. None of these hiding places measured up. The prison was a closed system, structured to leave no open ends or secret spaces. The only option was the one provided by the natural environment: we decided to bury the phone in the dirt at the edge of the compound.

When night fell, I wrapped it in plastic, dug a hole in a shadowy corner, beyond the full glare of the floodlights, and placed the buried treasure within. Retrieving it was as much a risk as putting it there in the first place. When I returned a few nights later, I found the handset no longer worked.

Moisture was the culprit, I assumed: we were close to the shore and just a few feet above sea level. I removed the battery and tried to air out the main circuit, but still the device wouldn't switch on. I even placed it in the midst of sachets of coffee, hoping they would suck out the moisture, but nothing worked.

The heat of the sun might help. Since I could hardly leave the device out in broad daylight, for anyone to see, I waited. When night-fall came, I shimmied up the side of MA2, high enough to slide the phone onto the roof. I knew this location well from my earlier leap into the unknown.

But when I climbed back to the same spot the following evening: disappointment. Our bootleg prize – valued at 800 cigarettes – was now a broken toy.

The following day I was called out by my number and marched to a small building outside the prison fence. Two expat guards sat me down and one started firing questions.

'Do you have anything you're not supposed to have?' he asked.

'Uh, no,' I said, playing dumb.

'If you have any prohibited material, now is the time to tell us,' he said.

'Well, no I don't,' I repeated. Maybe he had watched too many murder investigations on television: for some reason, he wouldn't mention the object by name.

'So you have nothing to report?' he persisted. 'Have you smuggled anything into the centre?'

This felt like a fishing exercise. Since there were at least four or five phones in circulation, I may not have been a suspect at all. In any event, the guards abruptly wrapped up their interrogation and escorted me back into the prison.

I was born a decade after the ruling military junta stripped citizenship from the Rohingyas and introduced increasingly draconian controls on our movements. Here I'm around a year old and learning to walk.

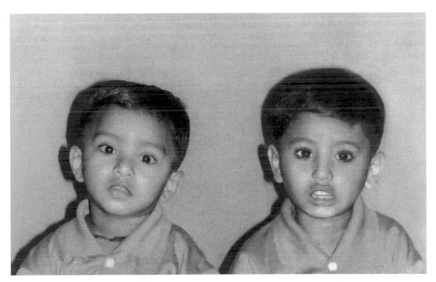

I'm about four in this photo and my brother, Shahed, is two. The two of us developed our own language, which conveyed as much through silences as words.

A still from a video taken onboard *Emelle*, the converted fishing boat I boarded in July 2013 to take me from Indonesia to Christmas Island (I was perched on the right-hand side of the wheelhouse, out of shot). Unable to swim, I was terrified of drowning.

In detention on Manus Island. My tropical prison uniform included a bright yellow t-shirt, which was designed to be easily spotted in the darkness.

A member of the Royal Papuan Constabulary on guard at the main entrance to the Royal Australian Navy War Criminal Compound in 1948.

Quonset huts from the World War II era were still being used to house detainees on Manus. This particular hut was used for various purposes: classroom, gym, common room and sleeping quarters. I briefly stayed in an identical quonset next door.

The sheds and modified shipping containers where we stayed. Note the makeshift window coverings, intended to provide shade and take the edge off the oppressive heat.

While most of the time our eyes were trained on the interior of the open-air prison, there was a sweeping view through the fence; a wild world of nature that lay just beyond reach.

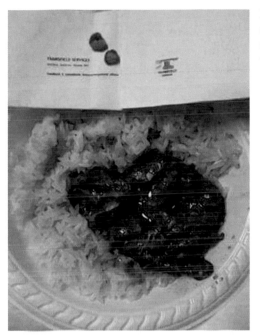

Detainees were used to finding stones and other debris in their food. On this day, dinner was laced with human teeth.

I tore the photo off my identity card because I couldn't bear to see my face on a dehumanising dog tag. I was eventually given a replacement.

This was my cell – a dark, hot, depressing steel box that was home for more than three years.

The view from my cell in Mike compound. The Papu dwellings were on the other side of the fence, just a stone's throw away – literally. During the attack on the prison, local civilians and G4S Papus threw rocks at detainees thinking we were terrorists, and we used mattresses as shields from the incoming barrage. The stones were followed by gunfire.

I was sitting with my back against this locker during the attack when a bullet was fired from outside the wire. Had I been standing rather than sitting, it would have hit me in the chest.

Prisoners put flowers on the fence next to a bullet hole.

The detention centre at night. The prison looked and felt like the scene of a horror movie about a perverse site for human experimentation; a floodlit laboratory in the middle of nowhere.

A detail from Mike compound, where I stayed the longest. At the bottom of the camera/light tower in the centre is a concrete base similar to the one I landed on after jumping off the roof.

The constant expansion of the prison was painful for us to witness, since it confirmed that the moment we were to be granted freedom would be denied indefinitely.

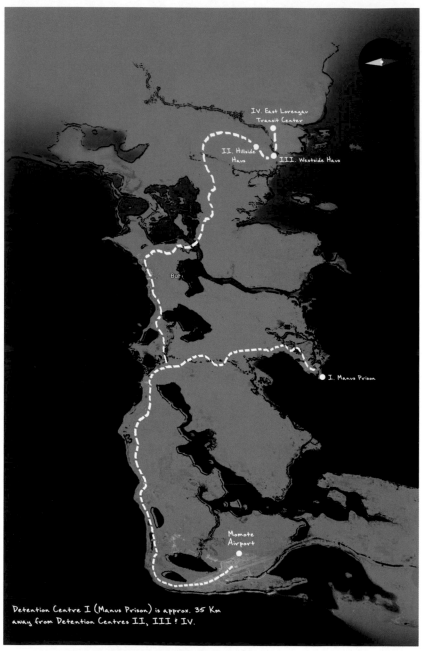

IV. East Lorengau
Transit Center

II. Hillside
Haus

III. Westside Haus

Buf

I. Manus Prison

Momote
Airport

Detention Centre I (Manus Prison) is approx. 35 Km
away from Detention Centres II, III & IV.

The original detention centre was expanded and then followed by the construction of three more prisons, spread across the narrow tip of Manus Island.

The four compounds of the main detention centre. The original, Delta (far left) and Foxtrot (in the centre), were followed by Oscar (next to Delta), where I first stayed, and Mike (far right). My shipping container, MA2-09, was at the edge of Mike (near the palms at the bottom corner).

After four years of imprisonment and torture, I spent some of my first days of liberty walking near the ocean in Port Moresby. Although finally free, I was a fugitive and found it unsettling to be in public because nobody was watching me.

I boarded a canoe and travelled across the Solomon Sea to the jungle outpost of Choiseul Bay.

The third of six planes I used to escape from Australia's so-called Pacific Solution: a Solomon Airlines turbo-prop, ready to take off from the grass airstrip in Choiseul Bay.

A rainy view of the aeroplane I took from Fiji to Hong Kong. Because of a gate change, I almost missed my flight, which would have been a disaster.

Time	Flight	Destination	Gate	Status
16:20	CX 542 / JL 7002	Tokyo/HND	15	
16:20	CX 840 / AA 8925	New York/JFK	49	
16:25	CI 679	Jakarta		Est 17:00
16:25	CX 532 / JL 7038	Nagoya	30	
16:25	HX 528	Hanoi	213	
16:30	AC 016	Toronto		Est 22:40
16:30	KA 974 / CX 5974	Beijing	508	
16:35	CX 502 / JL 7056	Osaka/Kansai	1	
16:35	CX 882 / LA 5634	Los Angeles	4	
16:35	UO 558	Da Nang	217	
16:40	CX 416	Seoul/ICN	43	
16:40	CX 448	Taipei	71	
16:40	HX 282	Taipei	212	
16:40	KA 454	Kaohsiung	510	
16:45	CX 703 / PG 4562	Bangkok	66	
16:45	UO 753	Chiang Mai	211	
16:50	CX 799 / AC 9796	Ho Chi Minh	64	
16:50	ZH 9096	Wuxi	214	
16:55	CX 731	Dubai	47	

A six-hour flight delay in Hong Kong put me – and Air Canada – under pressure. With time ticking down fast to Christmas Eve, the cabin crew let me on the plane but kept my passport. I took this picture at the time the first delay was announced.

I bought the thickest jacket I could find at Hong Kong's Chek Lap Kok Airport in preparation to face the full force of the Canadian winter, not to mention its immigration officers. An hour or so after I took this changing room photo I was airborne.

ZONE 5

Cabin/Cabine
Y

Flight/Vol

AC 016
TORONTO
Seat/Place

22J MIDDLE/CENTRE
Remarks/Observations

AIR CANADA

A STAR ALLIANCE MEMBER
MEMBRE DU RÉSEAU STAR ALL...

My final ticket to freedom: a stub of the boarding pass that took me from Hong Kong to Toronto, where I faced even odds of being accepted or sent back.

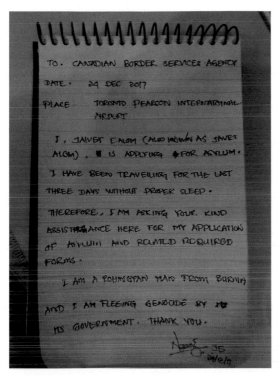

TO. CANADIAN BORDER SERVICES AGENCY

DATE. 24 DEC 2017

PLACE. TORONTO PEARSON INTERNATIONAL
AIRPORT

I, JAIVET EALOM (ALSO KNOWN AS JAVET
ALOM), IS APPLYING FOR ASYLUM.
I HAVE BEEN TRAVELLING FOR THE LAST
THREE DAYS WITHOUT PROPER SLEEP.

THEREFORE, I AM ASKING YOUR. KIND
ASSISTANCE HERE FOR MY APPLICATION
OF ASYLUM AND RELATED REQUIRED
FORMS.

I AM A ROHINGYAN MAN FROM BURMA
AND I AM FLEEING GENOCIDE BY
ITS GOVERNMENT. THANK YOU.

Having learned from experience with Australian immigration, I knew I needed to make a claim for asylum in writing. I scrawled this note during my trans-Pacific flight and took a picture under dim cabin lighting, to later send to my helpers as legal insurance.

In the main library at the University of Toronto. After all the horrors that went before, I finally found myself in a place I'd yearned to be all along – lost among books in a house of learning. PHOTOGRAPH COURTESY OF COLE BURSTON (www.coleburston.com)

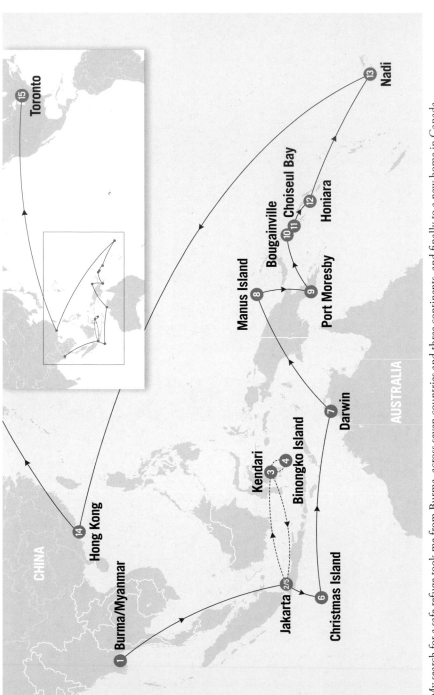

My search for a safe refuge took me from Burma, across seven countries and three continents, and finally to a new home in Canada.

Instead of returning me to Mike, however, I was taken to an administration office in Echo compound and made to sit in front of an oversized Australian officer. He was the guards' supervisor.

'We saw you on surveillance camera,' he said. 'Stop pretending. How did you get it?' Before I had a chance to reply, it was on to the next query. 'What did you use it for?' he pressed.

After a few more abrupt queries, I opened my mouth. 'I just wanted to be able to contact my family, because half the time, the calls here don't go through. Also, I know you're listening in on every conversation.'

'You know it's illegal to have a personal phone inside the processing centre? By bringing in a contraband object, you are putting everyone's life in danger.'

I nodded in agreement, imagining a scenario where my water-logged, inactive device attacked me in my sleep, or chased my fellow prisoners around the yard.

'You have to hand it over,' he continued.

'It's not even working.'

'I don't care,' he said. 'You're going to give me that phone.'

A spark of protest flared in my chest, bringing with it a scalding indignation. Who was he to tell me what I could or could not do, or what I could own, or have on my person? Who were these hyped-up security guards to lord it over us in this way?

Aside from the larger questions about rights and freedoms, there were the basic legalities. We were standing on the territory of Papua New Guinea. This man was Australian. He was as much a visitor as I was, and should check his claims accordingly.

He had no jurisdiction over this place, or over me. The fact that the other detainees and I had been taken here and held by a group of armed goons who had no proper business being in the country – how was that any different from a run-of-the-mill kidnapping?

Anyway, if I caved and handed over what he wanted, I would likely be sent straight to Chauka for a long stretch in solitary.

'I'm not going to give you anything.'

Fifteen minutes later, the guards pulled our cell apart. All our meagre possessions were tossed into the corridor. They found my phone secured to the bed frame with an elastic band. My second stint in solitary was coming after all.

During the long walk to Chauka, my heart was pounding, but there was a smile on my face. After all, they had not found the phone charger, which I'd hidden inside one of the hollow posts of the bunk bed.

A small victory that suggested a further advantage to come. My next phone, I promised myself, would never be found.

NINETEEN

'Friendship is born at that moment when one person says to another:
"What! You too? I thought I was the only one!"'

C. S. Lewis

Time was elastic on Manus Island. It twisted and elongated according to the state of sadness or physical pain you were in. It was easy to get lost amid the days when the absence of a clock was filled by the slow-dripping poison of indefinite captivity.

Ultimately, even the calendar I'd stuck to my wall proved a worthless tool for measuring time. It reduced years of anguish to neat lines and scribbled numbers on a page. But it wore out its purpose. When the days I'd marked off passed 600, I tore it down and threw it away. I had stopped writing in my journal too, though I managed to keep it (and still have it today).

Soon I charted my passage through time and space the way a bee does. I'd once read how they navigate, not by registering time and direction but by recording the obstacles they pass. Like a bee, I may not have known exactly where I was heading, but I knew how far I had come by looking at the wasted days piled up behind me.

Ironically the clockwork routines on Manus distorted time too. Years of lining up for food three times a day had homogenised existence to a point that each hour merged with the next. We were stuck in a continuous moment: a line that rotated in a pointless circle, with no terminus point.

Not even the seasons changed at our little dot in the Bismarck Sea. We couldn't say, 'Winter is coming,' or wait for spring. All year round, depending on nature's inclination, it was either hot and dry, or hot and very wet, the air choked with heavy rain.

Other prison routines were as dreary and unpleasant as the never-ending hot season. Twice a week, a contractor wearing a gas mask roamed the compounds with a noisy petrol-driven machine that blew plumes of white mist into the air. Our jailers called it 'fogging', but it was a large-scale fumigation operation aimed at keeping the bugs and mosquitoes, and therefore malaria, under control. It drove the locals – living just beyond the fence – mad.

The cloudy vapour was pumped into every corner of the prison: along fence lines, under buildings, out in the yards, and even inside the detention blocks. The insect population of the Manusian jungle was prolific, and after each dusting the ground was carpeted with thousands of tiny winged corpses. That was the power of DDT, a toxic pesticide banned in Australia since 1987, in the wake of the global outrage generated by the book *Silent Spring*, but apparently quite appropriate for our living quarters.

My background in industrial chemistry had given me a nose for the faint whiff of the killer chemical. One day I asked the Australian contractor why he used it, considering it had been outlawed by many countries for decades.

'There's no legal restriction on DDT in Papua New Guinea!' he replied chirpily. 'It's cheap and it works, so that's why we use it.'

Quite easily said with an industrial-grade breathing apparatus hanging around your neck. Every time I heard the man with the motorised blower approach, I'd run to get upwind of the airborne bug-poison. Plenty of detainees just ignored him, though, and breathed the stuff in. It will be worth watching to see if there turns out to be a cluster of medical disorders among Manus survivors from the intense and prolonged exposure to the toxin.

If you managed to avoid those fumes, there was no escaping the cigarette smoke. If smokers made up 15 or 20 per cent of the population outside of Manus, it was more like 50 per cent inside. People of all ages who had never even looked at a cigarette before became addicted to state-supplied tobacco.

Passive smoking was a serious problem: we lived in such cramped conditions there was no avoiding the poisonous miasma. Two of my cellmates were smokers, and although they usually indulged in the corridor, their blue-grey exhaust lingered on the air in a semi-permanent haze.

While cigarettes were the dollar bills of our black economy, some other gilded vice would have attained their purchasing power if given the chance. Chilli and sugar, for example, were eagerly traded for smokes: there might easily be a black market built around making the food taste slightly less disgusting. As it was, stockpiling cigarettes remained the way to buy a cell phone.

Which meant I stockpiled them too. Yet collecting enough smokes to buy another phone would take more months than I had the patience for. I needed a device of my own, and I needed it soon. Unwilling to wait, I borrowed from Zakaria on the promise I'd pay him back and let him use it to make calls in emergencies.

'You don't have to pay me anything. We are family.'

After greasing the palm of a tobacco-loving Papu, I got my hands on a decent quality Huawei with internet capabilities. By then, even more detainees had sourced their own cell phones – and the guards hated it. We kept a watchful eye on the corridors for the next raid, where our cells would be searched, one by one. When one room was checked, we would spread the word on Telegram, the encrypted messaging service, so the rest of us could start the hiding process.

Our success gave us a feeling of strength in numbers. After all, they couldn't fit 100 guys into Chauka at once. We used to joke that if we all did the abnormal at the same time, the abnormal would become the norm. Our sly stockpiling of phones showed there was some truth to it.

The arms race tightened. The guards would come any time, usually in the middle of the night. They would tear the rooms apart, pulling sheets off beds, and mattresses from bed frames. They left their muddy footprints on the floor where many of us slept to avoid the worst of the heat.

There were serious consequences for breaking the rules. One of my neighbours in the shipping container, a man from Iran whose toughness I admired, tried to hide his phone on his body during a raid, and was thrown to the floor, his arm twisted behind his back.

A few weeks later, he was summoned to court. Child pornography had supposedly been discovered on his cell phone, still held as contraband in Wilson storage. I accompanied him to court, along with a number of other men from our cell block, who were eager to bear witness to what had taken place. My English came in handy, and I helped make the case that the evidence had likely been planted by the Wilson guards. (One important, if unstated, point in his favour was that the pornographic images were a complete mismatch with his sexual tastes – and orientation.)

The guards didn't bother to show up and the judge threw out the charges.

As the devices proliferated, so did the places we found to stash them. Burying the Alcatel Pixi in the dirt, as I had done, was a rookie mistake. Guys placed phones in the ceiling, in the mesh screen that protected the fire alarm, and in bedposts and holes cut into mattresses. When all these places were discovered, they found new spots, like under the lockers in the hall, or in the gap between the storage containers.

Each time a new cubby hole was revealed, the guards would make note of it and go for that place in their next raid. They also shared the information with guards in the other compounds. For that reason, hiding spots became precious commodities. You did not tell others about yours, because if they copied it, and theirs were discovered, yours would be exposed as well.

It was generous, therefore, for Amir, my friend in MA2-11, to bring me in on a secret. In an act of ingenuity to rival that of a character from *Prison Break*, he had carefully removed a blade from one of the cheap plastic razors we were given to shave. You were only allowed a new razor if you turned in your old one, so taking out one of the two blades without obviously disfiguring the plastic took some work.

Using a lighter, he cooked the blade until it was hot enough to melt plastic, and inserted it into the side of a pen. And just like that, he had a cutting device.

The walls of our room were coated in a white veneer, with a layer of Styrofoam between the vinyl and the metal of the shipping container. Using his new tool, Amir carved a phone-sized hole in his wall, placed a poster (one of the ubiquitous food pictures) on top, and, like that, had a safe place to keep his phone. And then he did the same for me, using a portrait of biryani to hide the crime.

We kept the breakthrough to ourselves – and because of that, our phones were never confiscated.

The ban on cell phones in the detention centre made little sense outside the usual attempts to make our living conditions deplorable. The guards had the situation reversed. It was the phones that were ours by right, and the detention centre and its rules that lacked any legal foundation.

The clampdown was part of the larger effort by the Australian government to hide what it was doing on Manus Island, even as it tried to spread the news of our misery to other potential asylum seekers. That was a word-of-mouth campaign in which we were the unwilling agents, sharing our tales of woe in monitored conversations with friends and family.

That strategy fell apart if we were to build lines of communication with members of the wider public, and especially if we were to share actual pictures and videos of our lives in detention. Who could say where the evidence might end up?

*

Soon I had more to worry about than keeping my phone safe from harm. There was a new danger, which put a focus on my own survival.

Lately, as arbitrary and pointless as it seemed, the PNG immigration process had begun to show its teeth. Whenever a detainee was deemed a non-refugee, three or four PNG immigration officers would enter the compound with eight to ten guards to hand deliver the bad news in writing in accordance with PNG law. Knowing my time was coming, I would hide in another cell during their visits.

This was a legal trap that required a legal response. Around this time, a not-for-profit group in Australia had started collecting donations to top up the phones of refugees on Manus and Nauru, allowing them to communicate with social justice workers outside the wire.

One of my first calls on my new phone was to Tessa, the advocate who was helping Abul and his wife on the mainland. Tessa happened to be a migration agent, working for the authorities, as well as – ironically enough – being a member of the Darwin Asylum Seeker Support and Advocacy Network, one of the stronger refugee support networks out there. Our first conversation was friendly, with a touch of playing it safe on both sides.

'Hi,' I wrote.

'Hi friend!'

'I am Abul's friend, from Manus.'

'Yes, Abul told me. How are you?'

'Not too bad, surviving . . .'

'How is Manus?'

'Ahh . . . beyond words can express.'

From there, the friendship took off. As it turned out, I had found a kindred spirit in Tessa, who was all business, no bullshit, even as her honesty was driven by the strongest humanitarian instincts. Her approach was based on facts, logic, data, action and transparency – all things I valued too. The last thing I needed was someone to hold my hand and tell me how unfair things were. Or even more futile, to tell me that they weren't that bad. I needed a Tessa.

We got to know each other, during our long conversations. She had studied, remarkably enough, in China in the wake of Mao's cultural revolution, and saw the atrocities of that period first-hand. On a more familial note, she had a son about my age, who loved to play chess. This came up when I mentioned the rather ridiculous fact that I liked to pass the time by playing chess by myself, jumping from one side of the board to the other.

She took it in her stride. 'My son loves chess. He's also a lone wolf.'

It was the first time I heard that phrase, lone wolf, and after an initial twinge of resistance, I realised it was not a bad description after all. Sometimes it took a stranger to point out an aspect of yourself that was in plain sight the whole time.

Our camaraderie deepened despite the curious fact that we never actually spoke, just texted. If using a contraband phone was a risk, using one to talk to an advocate was perilous. It was much safer, as well as cheaper, to pull your blanket over your head and silently chat on Messenger. I mentally conjured a female voice to narrate the words Tessa typed to me.

Later I found out my impersonation was off the mark. The neutral tones I had been hearing in my head were replaced by a full-on Australian accent, which I usually associated with prison guards, rather than with a woman who would become one of my most essential friends and supporters.

Our early chats involved letting Tessa know exactly what was happening on Manus Island: the living conditions, the type of medical and psychological help available, and how the process of granting asylum was playing out. She became a confidante and my most trusted ally outside the detention centre.

She was the one to tell me about an official enquiry into abuses on Manus and Nauru, being conducted by a committee in the Australian parliament. Through texts to Tessa, I submitted seventeen pages of evidence, a detailed account of daily injustice. While I disclosed my identity only to the Senate's Legal and Constitutional Affairs Committee, I had little trust in any governmental body by this point, and feared the repercussions if my identity were to become known.

I did it in part due to my trust in Tessa. Ultimately, as far as I could tell, the committee's findings were ignored, if they were even released to the public in the first place. Still, at least the evidence was out there somewhere. It would not die with us. And it took away any excuse that the Australians simply did not or could not know what was happening.

Tessa provided a vital link, a live transfer of information between our remote tropical outpost and the sky-high echo chamber around the Australian mainland. Still, there was only so much she could do and know about, being on the mainland herself.

For that, I had two other amazing female allies based on Manus. Nina and Winiaka worked for Playfair, a company contracted to help detainees through the legal and bureaucratic requirements of PNG immigration, which seemed to take a perverse pleasure in throwing hoops into the air and watching us leap through them.

One morning, after a few cursory text exchanges, I was surprised when Nina showed up at MA2 to talk to me in person: the first proper outside visitor to my metal container abode. This was too easy. Normally you saw a lawyer after receiving an appointment slip, followed by a visit during office hours to Echo Block, the nerve centre of the centre. The visits were often unpleasant, as one of the requirements to enter Echo Block involved submitting to four body searches in a row.

Dressed as if she were going to a Saturday brunch in the city, rather than to my grubby cell, Nina had a gentle and elegant presence, and took a personal interest in my well-being. I had met a few lawyers before Nina, but she was the first to visit me, on my own ground, with no cavity search needed. Although she was comparatively young, I was struck by her quick grasp of our untenable condition. She explained the ins and outs of PNG immigration as it applied to detention, and how the processing of the paperwork and legal claims worked.

By visits three and four, Nina was bringing me contraband soup and probiotic capsules, hidden in stacks of paperwork, and asking after my mother. She clearly believed a person like me, slightly built and studious by nature, did not have a chance of lasting in this place. I knew this because she said as much, as the days went by and we got to know each other better.

In addition to the food and pills, she smuggled in pieces of intelligence, secrets that were risky for her to share, given her position as a semi-employee of the state. One of our private conversations was about a man she knew, an official in PNG immigration, who had flipped a decision on a man's asylum claim from positive to negative simply because he felt like it. A devilish move, by one who would play God.

Other officials were turning negative decisions on asylum into positive ones, if people agreed to leave the centre to live in the new settlement in Lorengau. It was a trading of favours, made for political expediency, that made a mockery of the concept and definition of legal principles.

The Australian government was playing a game of carrot and stick, or maybe a game of stick and stick. If you were declared a negative, or non-refugee, you were given a choice: either return to your country or take your chances with a detention centre on Papua New Guinea: the notorious hell hole known as Bomana Prison. No-one really knew what happened to the people in Bomana, since their cell phones were confiscated, along with any contact with the outside world. The rumours were that those held there were often beaten. Many had apparently gone insane.

The legal system was arbitrary and unfair, with lethal consequences. There was only so long you could avoid its reach. One day, the guards came to deliver their verdict on my case. In fact, they came for me at least four times, until at last they gave up and threw a package of documents, coldly addressed to EML 019, on the landing outside my cell.

My hands trembled as I opened it up. Inside was a PNG immigration decision stating I had been judged a non-refugee 'based on the evidence you presented'. Never mind the fact that no interview had taken place, nor any presentation of the evidence.

The result was this: I had either to allow the police to detain me or grant the PNG government the power to deport me at any time.

Deportation seemed an unjust option, both for obvious ethical reasons and for procedural ones. Any country, like Papua New Guinea and Australia, that had signed one of the iterations of the Geneva Convention should know better than to send an asylum seeker home to his death. The Geneva Convention, not that anyone appeared to care about it anymore, had a rule about 'refoulement', which stood against sending people back to a country they had fled for good reason. (Background: the WWII ships of Jewish asylum seekers, rejected at every port and then returned to the killing machines of Germany, had left a heavy burden of guilt on the global community.)

That was my situation. It would have been one thing if Burma had rolled out the welcome mat for its refugee diaspora. Instead, they were chasing us to the nearest border and killing those who were too slow to make it that far. And from the blood-curdling stories of genocide that filled the headlines in that period, things were getting very bad indeed for my fellow Rohingyas back home.

If PNG did somehow manage to send me back, there was no way I'd survive. The second best choice was to go to Port Moresby, and there be shut away inside Bomana, the country's worst prison.

In a heartbeat, time on Manus Island started to accelerate.

TWENTY

*'One who deceives will always find those
who allow themselves to be deceived.'*

Niccolò Machiavelli

Meanwhile, in the happy colonial centres that continued to make a wreck of our lives from afar, the Australian government appointed a new minister for immigration and border protection. Peter Dutton was an unsmiling ex-police detective with a predictable authoritarian stance on 'illegal' refugees. (On Manus, guys used to refer to him as Mr Potato Head, based on his appearance.)

Although some parts of the population had begun to agitate for the nightmare on Manus to be brought to an end, a majority of Australian voters, the ones whose lives revolved around barbecues and soccer matches, gave their complicit assent to the Liberal-National Coalition's offshore affairs. (It was not a one-time mistake, as the same coalition was returned to office in 2016 and again in 2019.)

The political landscape in PNG, however, was different. The country's opposition leader, a principled figure named Belden Norman Namah, had launched a challenge to the legality of offshore processing on Manus Island and brought it to PNG's Supreme Court back in 2013. The case went largely unnoticed in Australia, despite the fact that the Morrison-Dutton immigration department had paid millions to help cover the defence fees of the government of Papua New Guinea. Which, of course, was an autonomous nation with its own immigration laws.

Back on Manus, more than 1000 men sweated over the outcome. If our detention was found to be illegal, we might be sent somewhere better, like Australia; or to another offshore gulag.

On 26 April 2016, the PNG court at last announced its ruling: the detention of refugees on Manus Island was illegal and in breach of the country's constitution. Specifically, the arrangement that Australia had made with PNG to detain those who had committed no crime under the laws of the land was a breach of our right to personal liberty under national law.

The consequences of the ruling were clear, as spelled out by the court. Both the PNG and Australian governments were immediately ordered to move us out of detention.

For those of us affected by the decision, the news was slow to take hold. On the day of the court decision, communication across the detainment centre was shut down, with blame cast on technical difficulties. As always, these difficulties coincided with the release of possible good news. The bad news, on the other hand, played on a constant loop on our television screens.

There were by now enough cell phones tucked away around the detention centre to compensate for the media blackout. People went from one shipping container to the next, asking in low tones if someone had an update. I was stuck to the 2.5-inch screen of my Alcatel, my thumb on the refresh button.

When the headlines appeared, I was torn. As someone who had a phone and could understand English, it was my responsibility to share the news. Yet after years of disappointment, I was reluctant to spread false hope. Laws could be bent to suit political objectives, and heaven knows what dirty trick the Australian government would entertain next.

The response from Peter Dutton was telling. 'The court decision is binding on the PNG government, but not on the Australian government, so we will work with the PNG government to look at the situation and provide what assistance we can.'

A crafty statement, suggesting Australia really had nothing to do with the current circumstances. Yet it would be there to offer help nonetheless. A supportive if uninvolved friend!

'Those in the Manus Island processing centre found to be refugees would be able to resettle in PNG. Those found not to be refugees should return to their country of origin.'

How sensible these words must have sounded to those half-listening to their radios while turning the meat on barbecue grills across the sunburnt country. We seafaring refugees were being given a choice, and a fair one, according to this perspective. We could continue to hang out on our tropical island, tanning our shins near the sunny beach, or go home and receive a big hug from our loved ones. Maybe we could even enjoy our own celebratory barbecue when we arrived.

There were more treats coming. Two weeks after the ruling was delivered, the detention centre gates were opened.

'There you go!' we were essentially told. 'The door is open, so you're not technically being detained anymore.'

There were a few problems with this scenario. For one thing, the campaign, years in the making, to encourage the local community to view us as depraved criminals, in need of another beating. For another, to leave the centre would be to illegally trespass onto Lombrum Naval Base, which served as the outer ring of our fortified prison.

Our keepers had a solution to that too, offering to drive us just outside the fence of Lombrum, free to skip merrily through the jungle and into the arms of villagers who'd been threatening to cut our throats.

I knew the Australian government could act terribly, but its actions during this shameful episode, giving the middle finger to a Supreme Court ruling on a constitutional matter, were a new low. If there was ever any doubt about who was really in charge in PNG, we now had the answer. The court had turned the prevailing sentiments about guilt upside down. *We* were not 'illegal' – our detention was. Which meant the ruling should have changed everything.

In fact, its main practical effect was that it allowed us to use our cell phones with impunity. The result you might expect, that we would march through the gates of our prison and explore the world that had been opened to us, did not occur. By this point, we had seen enough violence to know we were safer inside, and no-one wanted to move from the shelter of our cage.

Given how much we had suffered inside detention, it was a testament to the unpleasantness of Option B and C – taking our chances with the locals in Lorengau, or going back to the death traps of home – that we chose to remain. For Option C, we just had to consider the case of Son Pham, probably the most well-loved of all the guys in the centre. He was pressured to return to Vietnam in 2017, and was stabbed to death weeks after he arrived. Men held a funeral in absentia for him in the detention centre to mark the devastating loss.

It was one depressing prospect after another, with no relief in sight. I still held out hope for a legal solution, despite seeing that even PNG's Supreme Court could not stand up to the forces of the country's realpolitik. It was a struggle to get back to the hard work of securing my freedom, part of which involved appealing to the mercy of the same legal system that had been used to betray us.

And yet, what other option did I have? The smart and smartly dressed Nina and I discussed the possibilities. On her recommendation, I requested PNG immigration to send me the files listing the rationale for their decision to declare me a negative, or non-refugee. If I had to make a choice between rolling the dice with a life (and possible death) in PNG or in Burma, at least I wanted a place at the table in my own refugee process.

A few weeks later, I received a twelve-page document that was sloppy and full of holes. They got my name, birthday, and nearly every detail of my story wrong.

We wrote back, arguing that in light of the errors in the rationale document, my case should be reopened, and the interview rescheduled. That never happened. After more than three years in immigration detention, I never got to speak face-to-face with an immigration officer about my asylum claim.

Instead, I was told the only person with the power to review the decision was the man who had signed it, Rimbink Pato, PNG's minister for immigration and foreign affairs.

We wrote to him too, and asked for a ministerial review.

He said no.

A few of those desperate enough to swallow their fears for a brief taste of freedom began making trips into Lorengau on a Wilson Security bus. These were sorry excursions to a poor seaside village, where we weren't welcome or wanted: hardly a triumph of liberation.

There was a strict daily quota of twenty people out of a population of roughly 1300. If you were lucky enough to be on the list and your number called, you were scanned with a metal detector and subjected to a full-body search before being put on a bus at 9 am for a half-hour drive to the market in Lorengau.

There we could hang around for a few hours and maybe sample some tropical fruit before being loaded back onto the prison bus and returned to detention. Nothing from the market was allowed back in the detention centre, and nothing from the centre could go out. Even cigarettes, as our only currency, were limited to one packet per person. We had to leave at the exact time we were told, and return by the next designated deadline, our hands empty at both ends of the journey.

Upon our arrival back at detention, we were searched, scanned, addressed as numbers and methodically stripped of whatever dignity and joy we might have recovered during our brief foray into the civilian world.

The gates were opened but we were as confined as ever.

With my mind set on building any leverage possible, I continued to trade cigarettes on the black market for ten to fifteen kina per packet (three to four Australian dollars). On one trip to Lorengau, I'd saved up enough to buy myself a soft-bristled toothbrush, plus proper toothpaste, some probiotics for my wrecked gut, and soap from a shop called City Pharmacy.

For me, the only other aspect of life that changed after the gates were opened was that now I had access to the post office in Lorengau. That was to prove more valuable than I may have guessed.

On one trip to Lorengau, I visited a local wharf, next to a market, with a friend from detention, to get some fresh air. After a while, a local guy came over and spoke to us. 'Papu!' he said urgently, using the term Manusians gave to foreigners as well as to themselves. 'Papu, can you make me a bomb please?'

'What? A bomb?' I was confused.

'Yes, Papu, a bomb. Please! I want to catch fish.'

The villager explained how he wanted to detonate an explosive charge underwater. 'The fish die and then float to the top,' he said, wiggling the fingers of his outstretched hands. 'Please, Papu, make me a bomb. Just one. Please, Papu!'

It was such a weird request I had no idea what to say. My friend and I looked at each other vacantly until the penny dropped. 'Ahh,' I said as the explanation dawned on me. 'This guy thinks we're terrorists.'

To this day, I have still yet to set off a firework.

While the opening of the gates of the detention centre left us exposed, there were some welcome visitors. There was one local, in particular, who became a regular guest, and later a well-loved member of our besieged community.

We had seen Tiger when he was a puppy, sniffing around with the other dogs that scouted out the sandy area that separated the prison from the ocean. The strays congregated in anticipation of finding a morsel of food tossed over the fence by the detainees. The detainees, in turn, fed the dogs in the hope of making an emotional connection.

As a scrawny puppy, Tiger had been able to squeeze through a depression in the hard dirt under the main fence. He would breach the perimeter, visit with us for a few hours, and then leave by the same route to rejoin the pack. We raised him on milk until he was old enough to share our semi-solid meals. His cheeky forays into the prison lasted longer and longer, until he was too big to squeeze through the fence, or too attached to us – as we were to him – to want to leave.

His favourite area was where the men from Sri Lanka lived – Tamil refugees in flight from that country's civil war. There was Shamindan, who had once been a vet-in-training, and whose care of the dog had a professional feel. And Ramsiyar, who had lost half his family to war before nearly dying himself. With their loved ones far away, or perished, these guys yearned for companionship, and their adoption of Tiger, who embodied pure joy and affection, filled a deep need.

I became a regular visitor as well, mostly to see Tiger, until I got to know the guys better as well. The mutt, who grew up to be a handsome creature, with a tan and black coat and intelligent brown eyes, became a pet to hundreds of men, loved by each and exclusive to none. He brought us closer together, providing a common focus and outlet for our devotion – for an outpouring of love that had nowhere else to go.

He was not the first pet of Manus. A year or so earlier, a wild, multi-coloured parrot with an injured left wing had fallen from the sky and into our midst. He stayed first in Foxtrot, splitting his time between a broken piece of roof and two small palms that had taken root in the compound's main yard. Someone called him Jafar and the name stuck.

He was fed and fussed over, until he was tame enough to sit on our shoulders. Soon he was making the rounds of the other compounds too, passed from one hand to the next. Because he was a parrot, there were efforts made to teach him how to talk, but with twenty-two nationalities vying for his attention, the poor bird had little hope of mimicking human speech.

Something else happened during these ill-fated language lessons. Men who had fallen out of touch with their families back home, or who had stopped telling their real stories, for fear of causing hurt, instead opened their hearts to Jafar. He was an ideal friend, who could take in any confession, no matter how sad or dark, with good humour and a lack of judgement or reproach.

Over time he recovered enough to make short test flights around the compound. These in turn became longer excursions to fences and nearby trees. His jungle home was calling him, and we were sad to see him go. Some men even spoke of clipping his wings to keep him from departing, but that debate did not last long. One man asked, 'How do you like being locked in a cage?' and that ended it.

A few months after he first visited, Jafar flew away and never returned. Tiger made his departure a few years after that, dying before his time, and was buried with honours, wrapped in a shawl and covered in flowers. Both of these dear friends left an aching absence in the lives of those they left behind.

By this point, seeing the reports of horrors back in Burma (a child being clubbed on the beach, his legs broken by the same laughing tormentors who shot and shared the video, was circulating on Facebook: don't search it), I decided that life among the hostile residents of PNG was almost manageable, in light of my new hope to stay alive.

With Nina and Winiaka advising, I put in hundreds of hours over many months to plead with PNG immigration and its minister to look at my case. Yet like everything else in Manus, the legal process was slow, and the levers of justice were hard to reach. If I wished to print a document and the internet was down, I'd have to wait two weeks for another chance. If I needed to speak to a PNG immigration staffer, a guard could refuse to let me through, especially if he happened to be having a bad day. If immigration were due to meet with detainees at a shopfront in Mike and it was raining, the meeting would likely be cancelled – because who likes to get wet? – turning the two weeks of wait time into a month.

Nina and Winiaka were as frustrated as I was that the authorities refused to hear my case, or address the mistakes they had made.

In early 2017, on the advice of Winiaka, I filed for a judicial review in the National Court of Justice in Port Moresby. Winiaka had lectured in law at the University of Papua New Guinea – one of the many milestones of her career – and was confident that my negative review would be overturned if reviewed by a judge.

It was an ambitious plan that faced two obstacles. Launching it would be expensive, and finding a law firm to take it on would be near-impossible. The biggest client of nearly every legal practice in PNG was the national government. A law firm that took on my case would be shooting itself in the foot.

Given my experience of the past few years, I was prepared not to bother, but Winiaka had a galloping optimism that might have long vanished in a gentler soul. She disagreed with Australia's immigration policy, and came to the centre because she believed she could make the best impact from inside the system. Drawing strength from her Christian faith and her pride in her PNG culture, she was principled, forthright, single-minded and unwilling to let go. She launched a GoFundMe page from her personal account to raise money for the application, and spent months searching for a firm who'd be willing to fight by our side.

Eventually, a legal practice in Port Moresby agreed to take on my case. Using the post office in Lorengau, I painstakingly collected and sent the paperwork necessary to present in the High Court. In the end, I was informed it would take at least six to eight months before we would secure a hearing date. It was time I didn't have. By then, the government would have put me on a plane to Burma or into a cell in Bomana.

Good thing I'd started planning my escape.

TWENTY-ONE

'Falsehood flies, and the truth comes limping after it.'

Jonathan Swift

Weeks after I'd been declared a non-refugee, Nina handed me a torn piece of a yellow Post-it note with these curious words written on it: 'The quick brown fox.'

As I knew from my early days of trying to type, they formed the opening of the pangram 'The quick brown fox jumps over the lazy dog', long used to test out the keys of a typewriter. They also happened to be the password to a prison wi-fi – the most valuable gift to be granted in custody, outside of full freedom.

There were three wi-fi channels: one for the guards, one for the welfare staff and one for the lawyers. Nina gave me the lawyers' code. The signal didn't quite reach into Mike compound, so to log on I had to stand close to the fence that separated Foxtrot from Echo Block.

The walk was worth it. The free wi-fi, on the most basic level, was a way of saving precious cigarette money, otherwise spent on data. The way it felt was something else, like having the curtains in a dimly lit room thrown open, revealing the sea. I was free to surf any wave I chose, to any destination.

It mattered to me, more than ever, to chart my own intellectual path through this hostile place where we'd landed. With every aspect of our lives treated to a poisonous fog of disinformation, the facts I trusted were usually the ones I discovered myself.

My research showed me how deep the deception lay. For example, back in 2014, in the wake of the riot on Manus, there had been plenty of reports about the problems with the detention centre, and how the current system was unsustainable. How did the government react? By quietly granting a $1.2 billion contract to Transfield, the asset management company, to run Manus for another twenty months and Nauru for another twelve. The investors knew the real deal, as shares in Transfield surged 26 per cent.

The policymakers and their cheerleaders in the media could be trusted to play fast and loose with the facts to serve their own ends – that was clear to anyone paying attention. A version of the same scepticism was needed, perhaps surprisingly, when talking about current events with the refugee advocates. Many of our supporters were consumed by the political battles back on the mainland, and by their optimistic belief that the government would soon be voted out of office, along with its fetid immigration policies.

The advocates tended to place their hopes on the fortunes of the Greens, who had taken the clearest stance against offshore detention. (The Labor Party was the waffler.) Judging from their social media feeds, these advocates existed in something of an echo chamber with others who shared their progressive views. Unfortunately, of the major political parties, the left-leaning one was least likely to win power, a fact that was demonstrated in election after election, despite the best wishes of its outspoken champions.

The refugees who spoke to these advocates naturally believed them, going along with their promises of better days to come in a desperate act of wishful thinking. They had been invited into the echo chamber without a clear understanding of how partisan rhetoric works in democracies – or, in the case of Australia, a corporatocracy.

The way the refugees were used reminded me of *yoke thé*, Burmese marionette puppetry from my childhood. The shows featured dolls, dressed in embroidered and colourful costumes, performing elaborate dramas to the music of a live orchestra. This was known as high theatre (as opposed to low theatre, which was live performance), and the dramas were often used to make subtle political points that would have been impossible in another forum.

The movements of the puppets were complex and required the puppeteer to use two hands, one to control the body and the other for the finer actions. And the political comparison applied here too. Much like those dolls, the refugees were being pulled on strings, by all sides of the democratic spectrum: playthings in an ideological theatre, for a purely Australian audience.

'You'll be settled one day soon,' we'd hear from the advocates. 'Just hang in there – this won't go on forever.'

The facts on the ground said otherwise. Thanks to Nina, I had the ability to scan the internet for the kind of information that directly affected our lives. Since the mass media was part of the problem, I tried to go straight to the source, to the news before it became news, in all its raw specificity.

I had always had a high tolerance for boring details. Amir, the Iranian who had helped me carve a hiding spot in the wall for my phone, used to make fun of my pedantic streak. While he and the rest of the guys were together, smoking and trying to make each other laugh, I could be found in my cell, reading the news, or – before I had proper wi-fi – anything really, including the fine print on the iTunes sign-up page.

Jokes were a typical way of letting off steam, and they got passed around like a common currency, bringing us together. 'Same shit, different day' was a phrase you heard pretty much everyone say, at one point or another. It was the mildest form of gallows humour, since in truth things kept getting worse. Whenever we reached what seemed like the lowest level, there turned out to be an even lower one waiting for us.

From *Man's Search for Meaning*, I understood that humour was a defence and means of protest of the powerless, and some of the shared quips were dark and cutting indeed. But still, something stopped me from joining the guys when they got together to pass the time.

Outside of law students and historians, I was probably the most avid reader of obscure reports and parliamentary notes. From the minutes of the Senate Estimates (Budget) Hearing, I learned that an additional $61.5 million had been pledged for the 2016–17 fiscal year to keep our detention centre running, on top of the original spend of $810.8 million.

Then there was a release from a group called No Business in Abuse that showed Australia had burned through almost $10 billion to keep its penal colonies in working order. The cost of housing a single refugee was $400,000 a year, in the form of $1.4 million a day spent to pay Transfield to run the centre.

By that point, the taxpayer had spent $1 million on each of us. A rousing show of support: they really valued our company! Yet most of us would much rather be working and paying taxes than draining the coffers of a government that despised us, and claimed, in other contexts, to care about the value of a dollar.

There was another detail in the report that stunned me. It showed a further commitment of $6 billion over the next five years. I took this in while leaning against the fence near Echo Block, my eyes watering as they scanned my phone's tiny screen.

Five years! This was both horrific and heartbreaking. Better to die in a botched escape than to wait that long. It was either going to be a flight from the detention centre, or from this world altogether.

The possibility of suicide was always close at hand, appearing as a plausible option each time I ran into a new and formidable obstacle. The only thing stopping me, besides my evident lack of talent for the requirements of the job, was the reassurance I had found in the pages of Victor Frankl's book.

He'd developed a theory, or rather continuous practice, he called logotherapy, which he explained with a cinematic analogy. Just as the story of a film could only be fully understood in its final moments, so it was with a person's life. It was up to each of us to find the meaning and purpose of each moment, each frame of the film. Only as such could we ensure that, by the end, our life had a significance we chose freely, rather than one that was forced upon us by circumstance.

In my case, taking back control meant getting the hell off of Manus. No-one could fault me for trying to take the easy way out. I had tried and exhausted every legal course of action, pushing my case further than any other detainee.

With the backing of my superhero team of experts – the sharp legal minds of Winiaka and Nina, and the support of Tessa, who was always my lodestar when it came to finding the unvarnished truth – I had sent my claim all the way to the immigration minister's desk and was granted a judicial review in the National Court of Justice.

And then . . . nothing. Again. With the legal options played out, it was time for a new strategy. I had done the thing I was supposed to do. If following the rules were the best option, I'd be back in Burma, getting my legs broken and dumped in a river, set on fire or shot to death, like many of my countrymen. Or facing the prospect of years in a detainment centre or refugee housing run by the IOM or UNHCR in Indonesia.

On Good Friday, while returning from a day trip to Lorengau, the bus was passing through the first exterior gate when we heard it: the air punctuated by the sound of gunfire. We froze in confusion, pinned to our seats, as the vehicle kept making its slow way forward. The detention centre drew near and the walkie-talkies on the hips of the guards on the bus snapped into range, releasing a barrage of warnings and codes.

The bus following us was able to turn back to Lorengau but we'd come too far. Behind us was the perimeter gate, firmly shut, and ahead was the shooting.

Our keepers, trying to regain a semblance of control, shouted at us to get out of the vehicle and hide in the bushes nearby. We did so, and one of the guards, seeing the wisdom of his own orders, joined us. The barrage continued, sending the security staff flying, from one detention centre to another, from tents to concrete structures.

It was dark when we got a green light for the bus to return to the centre. More than 100 shots were fired that night and nine people injured in the melee, including five detention centre staff, one defence force soldier, one immigration officer and two detainees.

According to later reports, the assault began when PNG soldiers, after arguing about the use of the soccer field next to the detention centre after curfew hours, went on a drunken rampage. The soldiers opened fire, assaulted an immigration official and tried to ram a car through the fence.

That was the summary of what happened, according to the witnesses interviewed by the investigators from the PNG police force. Yet Australia's immigration minister, Peter Dutton, weighing in from across the ocean, had his own account. He said the incident began a week earlier, after three asylum seekers were spotted leading a five-year-old boy into the centre. The residents of Manus Island, he suggested, were worried the boy had been sexually assaulted.

His account was refuted by none other than the commander of the Manus division of the PNG police force, Inspector David Yapu, who went on record to state that Dutton was wrong. The boy was in fact ten years old, and the catalysing incident had nothing to do with him – it was indeed over a soccer match at a naval base.

Rather than clarify the clear mistake he had made, Dutton demanded that ABC News apologise for covering the story. He then seemed to double down by turning to a friendly journalist, Andrew Bolt, a conservative commentator and the immigration minister's biggest supporter in the media. On his Sky News TV show, owned by Rupert Murdoch, Bolt said he had been given confidential access to what he said was a Border Force report on the incident and crucial CCTV footage of the incident.

The fact that the journalist would be treated to such sensitive evidence was just one of the odd and uncomfortable aspects of this story. According to Malcolm Turnbull, who had been prime minister at the time, Sky News had reasons to lend one of their reporters to do a favour for Dutton. Rupert Murdoch had taken a liking to the tough-talking immigration minister, and aimed to have him launched into the prime minister's seat. The false pedophile story helped burnish Dutton's conservative credentials, while having the side benefit of assisting Murdoch and his media proxies in their mission to demonise refugees: win/win!

For all these reasons, none of those involved in the sordid misinformation campaign – not the immigration staff, Dutton, nor his reporter pal – felt the need to address the incident further. The damage was done, and the lie had taken root in the public consciousness, where it would continue to grow, unimpeded by facts, retractions or apologies.

Back on Manus, meanwhile, there were other opportunities to be wrung from this incident. The building that housed the computers – used by the detainees to communicate with their lawyers and family members – was closed, and the East Lorengau 'transit centre' was expanded (from 298 to 440 residents) by doubling the numbers of bunks in some of the rooms.

This was the third or fourth violent attack on Manus detainees since I had arrived. What made this one unusual was that, this time, we were not the only victims. There were Australian detention workers who were running for cover from the gunfire, ducking into the homes of locals and taking shelter in our cells.

The attack was followed by a wave of resignations by guards and staff members, who told their sad stories to a receptive audience of journalists and the wider public. Those of us who had been on the receiving end of violence from those same guards, as well as from the locals and pretty much everyone else in this foul system, did our best to sympathise.

TWENTY-TWO

*'Each had his past shut in him like the leaves of a book known to him
by heart; and his friends could only read the title.'*

Virginia Woolf, *Jacob's Room*

I had been thinking about running away since the gates of Manus
were opened in May 2016. Leaving an island that was heavily
patrolled and lay hundreds of miles from the nearest shore, however,
was going to be difficult.

One way out was through a medical transfer to Granville House
in Port Moresby, where those refugees receiving medical treatment
were held. The sorry state of my mouth and gums was well known
by the medical staff by that point, and I tried to improve my chances
of being relocated by stating my family would pay for the treatment.

I pursued that line for months, knowing Australian Border Force
was likely to take a look at the request and refuse. True to form,
they did.

Time for a new plan. Borrowing a trick from my favourite show
Prison Break, I began taking detailed notes on the world around me.
I knew, for instance, the schedule of each guard, how long it took
him to go from fence A to fence B, how many seconds it took to walk
along the fence line, and how long the same trip took when cutting
across the yard at a 45-degree angle.

There were other, more gruesome metrics, like how long it took
the guards to figure out someone was sick or had committed suicide.

If the body didn't show up in an obvious way – in a surprise room inspection, for example – the guards were often alerted to the tragedy by counting up the unused meal tickets (though that became less of a warning bell after we were allowed to leave the centre for daytrips to Lorengau).

My tables of notes, featuring the hours of work and any other detail that seemed like it might be useful, were entered into my journal and checked against the data from the previous days. It was tedious stuff but it laid bare the graceless choreography of the guards' movements in and around the property – I had a better understanding of where their next step would fall than they did – and the mechanics of the centre itself.

The research was for more than satisfying my idle curiosity. From *Prison Break*, I had learned that most people, when planning an escape, tended to focus on getting past the next obstacle, and the one after that. With such an approach, they were likely to fail. If each new crisis point came as a surprise, they would be unprepared for it, leaving no obvious path to success. A better approach was to start at the end goal and work backwards, in the manner of reverse engineering.

The detention centre on Manus presented a fierce challenge. It was a prison inside a military base, on an island that was patrolled by the Land Rovers of the Australian Federal Police and the ships of the Australian Navy. There were circles within circles within circles to cross.

Realistically, the only way off the island was by plane, and the only flights from Manus went to Port Moresby, the capital of PNG. Taking that as my destination, I took a step backward, starting with a proposition: 'How might I get past airport security?'

Once the encounter with a customs or immigration official was clear in my mind, I considered the preparation required to make it that far. In this scenario, for example, I would need a good fake ID, as well as transportation to the airport, some suitable civilian clothing, a disguise and an airline ticket. Only in this way could I present myself as someone other than a Rohingya man in flight from captivity.

One of the odder ways the Australian government had thought to spend money on us was by offering lessons in Tok Pisin: perhaps to help prepare us for our exciting new lives in the backwaters of Papua New Guinea. I had sat in a few classes, mostly out of boredom. Now energised by my new plan, I became a star student, taking in every word of the regional dialect. While most people in PNG spoke English, it might be wise to have some local words in my kitbag. What if a Papu official preferred to communicate in Tok Pisin? It was good to think through each scenario and come prepared.

On the nights when I wasn't dreaming about guards chasing me down and throwing me into a cage, I'd lie awake trying to imagine the escape in detail. Part of that meant coming up with plausible excuses, in case I was cornered on the way out.

If I made it to the airport and I wasn't a fugitive, for example, then who was I? Aside from the Papus, nearly everyone employed at the centre flew in and out of Manus on rotating rosters. Yet I'd never be able to pass myself off as an Australian or a local.

There were two demographics that might work for me: interpreters and healthcare workers. An interpreter was a safer bet. Until that point, I had not had much interaction with the interpreters on the Island. Now I took a keen interest in their work. I watched them closely, recording their movements in my journal, alongside those of the guards. The pages also began to fill with their flight schedules in and out of Manus Island.

It was a slow process, since I could hardly walk up to an interpreter and ask, 'What day did you fly in and when are you flying out?' Reconnaissance had to be subtle: 'Hey, good to see you back! When did you come in?' If I asked the next interpreter the same question, and the following guy too – and their responses lined up – then I had a pattern to work from.

It took me about four months to be confident that interpreters flew in and out once every three weeks on alternating Thursdays and Sundays. In theory, an opportunity to pose as an interpreter and jet away from Manus presented itself in intervals of twenty-one days.

Drawing on my aborted medevac visit to Darwin, and on stories from those who had made similar trips – rehabilitated just enough to survive, only to be thrown back into detention – I knew the airport was patrolled by sentries of Wilson guards. Usually a pair of them, a Papu teamed with an expat. Running into a local guard at the Manus airport wouldn't pose much of a problem, but an encounter with an expat – who was more likely to recognise a Manus escapee, and less likely to accept a bribe and look the other way – would be a disaster.

Their busiest time was when flights landed, during the switch-over between arriving and departing passengers. In those moments, the guards were usually distracted, their hands full with the transfer of detainees returning from medevac. If I showed up at the airport during that window, I'd stand a better chance of squeaking through undetected.

After six months of quiet observation, I felt like I'd learned everything there was to know about flight schedules and staff movements – almost down to the minute. Taking the next step, however, I would require some help.

Winiaka was the first to hear of the strategy as it was shaping up. We met in her office one afternoon to discuss the progress of my legal challenges. She and Nina believed that, as a stateless person, without an official existence even in my home country, I was likely to be kept in indefinite detention on Manus. It was either that, or to the black hole of Bomana.

She was in the midst of laying out my unsavoury options when, overcome with excitement and nerves, I began drawing up my plans on a sheet of paper, a list of escape scenarios with arrows pointing to different options and courses of action.

'What do you think you're doing?' she whispered urgently. 'Stop it! Don't draw anything like that in here! Do you forget we're under observation?' Even here, in the office where she was tasked with providing confidential legal advice to detainees, we were being monitored by mounted CCTV cameras.

She could hardly give her blessing on the spot, since she, like Nina, was an employee of the state. And if the scheme went sideways, she would have to live with the guilt of whatever came next. At the same time, while she did not endorse the plan, she didn't say no either. Nor did Nina. In both cases, it was a silent yes that I understood without them saying a word. I pressed on.

To purchase an airline ticket I would need a high-quality fake photo ID: not an easy item to come by on Manus Island. Luckily, at that time PNG didn't have a uniform national identification system. Any card – like a drivers' licence or an employment ID – that carried a photograph and some kind of official seal could qualify the holder to purchase a ticket on domestic flights.

The plan evolved. Forging an ID in the guise of an interpreter was not much of a possibility. Airport staff would be familiar with those kinds of credentials and would easily spot a fake. Having never seen a local ID besides the ones that made it inside the detention centre, I was at a loss.

For that, I zeroed in on a Filipino guy named Richard, the pharmacist in charge of City Pharmacy in Lorengau. I was on good terms with him, thanks to my regular visits to buy toiletries and Tylenol to keep my wired-up teeth from driving me crazy. Richard wore an impressive-looking ID on a lanyard around his neck and I needed to get a closer look at it.

Since the products in his store – including the pharmaceuticals – were shipped in by plane, I hoped to pass myself off as a City Pharmacy sales representative, or maybe a visiting foreign chemist. Richard, after all, was a foreigner, and there were other Asian people working for various companies in Lorengau. Since I had interned as an industrial chemist back in Rangoon, I had a higher chance of impersonating one of them.

During my next trip to City Pharmacy, I engaged Richard in a long conversation at the counter, my eyes darting, now and then, toward the badge hanging from his neck. What I'd initially thought was a laminated photo stuck on paper was in fact a rigid plastic card with a high-resolution photo printed directly onto the surface. No facility on Manus could produce ID cards of such quality. It might be possible to have one made in Australia, but having it sent here would be difficult since our packages were delivered straight to the detention centre, where they were searched. I needed a better idea.

A few weeks later I was returning from town on the Wilson bus when I noticed a banner announcing the opening of the Lorengau branch of an IT school, impressively named the International Training Institute.

Back in the compound, I googled the company and saw it was run by IT instructors who appeared to be foreign-born. Since the business was new to Manus, the wider community – including people who worked at the airport – were unlikely to know what their employee ID cards looked like. This was my opportunity.

I searched online for their company logo and downloaded it. Next, I had a cellmate use my phone to take a headshot of me in front of the white wall of MA2-09. Back in Lorengau, a few days later, I visited a print shop, and had the portrait shot and logo printed onto extra-thick photographic paper that also listed my credentials as an IT teacher named Ian Vele – the most PNG-sounding alias I could think of.

Lastly, I had the card laminated – twice – to make it more substantial. The end result was pretty good by Manus standards. It even had an extra in-built detail that would help me avoid scrutiny. The birthdate listed on the card put my age at just a few months shy of eighteen, nearly seven years younger than my actual age. If I presented as a minor in PNG, there were certain things a parent, or adult guardian, could do on my behalf: like pick up a boarding pass.

Access to the Lorengau post office was a boon for the prison. For one thing, it brought the flavours of the world to Manus Island. Detainees began importing small parcels of their favourite dishes from abroad.

I joined in when some of my countrymen had some Burmese food called Lahpet – fermented tea-leaf salad – sent by Rohingya friends in Australia.

The post office was next door to my regular perch at City Pharmacy, and I made a point of being pleasant to the postal staff whenever we crossed paths. For some months now, I had been exchanging legal documents by mail with the law firm in Port Moresby that had been working on my judicial review. On days when a letter was likely to arrive, I made sure I was on the list to go into town by waking up before sunrise and lining up for hours to secure a spot on the bus.

My first attempt at intercepting a package at the post office failed.

'But it's addressed to me. I am Jaivet Ealom,' I implored the Papu woman on duty.

'Packages addressed to people who live in the centre are supposed to go there,' she said evenly. 'I can't just hand the mail over to you.'

'I know, but I am here now. This is my ID.' I showed her my identity card, complete with my misspelled name, matching the one on the envelope. 'Which means it makes sense to give it to me now.'

Wrong. When I tried the following week she rebuffed me again. The time after that, I went armed with the tracking number of the package, the name, address and telephone number of the sender in Port Moresby, along with a detailed description of the paperwork inside the envelope. 'Look, clearly this is my mail,' I told her. 'I really need it today – now – so can you please just give it to me?'

She relented and handed it over. From then on I was allowed to collect my mail in person from Lorengau, away from the prying eyes of the Australian guards.

I had been discussing with Tessa – who often had the most practical idea of what to do next – how best to go about purchasing a plane ticket. The money wasn't a major issue: I'd been busy squirrelling away my cigarettes. The challenge was how to buy a ticket in the name of Ian Vele without leaving a suspicious paper trail. Since I had no certainty the scheme would work, I began with the worst-case scenario – getting caught with the ticket – and backfilled it with a plan that hopefully would not land anyone in trouble.

Buying a ticket in person was futile. Although there was a travel agency on Manus Island, I worried the staff would spot me and inform PNG immigration. There were spies and accomplices everywhere on the island, and I was easily recognisable. From the post office to the fruit market, everyone knew what a typical detainee looked like.

Time was running out. My visits to the print shop and post office might get me in trouble at any moment. I'd placed my bets on a flight off the island, and needed assistance to make it happen.

'I have to be very, very careful,' said Winiaka. 'I can't be seen to be involved at all. The consequences would be huge for me too. But I will do everything that is in my power to help.'

As a dual resident of both PNG and Australia, Winiaka had influence with a wide circle of local contacts. When Nina also offered to help, I started to wonder if my plan might actually have a chance of succeeding. For the first time in four years, there was a stirring of hope in my chest, and the unfamiliar sensation kept me awake at night.

A makeover was in order. Since my tropical prison uniform – including the bright yellow t-shirts we had been provided with in detention, which were designed to be easily spotted and possibly shot at in the darkness – was unlikely to pass muster with airport security, Tessa sent me a blue button-down shirt and jeans, the sort of outfit you might expect from a professional on leave from the island after a three-week shift. She packed the clothes in a knapsack, and included the baseball cap I had requested, along with sunglasses and a pair of earphones for my Android: a poor man's disguise kit.

Meanwhile, I waited (and waited) for the credit card that Tessa said she'd sent me, the Load&Go Travel Visa holding the funds needed to cover the cost of my ticket. It usually took three weeks for parcels to come from Australia. As the days passed, the odds increased that the envelope might never arrive at all, another victim of the spotty PNG postal service.

Winiaka also advised me it would be a good idea to hold off trying to escape until after the PNG general election, due to begin on 24 June and run until the first week of July. 'Things can get quite scary when there's an election here. There's a lot of violence expected. It might be safer to wait.'

There were risks on both sides. Election chaos could tie up the staff who dealt with matters of citizenship and identity, leaving me relatively unscathed. On the other hand, it could also put the airport authorities on high alert.

A chance conversation with a staff member from Transfield, now rebranded Broadspectrum, dramatically raised the stakes. This was someone I had come to know while sewing together the pages of *Man's Search for Meaning* (he was in charge of the sewing sessions where we were supposed to be mending our clothes). Big changes were coming to the detention centre, he said. Those of us who were negatives were going to be isolated in our own compound and forbidden from leaving. They had tried to separate us twice before, but this time they were serious, and the changes were coming immediately.

He mentioned this in an offhand way, almost by accident, but for me the news was calamitous. If the gates were closed, my escape plan fell apart. It was time to move.

For weeks, Winiaka and I had been dancing around the timing of my departure, with her advising me to wait to ride out the PNG election, and me itching to leave. Now there was no question. I would depart first thing in the morning, before the gates closed on me, possibly for good.

There was much to organise, all at once. I asked Winiaka to book me on the next plane out, the 'interpreter flight' to Port Moresby on Sunday, 25 June 2017. Hearing the desperation in my voice, she agreed to do this against her own better judgement, since I would arrive right around the time when the pandemonium of the PNG election was gaining steam.

I gathered my legal paperwork and asked Zakaria, still living in Oscar compound, if he would mind holding onto it for a few days. If I were to get caught, I didn't want the authorities getting their hands on my records, and I needed someone like him, a trustworthy friend, to better cover my tracks.

'For a few days? Where are you going?'

'Oh, nowhere really. Just want to get these things off my hands. I'll come back for them.'

He looked deep in my eyes, suspecting that I was hiding something. Holding his gaze, I tried to arrange my face into a perfect blank screen, a mask of absence. For me to do this to a man who had been a friend of mine and my family's for years, and over as many continents, felt like treachery. But to tell him would be a risk for me, and dangerous for him too, if I were to get caught.

Back in MA2-09, I packed my bag, placing as little as I could in my knapsack, to avoid attracting attention on the bus ride the next day. In striving for minimalism, I forgot to include my most prized possession, the bound-and-stitched photocopy of *Man's Search for Meaning*, complete with my handwritten marginalia. Like the spiralling notes in the Talmud, the comments were almost as important as the original text, to me anyway, since it contained my reflections on what I had discovered in silent conversation with the author.

Of all the objects I've misplaced or left behind in my life, the loss of this book continues to bother me the most.

With my bags packed and ticket booked, I had one more important task. Taking my phone (which I could now use openly, thanks to the recent Supreme Court ruling on the illegality of the detention centre), I snapped pictures of every familiar sight. This was not just an exercise in nostalgia – it was an attempt to capture a visual record of a place I might never see again.

As I knew from my time in Burma, the past could be deleted at the stroke of a pen, and I was worried the same thing might happen to the centre. Whoever controlled the documents dictated the truth and history itself. There needed to be an eyewitness record of the detention centre before that erasure occurred.

For that reason, my pictures, some of which appear in this book, have an impersonal flavour, since I wanted to capture the facts of our physical surroundings, the fences, sides of shipping containers and the beach huts that doubled as sentry posts. Indulging my eye a little, I also took pictures of the oceanside, and plants growing in and around the compound.

The shrubs and flowers had largely been planted by Salim, a Rohingya guy whose journey paralleled my own. He had grown up in Burma, and travelled aboard the *Emelle* to Christmas Island, where we had our first proper conversation. His arrival on Manus had happened weeks prior to mine.

He had a first name that was distinctly Rohingyan, and a last name that was typically Burmese. It was a combination so unusual it was hard for me to wrap my head or tongue around, and I usually stuck to addressing him as Salim.

Other things that made him unique included his love of gardening, and his epilepsy, which ebbed and flowed as a source of affliction. His seizures, which had been less severe on Christmas Island, came hard and fast in detention on Manus. Nurses pushed to have him medevaced to Darwin. In the relatively humane conditions of the detention centre there, he recovered again, and the seizures stopped so completely there were some who doubted he'd ever had them in the first place.

Back in the hothouse environment of Manus, they returned at full strength. Still, he did his best to fill his time, finding calm in the act of getting his hands dirty. Many of the twigs he had planted years ago around Oscar had flourished, offering a source of comfort and relief to those of us tired of the hardscrabble grit of our surroundings. He had left his mark, and we were thankful for his efforts.

The plantings put more than just his personal touch on this place. They were a sign of the passage of time. Since we had come to Manus, the flowering plants had filled out and the shrubs had grown tall, much like the children who we were used to seeing pass by the fence. Time had passed, but not for us. We were still here, still the same.

My goodbyes that day were silent. When I saw people I knew, or cared about, I asked them how they were, and threw out a few of our well-worn jokes. The separation that lay ahead of us might be years long, but they had to believe I would see them tomorrow, like any other day.

To stop the farewells from hurting too much, I told myself that when we saw each other next, it would be under much happier conditions. This was not a goodbye, just a long build-up to that wonderful moment of reconciliation, and of getting to know each other again.

For some of my friends, that moment was never to come. Within a year of my departure, Salim jumped from the roof of a bus and lost his life. Whether it was his own internal troubles, or those inflicted on him from the detention system, he had decided it was time to end his journey.

His death triggered protests in cities and towns across Australia, by those outraged that his medical condition had been allowed to go untreated, to the point of mortality. In addition to the usual homemade signs and painted bedsheets, the demonstrators carried flowers, of every kind and colour, as a symbol of mourning and respect for the Gardener of Manus.

The only way out of the detention centre was on the bus, and it had one destination: Lorengau. By 11 am on 24 June, having lined up early for the privilege, I was on my way to town. It wasn't unusual for detainees to carry bags, which were searched on the way out (mostly for cigarettes, with only one packet allowed at a time) and again on the return to the centre later in the day (in that case, for food). Hopefully no-one would discover my own knapsack hid civilian clothes and a makeshift disguise.

The flight to Port Moresby was not until the following day, so when I arrived in town, I waited for the return bus to leave. Worried that my old phone might be traced, I bought a new one, then checked into a budget motel to wait for the morning.

The motel was crawling with cockroaches, and these ones were even more unpredictable than the usual surface-dwelling kind, with wings as well as skittering legs. With nothing but these insects for company I shifted to a white plastic chair outside the room.

The town was blissfully free of floodlights to block the view of the sky. It was the most clear and beautiful night that I had witnessed since coming to Manus, and it's one that still stands out in my memories. Rather than bothering to get some rest, I spent hours watching distant constellations slowly rotate overhead – and wondered how long it would be before I was captured.

It was past midnight when I pulled my old phone out of my pocket and deactivated my social media accounts – including Messenger, my sole means of communication with Tessa. I went further: destroying the sim card and disabling every function that might flag my GPS location. I'd spent weeks memorising the phone numbers and email address of everyone I knew and depended on, to prepare for this moment.

While the rest of the detainees on Manus slept, or paced the yard, I silently vanished from cyberspace. If only I could have deleted myself from the island so easily.

TWENTY-THREE

'The art of losing isn't hard to master.'

Elizabeth Bishop, 'One Art'

The flight was scheduled to depart Manus at half past one in the afternoon. Just after midday, Aaron arrived at my motel in Lorengau in a pick-up truck splattered in mud and sand.

Aaron was a distant cousin of Winiaka, who she had called upon to help me make the risky forty-five-minute journey to the airport. Risky, because for most of its length, it backtracked along the same road that I had taken from the detention centre. We were almost certain to pass buses full of people I knew on the way to Lorengau, and familiar guards in military vehicles.

Aaron was a quiet guy. He seemed eager to help, but I was unsure of how much Winiaka had told him about me or my situation. I kept the conversation light, in case something I said might contradict the picture that Winiaka had painted in my absence.

When I got in his pick-up, he looked at my knapsack and asked, 'Is that all you got?' He smiled, and passed me a water bottle to ward off the scorching heat. We were on our way.

Aaron, who was from a different part of PNG, had lived on Manus for years, and worked for an NGO focused on wildlife conservation. Neither he nor his well-known truck would raise suspicion. That was my hope, though on an island where the most natural mode of transportation was the boat, any vehicle stood out.

As the pick-up entered the jungle, my misgivings grew. Ten minutes into the trip, a Wilson Security car sped towards us from the opposite direction. I was sure they were onto me but it flew past, and showed no signs of turning back in pursuit. Ten minutes later a second Wilson vehicle appeared, setting off another alarm, then continued on its way. Another deep gulp of relief, along with the fear of the next chilling sign of my captors, and a reminder that my escape attempt might be over at any moment.

The road narrowed near the airport, and Aaron pulled to a stop. From this vantage point, we'd be able to see the plane come in to land, while staying at a safe distance from the gathering airport crowd.

The flight was late, and the wait wore on me. It was a little like being on Christmas Island again, listening for the lock to turn and for the angel of death to appear at the side of the bed. The tension was enough to make you wish for the end to come quickly.

When we eventually heard the whine of the rotary engines, Aaron drove closer to the terminal building. As the Air Niugini jet touched down and taxied to a halt, another car belonging to security forces passed us on the road and stopped in front of the main entrance of the airport. The driver got out, shut the door and headed inside, I realised who he was. Rex: a Wilson guard I knew quite well. He was likely to recognise me too.

I turned to Aaron. 'If that guy is posted at the airport today, I'm screwed.'

I hunched low in the seat and used the side mirror to survey the terminal doors. A few minutes later Rex emerged, climbed back into his car and left the airport.

Exhale.

With passengers already trickling onto the tarmac, it was time to move. Aaron drove up to the terminal and parked beside another truck. I handed him my ID and the booking confirmation to fetch the boarding pass.

'Okay,' he said. 'Wait here.'

Since I was booked as a minor, Aaron presented himself as my adult guardian to the airport staff. While people in PNG were generally trusting, he was in his early thirties, less than a decade older than me, so posing as my father was a stretch. I waited for him on tenterhooks, but a few minutes later he returned to the truck.

'Here,' he said, slipping me the strip of cardboard. 'One boarding pass.'

Following the plan we had drawn up on the drive over, Aaron returned to the terminal to case out the scene. He would call me when there were just a few people left in the boarding area. The idea was for me to join the line of travellers as smoothly as possible, without drawing attention for being the last to board.

An SUV parked next to our truck and two Australian immigration officers climbed out. A terrible wildcard. Although I'd been largely able to map out the flight schedules of the Wilson guards, medicos and interpreters, it had been impossible to get a read on the movements of immigration officials – because we rarely interacted.

I texted Aaron: '2 immigration coming. If they get on the plane, I go nowhere.'

I slid down in my seat, leaving enough of a view to watch the men, just a metre away, open the trunk and mess with their bags. They got back into the car, and then out again. For me, it all took place in slow motion.

Eventually, the two immigration staffers organised themselves and left on foot. Maybe they went to the airport – who knows? My vision had dimmed, as if I were having a stroke.

A few minutes later Aaron called my phone: 'Come on! There's only six or seven people left in line.'

Time for the disguise. My cap pulled tight, my sunglasses on and earphones plugged in, as if I were listening to music, I strode into the terminal with a feigned and brittle confidence. So focused was I on getting through the check-in that I made the potentially fatal mistake of cutting in front of the other passengers. While it was more of a loose gathering than a formal line, bypassing it meant drawing attention to myself, something I could hardly afford.

Realising what I'd done, I turned to face the woman behind me. She gave me the look that a queue jumper deserves. That's when I realised I knew her. It was Samantha: a Papu nurse who worked at the detention clinic.

In that moment she held my life in her hands. She may well have recognised me. In any case, she said nothing and let me go. I'm still thankful to her for that.

The tarmac was as hot as it had been on the morning of my arrival on the island. So long ago now: for the record, it had been 1284 days, or three years and six months. With each step my muscles tensed, flinching in anticipation of the hand of a guard to grip my shoulder and stop me in my tracks.

The air smelled of jet exhaust, both evocative and sickening, and vibrated with the whirr of turbines. My pulse thundered in my head as I climbed the metal steps toward the plane door. Could I really be leaving this terrible place?

The Fokker 100 had two rows of two seats on either side of the aisle. My assigned seat was on the right-hand side, next to a window, about two thirds of the way back. I put my knapsack on the empty seat next to mine to discourage company.

My senses were pin-sharp from a mixture of fear, dread and exultation. Buckling my seatbelt like a regular traveller, I continued to pretend-listen to the music on my headphones. Every word from the other passengers caught in my ears and grated on my nerves, as I waited for a voice to shout, 'That's him!'

The seconds slowed while I stared sideways at the cabin door from behind my sunglasses, willing it to close. A series of possibilities flashed through my mind, each more unpleasant than the last. Then a real worst-case scenario, as the two immigration officers from the carpark came up the aisle. They found their seats on the left-hand side of the cabin, four rows ahead of mine.

Inhale.

My design was flawed. This was supposed to be a flight of interpreters and healthcare workers. Instead, there were immigration officials onboard, and they were now joined by a man whose tattooed brawn suggested he worked for Wilson Security or another of the firms subcontracted to provide muscle for its immigration staff.

I didn't recognise him, and fortunately the lack of familiarity cut both ways. At one point, leaning forward from his seat, in the row behind mine, he tried to engage me in a chat; some palaver about the plane being late. Adjusting my earphones, I pretended not to hear and he left me alone.

'You're an interpreter,' I told myself. 'Remember? Try to relax.'

The door closed and the plane crawled toward the end of the runway. The engines rumbled with greater urgency, and we began to move. Faster now, then faster still, until the horizon tilted outside the window and we took to the air.

The ground dropped off, showing the tops of trees, and then the detention centre came into view. 'God, what a shithole,' I thought. The sprawling bullpen now dominated the landscape: the squat buildings and acres of treeless yards were an obscenity alongside the thatched huts of the locals and spectacular seaside jungle.

Distance can hide any flaw. The detention centre became a whitish-grey scar in the jungle. It was amazing that all we had been through – all that we'd suffered and survived in the past four years – had taken place on that cursed patch of land.

The scar faded to a white line on the green island. The island in turn shrank and became a green circle in the blue ocean. A mere dot, like a full stop at the end of a sentence. For my fellow detainees on Manus, like Zakaria and Amir and the rest of the guys I was leaving behind, and already feeling guilty about abandoning, it was a sentence still being written.

They were trapped, and would continue to be trapped. They had years of torment ahead of them, shipped from prison to prison, like manacled slaves on a slave ship. At the time of writing this, hundreds of them are still held in that hateful system, broken and robbed of the best years of their life. My heart ached for them, as it still does.

We were part of a group, a band of brothers. Coming from different places and life paths, we had been brought together on a unique odyssey of pain and resilience. And now I had left them without saying a word, not a single goodbye.

And yet, for the sake of my own survival, my eyes were already on the dangers ahead.

TWENTY-FOUR

'When I was a boy and I would see scary things in the news, my mother would say to me, "Look for the helpers. You will always find people who are helping."'

Fred Rogers

Time must pass very slowly in hell. The *drip*, *drip*, *drip* of the seconds during the ninety-minute flight from Manus Island to Port Moresby covered me in a sickening sweat, and took years off my life.

Midway through the trip, one of the immigration officers stood up in the aisle and walked toward me. I swallowed hard. He acted as if he were looking for somebody. The lines I'd practised came to the ready:

'Hello.'

'Yes.'

'What's the problem?'

'I'm sorry?'

'No.'

'I'm an interpreter.'

The conversation never happened. As he passed my seat, he gave me a lingering stare that went to the back of my eyes, putting my nerves on red alert. 'Why don't you just drag me off the plane and get it over with?' I wanted to shout.

My mouth stayed shut as he lumbered past. His glacial pace seemed intentional, designed to torment. A few minutes later, he returned from the washroom and took his seat.

Port Moresby appeared in the porthole of a window, and with it the first trappings of urban civilisation. Regular buildings – rather than modified shipping containers or quonset huts – proper roads, traffic lights and neighbourhoods, organised for actual living, not for warehousing the souls of the half-dead.

After I'd boarded the plane on Manus, Aaron phoned Winiaka to tell her I was on my way. She'd arranged to meet me in Port Moresby. Believing the airport to be too risky for a rendezvous, she'd given me directions to a shopping mall where she'd be waiting.

In the arrivals area I had to play a reverse game of cat and mouse with the two immigration officers. The plane stopped on the tarmac, leaving a ten-minute walk to the terminal. Trailing the officers at a distance of a few metres, I timed my movements to avoid being noticed and trapped in their claws. When they slowed down, I slowed down. When they stopped, I stopped too, and pretended to check my phone.

At last, they were absorbed into the crowd, perhaps on their way to the luggage carousel, which I bypassed to head straight for the exit. As I passed through the glass doors and onto the street, my blank face hid an explosive and disbelieving bliss.

Past the glass was another world. Here on the ground, the orderly grid of Port Moresby disclosed its true anarchic energy. Buses, cars, motorbikes and human beings moved with blind purpose and alarming speed. Engines revved, voices shouted and taxi drivers called for fares by leaning on their horns. After a lasting and acute focus on the squawk of walkie-talkies and the ever-present piping call of the chauka bird, Port Moresby crashed into my ears and set off a cannonade in my head.

Stepping into my first taxi in years, I told the driver the name of the mall, Vision City, where I was to meet Winiaka. An ordinary request, but it felt dizzyingly powerful. After years of being told what to do, from morning to night, I was giving orders to someone else.

When we arrived at the mall, I paid the driver three times what he was owed. Not because I was feeling generous or had money to burn, but because I'd forgotten how a normal cash exchange was carried out. On Manus, being caught with real currency could have you thrown into solitary for days. Money was handed over in a flash, in the toilets and shower blocks, out of the guards' sight. It was in the same clandestine spirit that I placed the wad of cash in the driver's hand and darted from the cab before he could inform me of the mistake.

There were two entrances to the mall, and I ended up at the wrong one. After fifteen confused minutes, I met up with Winiaka and her sister, Mipil. Winiaka and I shared a long hug that took in our relief and surprise that we were seeing each other in this place, against all odds. Since we were not allowed to touch on Manus – the only physical contact coming from the guards' searching hands – the embrace was heavenly.

The comfort was short-lived. By the time we let go of each other, the feeling of doom had returned and I had to keep myself from sprinting to the safety of her car.

Winiaka tried to match my pace. 'Jaivet, it's okay.'

'Yeah, I'm fine,' I said, feeling anything but.

We got in the car and closed the doors. She turned to me and put her hand on mine. 'Jaivet, stay calm, alright? You are not a prisoner anymore. Try to relax. You're safe. I promise.'

'Yeah, okay,' I said, exhaling heavily. 'Thank you, Winiaka.'

'Now,' she said. 'What do you want to do?'

'What do you mean?'

'You've been in prison for four years. What is it that you want to do the most in the world?'

What did I want to do? A question that opened doors. After thinking a while, I replied, 'Ohhhhh, you know what, can we go for coffee? Not like those instant sachets in detention – I mean a *real* coffee, freshly brewed using real beans. Also, I would love to have a warm shower.'

It was perhaps not the reply she had expected. Good sport that she was, she took in my wish and promised me a coffee after we were done checking into the place where I was going to stay.

We drove to a house on the outskirts of Port Moresby. On the drive over, I learned that Luther, my new host, was a former classmate of Winiaka's, from her high-school days. Now working as a flight attendant, he had agreed to let me stay with him for free until I figured out my next step. Winiaka had organised this in advance since she could not take the risk of putting me up herself.

Half an hour later, I stood under my first hot shower in four years. It was like falling into a warm and pacifying trance. After I dried myself and rejoined the others in the living room, Winiaka flashed her warm smile.

'How did that feel?' she asked.

'H-e-a-v-e-n-l-y,' I replied, flopping onto the sofa.

'I guess it's been a while. How long do you think you were in there for?'

'Oh, I don't know – ten to fifteen minutes.'

'What if I told you that you were under that shower for one hour and forty minutes?'

I felt like the man who caught the magic fish, my every wish granted. My next one came later that evening, at a nearby cafe. The first sip of coffee was better than I had imagined.

'Holy shit,' I gasped. 'I might be coming back to life.'

Winiaka told me her mom, who shared her Christian devotion, had been praying for my safe journey all this time. Having never met this woman, I was gladdened to hear I had a place in her thoughts. Winiaka said she had been talking about me with her mother since meeting me nearly two years ago and sharing her hopes for my eventual escape. Her mom would be so happy to know it had finally happened, she said. I began to understand where Winiaka's sunny and beautiful spirit came from.

We ordered a burger and French fries – a new type of heaven, even though each chew brought a jolt of pain to my wired mouth. The soda was too sweet for more than a sip. Just as my eardrums were trained on the soundscape of the island, and could not make sense of the general din of Port Moresby, my palette was accustomed to the bland flavours of the detention centre, where the main taste was one of decay. I finished the meal but left the plastic cup almost untouched.

Back at Luther's place, he and Winiaka teased me a little more about my marathon shower. 'Seriously, though,' he said, 'after what you've been through, you have earned as many showers as you want.'

That night was an embarrassment of luxuries. I took another shower, maybe not quite as long but still amazing, and fell asleep in a comfortable bed in an air-conditioned room. It was a dream that might end at any moment, dropping me back in the dirt of the island.

Waking up in the dark, I replayed the day's events in my head. Had I really just escaped from the detention centre? What in the hell was I going to do now? Despite all my calculations, I found myself without a clear objective. The real energy came from behind, the return of the invisible wall at my back, pushing me relentlessly forward. The desperation that kept me running from Burma and Indonesia, that put me on a boat and launched me across the ocean, was now directing me toward an unknown destination.

Over the next few days, I tried to relax and take in what was, after all, an average influx of sights, sounds and sensations. I was, in the parlance of medical health journals, institutionalised. It was a struggle to take a simple walk around the block. I was so used to being watched that the absence of an overlord was unsettling.

The other big change I noticed was the quality of the air. Behind the wire, the atmosphere was filled with so much tension and sorrow it entered the nose with a certain scent, a chemical steeped in human desperation.

Port Moresby had its own flaws. One of its claims to fame was that it was said to be among the world's most dangerous cities, a place where carrying a cell phone in public could be a life-threatening act, and where you might find yourself stripped to your underwear if the locals liked the look of your outfit. (The same thing, to be fair, happened in Lorengau.) Many locals had slash marks on their chests and shoulders, scars left from prior knife attacks.

For someone like me, however, having lived for four years in a tropical concentration camp, this new city was a Xanadu, a stately pleasure dome. Instead of carrying a whiff of fear and desolation, the air was a soft and inviting blend of local fruit and kitchen scents, carried on the breeze. I liked the way it touched my nostrils. It smelled of freedom and release.

The fairytale continued, as the clock ticked. I made a coffee, and bought a round cup of espresso-flavoured ice cream.

Next, I called my brother. 'Shahed. I made it, I'm here.'

'Thank God. Mom and Dad will be so relieved.'

'Wait. Don't tell them too much, until I know what I'm doing. You'll just make them worry.'

'I don't get it. Where are you?'

'It's . . . a city. Where I don't think I can stay.'

The next step could wait. Still floating on a wave of warm showers and fresh coffee, I was able to put off my deliberations a little longer. Any place was paradise, as long as it was not back into custody.

Winiaka suggested I find a retreat outside the capital, since it was likely the news of my escape would trigger a manhunt. There had been one other detainee who had fled Australia's offshore system of detention. He had made it as far as Fiji when he was apprehended. The authorities of Fiji, a country under the same colonial sway as the other islands in the region, handed him back to PNG officials, who threw him into the black hole of Bomana Prison.

Winiaka was determined to keep me from such a betrayal. She had friends and family in Mount Hagen, a one-hour flight from Port Moresby. A city of about 50,000 people, it was located in the rugged western highlands of PNG, where tribal cultures still thrived.

'It's a mountainous region and easy to hide. You could live there for years without attracting notice,' Winiaka explained. 'We'll be able to figure out a way for you to get out of PNG eventually. Until then, your home is a farm in the hills where the outside world will feel far away. And my mother will be so glad to meet you.'

A few months in the mountains sounded like a welcoming option. Before I went anywhere, though, I had to get the braces on my teeth fixed.

Winiaka helped arrange an appointment for me at a local clinic called Lamana Dental. After a glance in my mouth, the dentist delivered the news: the braces had to be removed immediately.

'Infection is out of control,' she said. 'It has spread from your gums into the lining of your mouth.'

She wasted no time, and within half an hour dismantled the tiny metal scaffold that had afflicted me from the day I'd set foot on Christmas Island. I was prescribed a course of antibiotics and told they should take care of the infection.

The relief was indescribable, and fleeting. On the street outside the clinic was an SUV with four Wilson guards milling around it. 'Shit! They're shadowing me!' I thought, frozen in fear. Going back into the clinic would attract more attention. Reaching deep for a source of strength and serenity, I levelled my gaze and walked past them.

When I climbed into Winiaka's car my breath was ragged. 'Just stay calm,' she urged me. 'They could be here for many reasons. If they had recognised you, they would have grabbed you already.'

That night I was almost able to chew my food properly.

There was a version of reality in which I managed to make it to Mount Hagen, and reinvent myself as a rural guest, living simply among the hill tribes. There I could take refuge from the political storm that was about to engulf Papua New Guinea in advance of the general election.

As it turned out, that election, held in the summer of 2017, put a stop to my bucolic fantasies. There were reports of widespread voter intimidation, ballot-box tampering and outright political violence during the three-week period. By the time the polls closed, more than 200 people had been killed in the unrest.

With all this going on, Winiaka and Tessa both advised against travelling to the mountains. A Plan B to hide in the northern city of Lae – where Winiaka also knew some people – was forwarded and then shelved. For the time being, I was stuck in Port Moresby, at the heart of the conflict. At least by staying, I was able to take advantage of a follow-up appointment with the dentist. She said my mouth was healing well.

Although I was living a low-key, semi-normal, semi-safe existence in the capital, it was risky to stay in Port Moresby, which was crawling with Wilson guards. I was stateless, a jailbreaker on the run. The longer I remained in the capital, the higher the probability I'd be grabbed by the neck and either shipped back to Manus or tossed into the local prison system. Or sent back to the killing fields of home.

Throughout all of this, Luther had been fantastic. I'd become a fixture at his house, welcome to stay even as he left for days at a time for his work with the national airline, Air Niugini, as a flight attendant. When he was home, he would ask what I wanted to eat before every meal. He even helped me prepare a Burmese dish with improvised ingredients. 'Stay here as long as you want,' he advised. 'Feel at home. Feel safe.'

All I could do instead was worry. Port Moresby was starting to feel a little like the open-air prison of Maungdaw, or even Manus. I was free, relative to living in a shipping container under armed guard, but I definitely didn't have the same liberty as a normal person. I might have physically escaped the island but it still had a hold on me, like a tentacle wrapped around my ankle just as I was trying to pull myself loose.

I don't know if it was Winiaka or Tessa who first made the suggestion, but eventually Bougainville was floated as a potential hideaway. The remote island province belonged to an autonomous region that lay to the east of Port Moresby. While officially part of PNG, its administration is entirely separate from the rest of the country, from its immigration and customs down to the police force. Winiaka had a friend in the Bougainville town of Aropa. An elementary school teacher named Mariam, she said she was happy to take me in for a few days.

The next consideration was the plane ticket. Papua New Guinea was in the process of implementing a nationwide database of its citizens to improve electoral processes. The national ID (NID) card was also required to apply for passports and drivers' licences, and even to buy a sim card or a plane ticket. The rollout had begun in Port Moresby where almost everyone now had a NID card. My fake credentials weren't going to cut it at the national airport.

Since the NID was a recent measure, I reasoned that some PNG nationals might not have received their cards, because they were out of the country during the rollout, or hailed from a remote province – like Manus. I hoped to pass myself off as such a person. After making some enquiries, I learned that, prior to the introduction of the NID, people who didn't have identification could simply apply for a temporary photo ID from Air Niugini.

The next day I went to the Air Niugini offices in Port Moresby and tried to play the role of a local. Spooked by my earlier encounter with the Wilson guards, I asked Mipil to come with me, since her sister Winiaka was back at work on Manus Island.

With Mipil standing at the ready, I approached the airline counter and explained my need for a temporary ID from the airline, which would allow me to buy my ticket to Bougainville.

'I'm sorry,' said the woman at the counter. 'We don't issue IDs anymore.'

'I was out of the country when they were being issued.' My accent was English, with a smidgen of Tok Pisin.

'Once again, I'm sorry.'

As I left the Air Niugini offices I felt the grip of Manus tighten around my ankles. I couldn't even buy a simple airline ticket for a local flight!

While Luther was a kind host, I couldn't stay at his place forever, with no job and no future, and with the threat of arrest hanging over me – along with the possibility of Luther getting in trouble too. Nor could I go back to Burma and expect to keep my life or liberty for very long.

There seemed no option but to turn myself in to the PNG police and tell them everything. That night I steeled myself to surrender.

It was Luther who came up with the breakthrough. As an Air Niugini employee, he had inside information about special tickets for staff. Airline workers – from the pilots to mechanics and ticket sellers – had access to discount fares for family members, a common perk for airline workers around the world. The arrangements were all made in-house, so there was no need for ID.

Luther found a colleague who was willing to sell me a discounted family ticket. Suddenly the door out of Port Moresby opened a crack.

I researched Bougainville online and was relieved to find it hosted a sizable expat population, thanks to a major gold mine that had attracted foreign workers. On Manus, my lighter skin colour was a neon sign that I had no business being anywhere but in detention. On Bougainville, I had better odds of blending in.

The next morning I said goodbye to Luther, thanking him for his support and friendship. I felt buoyant but nervous too. There was every chance I was on a watchlist at the Port Moresby airport, so Winiaka called her sister and asked her to drive me there in case.

As we pulled up at departures I shifted into a private atmosphere of panic. The Port Moresby airport was my escape route: it was also, potentially, a portal back to hell. So far, it had only led me to or from Manus Island. It was also teeming with security, military and immigration staff armed with two-way radios.

The security staff were dressed in the uniforms of G4S, the same company that ran Manus before Wilson took over the contract. For me, they were most immediately familiar from the prison attack, since it had been G4S staff who beat us that night, and then kept us on the concrete as further punishment. And here I was, walking among them, like I was just another of the good citizens they'd pledged to protect.

Since it was a domestic flight, I was spared the rigours of a full security screening. Regardless, my palms were wet and my mind raced behind my holidaymaker's disguise of earphones and sunglasses.

I checked in and took a seat in the waiting area, only to catch an announcement over the PA that the day's flight to Bougainville had been cancelled. That undersea monster again. Each time I batted it away, it returned to drag me under.

With my recent spate of misfortunes, I was becoming a burden on my friends and collaborators. Mipil had to return to the airport and drive me back to Luther's place, where I'd already said my emotional farewells.

Rolling with the changes with their usual good spirits, my team helped me rebook the ticket for a flight in two days' time. Mipil, who had already done far more for me than my connection to her sister warranted, offered to take time off work to drive me to the airport again.

Had it not been for the backing of these selfless people, I likely would not be in a position to share my story – and thank them for their lifesaving efforts – as I am grateful to do today.

TWENTY-FIVE

'The only way out is through.'

Robert Frost, 'A Servant to Servants'

On the flight from Port Moresby to Bougainville, I caught a
break. For once, there were no guards onboard. Either this was
a rare stroke of luck, or I was moving beyond the direct grasp of the
Australian refugee system and its sticky network of penal outposts.

This time my comfort grew as the flight wore on. We had a stopover
in Rabaul, where some passengers got off and others replaced them –
white people, but not the overstuffed tattooed types who guarded us
on Manus. Relieved, I sent a text to Mariam: 'An hour away from you
guys. See you soon.'

It was as if my reserve of good fortune and personal safety were
loading up like a piece of computer software, a sliding bar gradually
moving to 100 per cent. The sight of Bougainville through the tiny
airplane window added a few more precious pixels to the buffering.

The island was not only autonomous from the rest of PNG, it
occupied a different time zone – aligned with the neighbouring
Solomon Islands. Now 1000 kilometres east of Port Moresby, I had
traversed a small but meaningful arc across the globe. The doorway
that led back to Manus was closing.

My welcoming party at the Aropa airport was Ronald, boyfriend
of Mariam, who in turn was the elementary school teacher in touch

245

with Winiaka. Ronald was the friend of a friend of a friend. In other words, by this point I was learning to place my life in the hands of strangers. I had no choice.

He handed me a bottle of water as we climbed in his car, and merrily bounced along the dirt road that followed the eastern coast of Bougainville Island. We swapped small talk on the drive but already my eyes were scanning the new environment, taking note of the local signs, the placement of landmarks and the direction of the nearby mountains. It was too soon to lose this habit of watchfulness, of looking for clues and exit points.

As hospitable and kind as Mariam and Ronald turned out to be, I never told them I had just escaped from immigration detention. My alibi: I was a friend of Winiaka's who'd come to explore the islands of the region. I believed – and Winiaka agreed – that whenever I interacted with people, I should spare them the details. It was a precaution for their sake as much as mine. If they didn't know much, they could realistically claim innocence if authorities came asking questions. They were being offered one isolated point in a bigger game of connect-the-dots, since the full sketch, if it were to emerge, might get them into serious trouble.

Mariam and Ronald showed me to a spacious guest room in their home in Arawa, the largest town in Bougainville. The room was on the top floor and faced the backyard. The houses on the island were grander and more solidly built than the ones on Manus. This one had two storeys of living space, including a flush toilet and a television.

When I arrived Mariam was in the living room, with her children, both below the age of five, playing nearby. She was in her early thirties, cheerful and attentive to detail. Ronald had a contrasting personality: loose and breezy, with a touch of swagger. They were both wonderful cooks and treated me to a meal of smoked fish and taro, the ubiquitous root vegetable of Papuan diet.

And all this for me, a stranger. It was wonderful to discover such people after the dog pit of the Manus detention centre. It gave me hope that there might be an entire network of helpers out there, ready to put their own comfort and security at risk for those in need. And they did so quietly, their efforts going unmarked and unheralded. Out of modesty or self-preservation, they did their good works in a secret realm, beyond the prying eyes of the government officials or news media.

They didn't ask where I'd come from or where I was going. Either they had been tipped off by Winiaka, or had figured out for themselves that I was withholding the truth. Their lack of curiosity, mixed with their warmth and generosity, was a gift. Yet even with their unspoken consent, I regretted that the real reason I needed their hospitality was so I could scope out my next move.

My first walk that evening along the streets of Arawa was both uplifting and strange. It brought to mind the sensation of having handcuffs removed. That's how my entire body felt, as well as my heart and mind: liberated, but with a sting of absence – the unfamiliar feeling of being free of constraints – that would take some getting used to.

Here in this low-key town, which had its own supermarket and a bank branch, and where the clouds rubbed up against the buildings like friendly pets, the people let me be. There was no-one to search for me or shout the code on my prison ID to get my attention. If I wanted to eat the fish at the local market, I could. If not, I could choose something else. I could find a place in the grass and watch the ocean without a steel fence destroying the view. My first few hours in town, I did just that.

After a day or so of checking out the sights, I came across a pop-up seaside market a few hundred metres from Ronald and Mariam's place. A dozen or so long, narrow canoes with outboard motors were beached on the shore. Nearby, traders and locals bartered over fruit, vegetables, woven baskets and other hand-crafted wares. The morning slipped by pleasantly in view of the laid-back commerce of the tropics. Around noon, some of the traders loaded up their canoes, started their engines and headed east on the quiet sea.

A conversation with some locals explained it. Each Saturday, traders travelled by canoe from 'the other side' to do business with their peers in Bougainville. They came from Choiseul Bay, a remote outpost in the northernmost part of the Solomon Islands. The two places were so geographically close that people on both sides of the water could tap into each other's cell phone networks.

The division between the island nations was a modern invention, the product of colonial adventures that led Europeans to draw lines on the map for their own economic advantage. The seaside market and the maritime trade, meanwhile, had been going on for millennia, between ancient clans who paid little attention to borders. As such, there was no security checkpoint, immigration officer or coastguard involved, and no paperwork needed to move from one country to the next. The lazy seaside market represented a wide-open back door to another land. I wondered if I might be able to step through it.

That night I phoned Winiaka to suggest I might have found a way of getting out. She understood what a breakthrough this was. As someone who had been born and raised in PNG, and seen it become overrun with Australian security and immigration agents – a proud nation forced to become the host of prison colonies – she knew I could never be safe until I left for good. The Solomon Islands, in her reckoning, were just beyond the boundaries of Australian inter-ference and control.

'I should have thought of it first!' she said. The boat trip from Bougainville to the Solomon Islands was familiar to her. She had made the crossing herself, years earlier, with some adventure-seeking friends. As an added benefit, there was an airport in Choiseul Bay, which many travellers from Bougainville used to fly on to Honiara, the capital of the Solomon Islands. The plan, she said, had a decent chance of success.

The idea of passing through another airport worried me, given the documents and security checks involved, until an online search revealed that the Choiseul Bay airport was essentially a tent beside a grass landing strip.

Next, I talked to Shahed in Burma. Pulling together the very last of his dwindling funds, he managed to find enough to purchase an online ticket from Choiseul Bay to Honiara for the following Saturday.

There was a motel near Mariam's place that could print it out. In a positive sign, the receptionist happened to speak perfect English and didn't seem to think there was anything suspicious about what I was doing. The ticket she handed me, however, was a coupon with just a reference number printed on it. I had to take her word for it that the scrap of paper would get me all the way to Honiara.

The following day, I asked Mariam how someone might hitch a ride on one of the Saturday trading boats. In another stroke of luck, it turned out that Ronald had been planning to make the trip that week to pick up some items from Choiseul. My confidence in the plan grew.

Then, like a rogue wave, the fear hit me, coming in the form of a memory that was so strong, it threw me back to another place and time. I was on the tilted deck of a sinking ship off the shore of Binongko Island, soaked in sea water and smeared with engine oil. The image of the baby plunging into the water was as vivid now as the day it happened.

A sea journey was a mistake I had hoped to never make again.

This time, at least I'd have a chance to take a close look at the transport before trusting my life to it. The traders' canoes were finger-like craft with outboard engines on the back, and sides that rose just a foot or two above the hungry waterline. I imagined they'd sink even lower once loaded with people and baskets of goods.

The dilemma involved two sets of anxieties that were at war in my nervous system. On the one side was the apprehension about what lay ahead: an ocean journey, possibly ending at the side of another sinking boat. On the other was the dread of what could happen if I stayed in this country, where I was always just an intervention away from being tossed into detention on Manus Island or Bomana Prison.

A trip to the Solomon Islands was a wide-open possibility. It was a new country, with its own rules and systems for dealing with people like me. The ID I carried was fake, and I had no passport or visa, or legal right to be there. And if I managed to fly to Honiara, what then? I lacked a destination and even a sketch of a plan, and the lack of knowing left me vulnerable.

The path backward was fairly clear, as it headed into the dark past I was trying to escape. In my world of limited choices, hope prevailed.

I asked Ronald about the seaworthiness of the local canoes. When I revealed I could not swim, he stifled a look of disbelief. Having grown up on an island, he had learned to tread water around the same time he learned to walk.

'Even though you're in the sea, it is not wide open. There are little islands along the way,' he assured me with his easy-going smile. 'If something happened to the boat – which is unlikely, by the way – you are still not going to die.'

Easy for him to say. Still, his confidence tilted the battleground in one direction. I made up my mind to set sail for the Solomon Islands that Saturday.

I was relieved to have Ronald beside me in the canoe. If we capsized, I at least knew he was there to help. We left Bougainville mid-morning – me, Ronald and the merchant skipper, along with a load of handicrafts, including a collection of woven baskets to be sold at the market on Taro Island. We motored across a relatively calm surface for about an hour when a small landmass appeared on the horizon. We may have still been in the waters of PNG, or the canoe may have already pierced the imaginary boundary that surrounded the waters of the Solomons. The engine slowed and we drew nearer to the mysterious outcrop, revealing the most inspiring view.

The wide apron of sand that ringed the island was as white as icing sugar. Coconut palms flanked the shoreline, backing against jungled cliffs. Where the sun reflected off the sandy shallows it turned the water a luminous pale blue. I had never seen a more beautiful place, let alone set foot on one.

Close to the shore was a collection of thatched huts, perched on poles high above the sand and connected to each other by ribbons of ramshackle elevated walkways. Ronald explained that the community had built their homes this way so that when high tide arrived they could continue to go about their lives without getting wet. As we drew closer, we could see the greenery beyond the huts was alive with birds, darting in and out of vegetation so thick and vibrant it seemed to pulsate.

I was never told the reason for the stopover – whether it was to refuel or trade goods, or so the skipper could drop in and say hello to family or friends. But it lasted long enough for me to get my hands on a cracked-open coconut and enjoy its sweet insides in the shade of the palms.

The journey was already turning out quite differently than the people-smuggling operation aboard the *Emelle*. I was assured by the competence of the skipper and the integrity of the skiff. As we buzzed across the Solomon Sea my thoughts turned to the next leg of the trip, and the challenge of getting on the plane in the Choiseul Bay airport.

The plane was scheduled to depart that day at 3 pm. Since we'd left around 10.30 am, I figured the two-and-a-half hour trip from Bougainville would leave me with plenty of time to get to the airport.

Booking a flight for the same day as the canoe ride had been a calculated risk. There were only two flights per week: Saturdays and Mondays. After doing some research I'd decided on Saturday. Supposedly, there were far fewer non-locals in Choiseul than there were in Bougainville, so someone like me, with unusual skin tone and facial features (by local standards), would attract attention. And for an undocumented person like myself, that could be lethal.

Better to climb off the boat and board the plane to Honiara as quickly as possible. Once in the capital, I'd be able to melt in with the mixed crowd that Winiaka had told me to expect there.

The canoe closed in on Choiseul Bay with plenty of time to spare. The skipper had agreed to drop me ashore near the airport – the long strip of grass in the Google Maps photos, at a place called Taro Island – before he and Ronald continued on to Choiseul's own seaside market.

As we approached the shore, I discovered one of the most impressive, and problematic, aspects of the Solomons. The islands were surrounded by elaborate coral reefs, starting close to the surface and extending into the depths. The enormous aquatic cities were teeming with tropical marine life, and provided a protective barrier between the sea and those who lived onshore.

The reefs also caused problems for maritime navigation. I had insisted on approaching the island from the side that faced the open ocean, since that lay closest to the airport, rather than taking the usual route of docking at the pier inside the bay.

But it was low tide, and as we drew toward the shore, the underbelly of our canoe scraped across the razor-sharp coral, making a terrible crunching sound.

We were stranded. By this point, it was around two o'clock. The plane was scheduled to depart at 3 pm.

The skipper told me the boat was going nowhere until 5 pm, when the water levels would rise again. He must have known this was coming, but I had insisted, and the customer was always right.

'Looks like we're stuck here,' said Ronald, with a grin that I'd already come to recognise from my brief exposure to Solomon Islanders. 'Just *chill*,' this smile said. He had no way of knowing how much I had at stake. I was playing the role of a wandering tourist, with little in the way of plans – or sense – and he was taking me at my word. Meanwhile, I was sweating. My *insides* were sweating.

I had an idea. 'How about I get off here and walk to shore?'

'Out there? Walking is rough. I hope you can swim.'

As the skipper voiced his caution, Ronald caught my eye. He knew what my answer would be.

'Swim. Hmm. Maybe I'll stay after all.'

Since I had long ago given up on asking God for favours, I grasped at the possibility that the flight would be delayed long enough for a last-minute reprieve.

About an hour later we heard the buzz of an approaching engine. From my wooden bench in the canoe, I looked up and watched the plane come in for a landing.

An hour later I watched it take off again.

TWENTY-SIX

'Travelling – it gives you home in a thousand strange places,
then leaves you a stranger in your own land.'

Ibn Battuta, *The Travels*

Sitting in the boat for hours, perched like fools on the coral reef, left plenty of time to think. For me, it was like being stuck in a metaphor, an old one. We were at the bottom of the wheel of fortune, waiting for it to rotate and lift us up again.

The sun moved lower and cast the sky in purples and pinks. The sea responded in kind, creating a rippling canvas of deepening shades that had no top or bottom, and no edge but that offered by the nearby shore.

At last, five o'clock rolled around, and as the skipper promised, the tide turned and freed us. Our luck didn't get any better, though – not yet. When Ronald and I arrived at the terminal, there was only one person left, a man in a yellow vest with reflective straps. He was in the process of closing the door to the tent, which housed – or rather *was* – the terminal.

'I am here for the Solomon Airlines Flight IE 353 scheduled for 3 pm.' I thrust out my hand and gave him my dubious ticket confirmation.

'You are late. This plane already left.'

'Are you sure? Aren't there any more flights to Honiara?'

'I'm sure.' He looked annoyed. This man appeared to be the air-traffic controller, baggage handler, janitor, ticketing staff and airport manager rolled into one. 'That was the departure for Honiara and there aren't any more scheduled for today. I am shutting down.'

Although I was getting used to things going wrong, missing a flight was a new one. Returning to Bougainville was not an option in my contingency plan. The news caused me to freeze as my synapses misfired, looking for a pattern in the storm. I turned to Ronald but he had walked away, and was texting on his phone, probably sending messages to the merchants he had planned to meet hours ago.

The airport manager took in my stricken expression with curiosity, and then compassion. He had seen enough to feel some pity for a stranded passenger on a remote island.

The multi-purpose airport worker opened a small wooden cabinet attached to the wall and removed a dangling keychain of colourful tags. One of the keys opened the padlock to the tent. Inside was a simple desk equipped with an old computer and fat off-white CRT monitor, marked with fingerprints. After a few loud keystrokes, he said there was nothing available the following day. The earliest trip was two days later, on Monday at 7 am.

My heart sank as I considered my two options: return to Arawa on a canoe that night and try again the following Saturday, or stay in Choiseul Bay – assuming there was a place here for me to stay – in the hope of catching the next plane out.

The hitch was I didn't know if my ticket would be valid for the plane that was due to leave on Monday. Ronald, for once, was at a loss for answers, and the man at the desk, despite his assortment of airport responsibilities, refused to confirm either way.

Places like Choiseul were far from the usual travel routes favoured by backpackers and suitcase tourists, and had little to offer foreigners who turned up out of the blue with a bag and no clue. A person like me would stand out like a mirror pointed at the sun on this under-populated island.

Erring on the side of caution, I decided to risk losing the money I'd spent on the ticket and return to Bougainville to try again in a week's time, when the next floating market took place, sending skiffs back to Taro Island. I made a mental note: on my next attempt, pay better attention to the movement of the tides. Perhaps another chart in my notebook was in order.

There was a new wrinkle. As Ronald explained, the canoe we'd travelled in wasn't from Bougainville. It was a Solomon Islands boat and it wasn't going anywhere.

'Okay then, what about a canoe from the Bougainville side?' I asked him. 'Can you find me a spot on one of those going back tonight?'

'You've seen our boats. They're narrow, they're packed with stuff. It's impossible to secure a spot unless you reserve in advance. Even if I can ask around, they'll be loaded to capacity this late in the day. By the time we get to the dock, they'll be long gone.'

Ronald didn't understand what a problem it was for me to have missed the plane. In his eyes, I was a plucky, self-sufficient traveller who would take the setback in my stride and find a solution. He saw me as a kindred spirit, relaxed and unbothered; not because I lacked common sense, but rather because I had faith in my own ability to handle any challenge. This was the downside of turning people into dots.

He bid me farewell and stepped out of the tent. While he had been glad to make the ocean crossing at my side, this was a working trip for him, and he needed to finish his business before the sun set. Through the open flap, I watched him walk away – to make his way into this tiny fishing outpost.

With no option to return to Bougainville, I needed a Plan C . . . or D (I had lost track). The airport manager, still watching my face with curiosity, waited for my next query.

'Do you have a way to check if my ticket is still valid for the flight on Monday?' I asked.

He typed the confirmation number from my ticket into the vintage computer, and said he could switch my booking to the Monday flight at no extra cost – but I would have to make up my mind quickly, since it was time for him to close down the system.

Two nights on Taro Island until Monday. The synapses whirred. By then, the kind airport manager had run out of empathy and was ready to leave. Seeing my options dwindle, I agreed to switch the ticket to Monday's flight.

He handed me a slip of paper with a series of dashes printed on it. I was to return with it on Monday when, he assured me, he would get me on board the flight to Honiara.

'I guess I'll just wait here then!' I said, doing my best impression of a seasoned tourist who was accustomed to waiting in transit.

'Uh, no.' He shook his head. 'You're not staying here. Not allowed.'

'Okay, is there any transit lodge or airport hotel nearby?'

'Have you been to Taro Island before? It's not that kind of place.'

'So . . . I can't go to Bougainville. I can't stay in town, because there *is* no town. And I can't stay at the airport. That puts me in a tough spot, wouldn't you say?'

'There's maybe one thing you can try . . .' As he closed the padlock on the tent door, he described a fisherman's lodge where I could possibly rent a room. His directions were more like cryptic clues. 'Go left, then right, past the big tree, left again, then past a little tree, up a hill and turn right . . .'

Taro Island was lacking in street signs or house numbers. Doing my best to keep his words clear in my mind, I cut a zigzagging route across the island, which was actually more of a coral atoll, topped by greenery and fishermen's huts, the low terrain marked by a tangle of laneways and dirt tracks.

I was alone, and nearly broke, with just a few dollars of the local currency in my pocket, thanks to a gift from Ronald and Mariam. I was also lost, since my phone had no connectivity. The sun was now starting to sink below the western horizon of the island. The prospect of wandering aimlessly around a remote outpost – in the dark – was making me quietly panic.

Following a dirt road toward what looked like a radio tower about a kilometre away, I came upon a chain of small businesses, really just shacks lit by tube lights and dangling bulbs. There was a shop that sold a range of snacks and consumer goods, most of them hanging from strings. No-one spoke English and when I tried to buy a sim with PNG money, I was waved away. I found a kiosk that exchanged currency, returned to the first shop, and bought the sim card with Solomon dollars.

'Winiaka! It's me.'

'I can tell. Where are you?'

'Solomon Islands. And I'm stuck.'

'Oh dear, Javey. Nothing gets easier for you.'

As she took in my story, her sympathy was palpable through the tinny handset. But this time, her consolation and compassion were all she had to offer. Her magical ability to find valuable local connections and fix my problems had reached its limit the moment I crossed the maritime border. From this point forward, I would have to figure things out on my own. I asked her to tell her mom to say a prayer for me.

The late-afternoon shadows lengthened, bringing out the night creatures. The feral cats of Choiseul Bay were unlike any I'd seen before. They were unusually large, with puffy faces and menacing eyes. And they were everywhere: lounging on verandas, draped imperiously on the branches of trees, and creeping out of the roadside wilderness. Apex predators, they walked with the swagger of street gangsters. They scared the shit out of me.

As I searched for the fishing lodge it was clear the feral cats weren't my only worry. Some of the locals were getting drunk. Their angry voices came out of dilapidated fishing huts, loud with an escalating edge of aggression. It was a matter of time before someone took an unhelpful interest in me.

I held my head straight and kept walking. Finally, by a small miracle, I found the fisherman's lodge. It was just that: a hut that provided a communal area for fishermen to sleep, rather than a hotel where a stranger might rent a room. The owners took pity on me, sizing me up as either a tourist who had wandered far from home, or a fugitive. There was a space upstairs where I could sleep in exchange for a couple of Solomon dollars.

To my grateful ears, their grudging offer sounded like a kind welcome.

When I woke up the next morning, the cats had fled from the daylight, receding into the shadows of the jungle. In the glare of the sunshine, the island put on an astonishing pageant of natural beauty. The flora was rich and prolific with tropical birds, filling the air with their song, and the clear waters bubbled over with the mysteries of their depths.

There was so much life here, it turned the presence of a solitary human being into an incidental detail. As someone who had experienced enough of the human jungle lately, this primeval Jurassic Park was a glorious place. For two days, I took pictures of the ocean from every angle, and sampled the local dishes from the seaside food huts, quite aware I stood out as the island's only tourist.

By Monday at sunrise, I was back at the airport. It was a 7 am flight, but I arrived hours early. By now I knew to give myself time to deal with the unexpected, since anything might happen.

This time, it didn't. The plane stood at the ready, and my ticket was accepted by the airport staff, just as my jack-of-all-trades friend said it would be. (He was here too, helping people to load their bags of vegetables into the cargo holds.) To be safe, before boarding I put on my disguise of baseball cap, sunglasses and headphones, set to silent, creating a magnetic field that warded off any unwanted conversation.

The plane, waiting for us on a grassy field, was a fifteen-seater, about the length of a transport truck. It was a plain creature, with a door that opened in its nose to stuff in the luggage, and another in the midsection for more storage. The flag of the Solomon Islands was painted on its oversized tail. The door, which doubled as a staircase, had four steps to let us inside.

Because it was a small plane, every seat offered a clear sightline to the surrounding scene. We pulled off the grass runway, rising over the same coral reef that had toyed with our boat a couple of days earlier. The windows on the other side revealed the green hill, which faded to turquoise as we gained altitude in the rich, wet air. The mountain rose beside us, a continuous slope that plunged deep beneath the water's surface, shifting from bright to cobalt blue.

The plane barely reached 3000 feet for the entire journey, which followed a route south-east along the Solomon Islands archipelago. We flew low enough that there was a cell connection onboard, something I knew because the pilot was on his phone during the entire flight. So much for 'Please turn off your mobile devices' to avoid messing with aircraft navigation.

After a couple of hours, we had a refuelling stop at Nusatupe, at another make-do terminal, a one-room concrete shack on a battered golf course of a runway. And then it was back in the air for a few more hours, until our final resting spot was announced by the low mountains of Guadalcanal island.

Skirting the base of the mountain range was a city of considerable size. My chest tightened. Boarding a plane on a grass field was one thing, but this was actual civilisation, with a proper airport that would be equipped with all the standard security and screening measures. As the plane began its descent, I prepared a portfolio of alibis, in case someone on the ground felt a need to pry.

'Pleased to meet you,' I rehearsed. 'I am Ian, the backpacker who has inexplicably fallen in love with your fair city of Honiara.'

Fortunately, perhaps, the world was spared my masterful performance. The disembarking process went as smoothly as in any tourism video, and soon enough I was in Honiara, the capital of the Solomon Islands, on my way to the Airbnb that Nina had booked. Just like a real tourist! My alibi had started to merge with my real life. One day soon, I hoped, I could stop with the stories.

In the meantime, there were more tales to tell. On the drive to my homestay, I told the mother of the Fijian family who were to be my hosts – they had kindly picked me up at the airport – that I was returning from a short tour of the natural riches of Choiseul Bay. Busy tourist that I was, my intention was to stay in Honiara for just a brief visit.

I never imagined I'd still be there six months later.

TWENTY-SEVEN

'Good luck to you, even so. Farewell! But if you only knew, down deep,
what pains are fated to fill your cup before you reach that shore.'

Homer, *The Odyssey*

In one sense, human beings are made out of paper: birth certificates, passports, drivers' licences, identity cards, tax records, marriage certificates and university degrees. When it's not printed on a form, our existence is conjured by keystrokes and spun into codes to be stored alongside billions of other souls in databanks.

It's only when you're wiped from the system, or your pieces of paper are scattered across the seas, that you realise how much this stuff means to you. Without paper, in the eyes of society you don't exist.

By the time I landed in Honiara, I was as close to a human zero as could be. It was a somewhat familiar condition. For much of my life, I had skirted the void of legal selfhood. In Burma, my identity was registered on the census, but not on the roster of citizens, where I was classified as a Bengali. On Christmas Island, my name was misspelled and replaced by the abbreviated version of a boat.

The fact that I had managed to make it as far as Guadalcanal island was largely thanks to the help of those whose credentials were intact. They had the connections and legal clout to make things happen for me. But now, having travelled too far from their friendly orbit, I was stuck again, trapped in the dead end of a one-way oceanic wormhole.

The old familiar pressure was at my back. If I wanted to go further, I needed to be resurrected on paper.

The countries whose hands I had passed through so far – Burma, Indonesia, Australia and PNG – were too hostile to this project to call on for help. Coming to the rescue, once again, was Nina. She said if I wanted to be treated as a legal and legitimate person again, it made sense to seek the intervention of the UNHCR. And she happened to know someone in Canberra who might be of service.

I was sceptical. From my own experience, I knew how hamstrung and compromised the UNHCR was as an organisation, both in its role as an advocate and as a resettlement agency for refugees. It could only operate in places where it was permitted to do so, and only earned that approval by agreeing to abide by the local government's rules.

Such was the case in Indonesia, at least, which had been turned into a nationwide holding pen for the refugees who might be otherwise headed to Australia. As had Malaysia and Papua New Guinea.

And who had the keys to those holding pens? The local immigration departments, sure, but also the UNHCR itself, as well as its sibling, the International Organization for Migration. Willingly or not, they were as complicit in this grimy system of keeping refugees stuck in limbo – with no access to work, education or hope – as the local governments. In fact, they *ran* the grimy system in Indonesia, with Australia – as far as I could tell – ultimately footing the bills.

It was hard to know who to trust, and if I got caught that information could easily leak out. I'd learned the hard way how much influence Australia wielded over the region. Australia boasted the dominant population, the biggest military and the richest economy. A shark among minnows, Australia would move quickly if it caught my scent, shifting me to a jail in Honiara or shipping me back to one of my earlier sites of detention.

Nina's UNHCR contact in Canberra was a lawyer named Chanelle. It turned out I'd met her when she visited Manus Island as part of an investigation (which went nowhere, of course) into the conditions of our detention. At that time, we'd had a long talk about my case: the procedural blunders, the immigration deceits and complications, and the cancelled medical transfer.

Nina reminded me that Chanelle had integrity and a good heart. 'She works in the interests of refugees,' she said. 'You don't have to worry about her, Javey. It's an avenue worth trying.'

If Nina thought someone was a good person, I trusted her, because it took one to know one. She said she would talk to Chanelle to see if there was any way the UNHCR could put me on an official piece of paper. The response was not encouraging: I could only be processed into their system if I met face-to-face with a representative from the organisation. Yet they had no office in the Solomon Islands, nor plan to send any staff there in the near future.

For my part, I lacked any means of travelling to a country where the UNHCR had a foothold. Back to zero again.

My Airbnb arrangement with the Fijian family was too expensive to sustain, so I searched for another place to stay. Winiaka had a family friend named Jennifer who stepped forward. She found a sublet for me in the foothills of the mountains that I'd seen from the plane a few days earlier. It seemed my fantasy of becoming a country squire and hillside dweller was about to come true after all.

When we arrived, however, the area was a slum. While I was not overly delicate about my living conditions, this place seemed like a magnet for trouble. Drunk people hung off balconies, breathing danger into the air. It was not hard to imagine the police coming by, and often.

Back in the city, I felt dejected. I had run out of the sleeping pills and antidepressants I'd been prescribed on Manus, and had no way of obtaining another script. This not only made getting proper rest a challenge, it also led to withdrawal symptoms. My hands shook from time to time, and I struggled with strong and abrupt mood swings.

Deciding it was worth paying a little extra for the company during this difficult time, I ended up spending another week with the Fijians.

The two (attractive) daughters in the family did not talk to me, sadly enough, but their parents did. Kept airborne on their good jokes and amazing food, I felt strong enough after seven or eight days to shift to the cheapest Airbnb, on the outskirts of the town, near the airport.

Accommodation was quickly becoming a problem. Without a longer-term fix, I'd soon run out of a way to pay for my meals, let alone find a roof over my head. Shahed had sent all the money he had left, and that was now dwindling. I faced the prospect of being homeless, undocumented and erratically moody: not a great combination.

Compared to Choiseul Bay, Honiara was abuzz with activity. The low-built city was crouched beside a busy port crammed tight with fishing trawlers, freighters, motorised canoes and sailing boats. The capital was home to around 80,000 people, as well as the country's parliament, its administrative branch and judicial system.

And while it didn't quite feel real – maybe because, a week or so earlier, I had never heard of it – Honiara was still a part of the world I lived in, the one I was trying to leave behind.

I was flicking through a copy of the *Solomon Star* newspaper when a photo caught my attention. It was a black-and-white picture of men trapped behind a high steel fence. I knew that barrier and I knew the men. Under the headline 'NZ still wants Australia's offshore detainees', the accompanying report described the bid by New Zealand to take in 150 asylum seekers a year from Manus and Nauru.

The offer had first been made in 2013, around the time I had arrived on Christmas Island, only to be overturned by Australia, which apparently had the same power over its small-but-rich neighbour as it did over the other client states of the region. A number of excuses, none of them particularly convincing, were offered by Australia for blocking the deal. It was claimed, at one point, that allowing the New Zealand offer to go ahead might encourage the resumption of boat migration through the region, and at another that doing so might interfere with the negotiations with the United States to transfer the Manus refugees there.

Had the plan gone ahead, more than 750 refugees – nearly the entire population of the detention centre – would have been resettled in New Zealand by 2017, the time of the news story. Instead, Australia chose to keep spending billions of dollars on building its gulag empire, including the expensive deal with Cambodia that flamed out.

New Zealand's offer, first made by Prime Minister John Key, was kept on the table by his successor, Jacinda Ardern. Ms Ardern received mail from detainees on Manus and Nauru, in which they respectfully asked for a chance to build a future for themselves. (The careful effort that went into these letters, which I still have copies of, is heartbreaking.) And still, the offer was blocked by Canberra, year after year, right up until the time of the writing of this book.

Australia's move to kill the deal was only confusing if you actually believed the talk about 'stopping the boats'. By now, the government had made a serious commitment to building its federation of penal colonies across the South Pacific, and that federation had developed a life and economic logic of its own. There was too much money to be made and political points to be scored to throw it all away for the sake of New Zealand, that easily ignored younger sibling of a nation.

As I read and reread the *Solomon Star* article, my intrigue turned to dismay. I wasn't surprised the Australians could be so heartless – that was old news, although rejecting an offer of asylum from a peer country was depraved, even by their low standards. What seemed remarkable about the story was that it had been published at all. That such a far-flung newspaper even knew what was happening on Manus and Nauru, let alone reported on the political dynamic, for some reason impressed me.

Clearly, I had not done enough research into the ties between the Solomons and Australia. I knew the so-called 'Pacific Solution' was the brainchild of the Howard government back in the 2000s: that was the extent of my understanding.

An online search, made from the comfort of my bed in the Airbnb, set the record straight. The Solomon Islands had actually offered to host Australia's offshore detention centres when the idea of building them was first floated. Eventually Nauru and PNG claimed the dubious honour, but the Solomons' bid spoke for itself.

The virgin jungle I had admired from the ground and the air as I flew in from Choiseul could have easily been bulldozed to make way for a prison just like those on Manus Island. The realisation that I was the guest of a government happy to lock up persecuted people was a cold fist squeezing my heart.

Sleep became impossible, and the more I read, the more alarmed I became. Australia was at the forefront of an operation called RAMSI: Regional Assistance Mission to Solomon Islands. The project's moniker brought to mind the name of the Tamil friend of mine on Manus Island, Ramsiyar, who had lost half his family to persecution in Sri Lanka before trying to flee to Australia.

This RAMSI was quite a different creature: a fourteen-year-long effort of Australian troops and federal police to bring a forceful end to the post-colonial unrest and ethnic conflict across the island chain. It was the colonising strategy, at least as old as the Roman Empire, of pacifying a region in order to exert control over it.

From 2003 to just one month before I'd arrived in 2017, Australian forces had played a major role in steering the fortunes of the Solomons. Whatever pleasure I'd taken in wandering the streets of Honiara to that point shrivelled and died. Each step I took might place me in the grip of the enemy.

If that happened, as I've mentioned, I wouldn't be the first person to escape from Manus only to be returned. Loghman Sawari was a very frightened, very sensitive seventeen-year-old boy when he was first thrown into the adult jail on Manus Island in 2013. I didn't know Loghman in my early months, since he was separated from the rest of us. Despite carrying a photocopy of his Iranian national ID that showed he was underage, he was registered as eighteen years old in the Australian immigration database. That meant he was detained with the adult men on Manus, rather than being sent with the other families and minors to Nauru.

When Australian immigration realised their mistake, they simply plucked Loghman out of the prison population and held him in an isolated cell in a different section until he turned eighteen. Just like that: problem solved!

Once termed an adult, he was placed in the main prison with the rest of us. I used to see him around, usually waiting in the never-ending line-ups to use the phone. Maybe he thought hearing a familiar voice from home would get him through the rest of his day. He may have also wished to reassure his mother, who was under the impression he was living happily in Australia.

Desperate and depressed, he was one of the first prisoners to apply to move out of Manus detention centre, once granted refugee status. His new home was the freshly constructed East Lorengau Transit Centre, designed for those who had agreed to claim asylum in PNG. (Claiming asylum, as we've seen, implied you were to be stuck in the country indefinitely, the reason myself and others had taken a pass on the option.)

Australia used its shiny new prison to show the taxpayer its successful integration of refugees on the island. Although the detainees were offered a small range of extra liberties, including the ability to wander freely until the 6 pm curfew, they were also subject to regular attacks – stabbings and violent robberies – at the hands of the locals.

Given all this, it was unsurprising that Loghman, still a delicate teenager, did not last long in his new home. Within the first few months of his transfer, he tried to hang himself using a towel knotted into a makeshift noose.

When the Wilson guards saw his body dangling limply by the neck, they rushed into his room, cut him down and moved him – not to a medical facility, but to the local police station, where he was locked up for twenty-four hours with twenty local men. Loghman's transfer back to the detention centre came with a warning: 'Try to suicide again and you'll spend a longer stretch in the police cells.'

He was later allowed to resettle in PNG, but was told it would take eight years before he could see his mother. He ended up homeless and destitute in the city of Lae.

In February 2017 Loghman somehow got his hands on a fake passport and a plane ticket to Suva, the capital of Fiji, 3700 kilometres from PNG. There, he stayed with a Fijian family and applied for asylum. The friendly welcome he first received turned to one of hostility when some of the locals decided this gentle young man from Iran was somehow connected to Arab terrorists.

He was on the way to the Fiji immigration office to lodge his claim when he was ambushed by security officials, who had caught wind of his movements. His bid to register as an asylum seeker was over before it could begin, despite the fact that he already had refugee status from PNG, and that his seizure and deportation went against the rules of the Geneva Convention that Fiji had signed.

He was sent back to Port Moresby where he was arrested again, this time for travelling on a false passport, and thrown into Bomana, the black hole. He was kept there for the longest time, before being released and disappearing from the public eye.

My most enduring memory of Loghman came from the footage of him at the airport in Fiji as he was arrested – visibly broken, his dignity stripped in front of the thirsty camera lens.

He was crying like a child.

TWENTY-EIGHT

'No word of truth is beautiful without the touch of a lie.'

Burmese proverb

By sunrise, I was convinced I was in danger. With the government of the Solomon Islands – like that of Fiji, and the other territories of the region – being in thrall to Australia, one call to an embassy and I might end up like poor Loghman, hunted down and apprehended.

As long as I was an undocumented visitor to the country, I was especially exposed. For my protection while I was here, and for the sake of finding a safer harbour, I needed some kind of identification to prove my legal status.

Winiaka knew someone, a former student named Eliza, who now worked for the government of the Solomon Islands. Since this was a delicate topic – asking a government staffer to help secure what amounted to a fake ID – it warranted a trip to Honiara to make the request in person.

Soon after she landed, Winiaka met me near the central market. Her legal work on Manus Island was winding down. Most of the staff had left and been flown back to Port Moresby or Australia. The detention centre, she said, was being abandoned.

With that bombshell left for me to digest, we moved on to the matter of the day, and the reason she'd flown here: our meeting with Eliza. An hour or so later, the three of us met for lunch at the Market Street

Kitchen, west of the commercial area. After making introductions, Winiaka told her former student that I needed a local ID to get off the Solomons. She implied that my own background was from PNG.

'Why bother with an ID?' asked Eliza, taking the request in her stride. 'What you need is an actual passport.'

'Works for me,' I said. 'What can I do to make that happen?'

'To get one in this country, I don't think you even have to go to the passport office. There may be an option where they mail it to you.'

If the process were as easy as she described, it could be my salvation. After we finished lunch and went our separate ways, I did my research, and the more I read, the more my optimism grew. At that time, like most of the island nations in the South Pacific, the Solomons had yet to develop a fully-fledged national identification system. Just as the maritime borders were porous to any canoe, the usual trappings of ID cards and headshots meant little to the local people. It was a high-trust society, where people mostly believed you were who you said you were.

For me to get my hands on a passport, all that was required was for two Solomon Islands citizens to sign statutory declarations that they had known me for at least five years, and that I, too, was a Solomon Islander. Those affidavits were to be mailed along with a passport application form and two photographs to the Ministry of Immigration, along with a receipt for the processing fee. The ministry would then send me a passport in the post.

A new door opened. Step one would be finding and enlisting two people to vouch for me. Eliza couldn't be one of them, since she worked for the government. She did, however, have two friends who, for a small fee, could be trusted to do the favour.

One problem was my face. I simply did not look, at a glance, like a native of the Solomon Islands. My features were out of place, and my skin was the wrong shade.

Thankfully, a loophole lay in the history of the region. Since arriving in Honiara I'd noticed a number of people who stood out from the Melanesian locals. Many even looked like they might be of

Indian descent, with origins closer to the part of the world that I came from, and with features similar to my own.

A quick history lesson from Eliza revealed that the first Indians had been brought to Fiji in the nineteenth century as indentured labourers. By the twentieth century, Indo-Fijians accounted for more than half the population of the islands. From Fiji, these former labourers, now successful traders and business people, had migrated to other parts of the Western Pacific, including to the Solomon Islands. Some married locals and raised children who looked a lot like me.

It was among this cohort that I planted my new fake identity. 'Michael' was a boilerplate moniker among Solomon Islanders, and Waradi was the most Fijian-sounding family name that Eliza could think of during our second meeting. In the new biography I hatched for myself, my father was himself mixed, an Indo-Fijian, and my mother was a Solomon Islander.

Eliza gathered the application forms and Winiaka helped me fill them in. I had photos for my new ID taken at a shop in Honiara.

'Bye bye, Ian, good luck, Michael!' Winiaka wished me, as she left Honiara.

My old name, Ian Vele, the IT specialist from PNG, was of no use in this country and it was time to get comfortable with my new alias. Still, an invented name and family tree only got me the passport. If I were ever to come face-to-face with a customs official at the airport, I would need to do a credible job of acting like the real thing.

The language lessons in the tent back on Manus finally proved their use. While they did not make me fluent, they had trained my ear to understand the dialect of the Solomons, Pijin, and the subtle ways it differed from the Tok Pisin spoken in Papua New Guinea.

My peregrinations around Honiara, visiting the shops and making casual small talk with the locals, had a new, secret purpose: to help me sound like one of them.

My wardrobe had to change too. The jeans, shirts and shoes that had followed me from Port Moresby were replaced by the rubber flip-flops, shorts and t-shirts that were the daily uniform of the Solomon Islanders.

If I were to fully inhabit the role of Michael Waradi, I had to believe the lie. I approached the challenge with the zeal of a method actor. Soon, with practice and deliberation, I felt confident to appear on the main stage.

Once ready, I put the application in the mail, and waited for the passport to arrive. At last, I would have a legal existence, captured on paper. And even if that existence was a fiction, it would help get me off this island and to a safer place where real life could begin again.

The moment of release never came. Instead, weeks later, I received a notification that the policy on passports had changed. Just one week after I had heard about the mail-in option, that option had evaporated. Now all applications had to include biometric data which could only be shared in person.

It was possible, in this case, that I had been too careful. Had I applied earlier, my application may have made it through under the old system. Now I was stranded. While my preparations might be convincing enough for a two-minute chat on the way to boarding a flight, no trained immigration officer would believe I had been born and raised in the Solomon Islands.

For the next two weeks, I considered my options, as my ability to think through them was eroded by lack of focus, since I was too nervous to eat or sleep. I had no way of supporting myself other than with the evaporating funds that Shahed had sent, and no way of registering with the UNHCR.

That left one option: to fly back to Choiseul Bay, beg a ride on a canoe and sail back to Bougainville. Maybe I'd even need to retrace my steps to Port Moresby. Life was going backward, into darkness.

Winiaka was devastated to hear the news when I phoned her that night.

'I think I have to come back,' I told her.

'I don't think that's a good idea,' she replied. 'The violence is actually heating up. As bad as it may be, you're better off staying.'

Around the time I arrived in the Solomons, I'd begun monitoring the conversations on the app that we had used on Manus to share news and updates. This was an encrypted messaging service, which allowed us to chat free from the unwanted scrutiny of the immigration and security staff, who listened in to our phone calls.

And now I was the one listening in. It seemed wiser to keep my return to the app to myself, since announcing where I was – and how I got here – would trigger questions and further explanations that might make trouble for all of us.

One afternoon, I found a quiet moment in a coffee shop, the Breakwater Cafe at Point Cruz, which overlooked the water and a handful of moored sailboats. More relevant to my situation, the cafe offered free wi-fi.

This time, when I opened the messaging app, rather than the usual quiet complaints and the occasional dark joke, my phone blew up with a rapid-fire exchange of alarming updates. As Winiaka had indicated, the Manus Island Regional Processing Centre was about to be closed.

The headlines, this time, confirmed what the guys were hearing on the ground. After months of dancing around the Supreme Court ruling on the detention, providing excuse after excuse, delay after delay, and prevarication after prevarication, the government of Australia had reluctantly given in, and had set a deadline to close the main prison on Manus Island for good.

The government of PNG, doing the bidding of its political master, had told the detainees they had to move out by the end of the month. The 'negatives' were ordered to relocate to a centre called Hillside Haus, also on the island. These were the guys who had been classified as non-refugees, either because they had exempted themselves from the process (as I had), or they had seen their cases rejected for whatever arbitrary reason. Their road ahead was a desolate one. From

Hillside they were to be held indefinitely, to later be deported, either willingly or not, back to their homelands.

The rest were to be sent to one of two spartan accommodation centres, the new one called West Lorengau Haus, or the existing transit centre in East Lorengau.

Haus: the name was an odd choice. A word in Tok Pisin for house, it was perhaps used here to suggest a Swiss cabin in the mountains, rather than the dwellings in question: shipping containers dumped in a freshly-cleared jungle. Minimal effort had been made to turn the containers into living quarters. The longest wall on each container, for example, had a single door but no windows.

Also odd was the company that had signed the contract to run the new steel cell blocks in Lorengau. The Australian government had put out a limited tender for the work, inviting just one firm to bid. Paladin was the riddle wrapped in a mystery, inside an enigma. This previously unknown outfit, registered to a beach shack on Kangaroo Island, off the coast of South Australia, with a PO box in Singapore, was the lucky recipient of $423 million over twenty-two months, the supposed cost of providing housing and security for the refugees in Lorengau.

This amounted to around $1600 per day to house each detainee, more than the daily rate for a five-star hotel room overlooking Sydney Harbour. A retired logistics manager told the *Australian Financial Review* – which had investigated the deal – that the real cost of keeping the men in Lorengau was $108 per day. On that metric, Paladin was pulling in around $17 million a month in pure profit. How to explain such a one-sided transaction? There were rumours of backroom deals, and well-placed friends.

The men still stranded on Manus had no way of knowing their distress was about to be used to line the pockets of a shifty corporation. Their only concern was the coming mass eviction. News of it spread quickly, sending tremors of dread through the detention centre population.

Life in our island prison had been bad enough, but Lorengau was considered an even less palatable option – an indication of how much the men feared being placed amidst the knife-wielding locals. Refugees were routinely assaulted and robbed in Lorengau by Papus who had been taught to view them as terrorists (thanks, Australia!) and were outraged these dangerous criminals were being sent to live among them.

In their defence, the anger felt by the locals was more than the effect of a brainwashing campaign. They had legitimate and long-standing grievances. Thanks to the Australians and their grand experiment in prison building, the Papus were losing their island paradise. There was the river of sewage that had been pumped out of the facilities into the local waters, and the mountains of plastic and waste that piled up in a community totally unequipped to handle the discharge. The naming of the most notorious detention block after the chauka, a bird so beloved it appeared on the national flag, was a crowning insult.

As the evacuation deadline drew nearer, I learned, via my covert access to the encrypted app, that the authorities had recently done a headcount. Finally – some four months after my escape – the guards noticed I was missing. Or rather they discovered that EML 019, that code in a registry of other lettered-and-numbered prisoners in their possession, was unaccounted for. My chances of getting caught and sent back to detention had inched up a notch.

The deadline and the anxieties it triggered had a mortal impact on some of the most emotionally fragile of the detainees. One man hanged himself in Lorengau hospital, where he was being 'cared for' after a previous attempt on his own life. Rajeev Rajendran was a Tamil refugee from the civil war in Sri Lanka and from the subsequent campaign of terror against his people. His death took the tally of refugee suicides on Manus to six.

The tragedy barely caused a ripple in Australia and brought no response from the government. Trying to have it both ways, as always,

Canberra contended that such events were a matter for PNG to deal with.

As efforts to shutter and demolish the detention centre intensified, the UNHCR released a statement, warning the Australian government that it risked unleashing a humanitarian disaster. 'Having created the present crisis, to now abandon the same acutely vulnerable human beings would be unconscionable,' said Thomas Albrecht, UNHCR's regional representative in Canberra. 'Legally and morally, Australia cannot walk away from all those it has forcibly transferred to Papua New Guinea and Nauru.'

But that's exactly what Australia did. Faced by the choice between one terrible dungeon and another, the detainees held fast, staying in the compounds even as the bulldozers were sent in to knock them down. When the 31 October deadline passed, the local authorities cut the power, water and food supplied to the centre. The 600 or so men who remained refused to leave, in the hope their peaceful protest might spark some compassion.

From across the sea, I wanted to shout out a piece of Burmese folk wisdom, 'Never expect mercy from your oppressor.'

As I read about the unfolding saga from Honiara, my heart broke for guys I had left behind. Even from a distance, I could imagine the extent of their anguish. When I saw the headlines, the siege of the detention centre had just begun. I did not know if the men would survive it, or succumb to a violent dislocation to Lorengau.

Also unknown: if I would end up joining them, given my lack of a way forward. I had crossed oceans, only to find myself pacing the rented room and feeling the walls closing in on me.

Twenty-five years old and still a tadpole in a drying puddle, my time was running out.

TWENTY-NINE

'A mask tells us more than a face.'

Oscar Wilde

As the walls pressed in, my mental health began to suffer. My sleep had been fitful at the best of times but now I found it difficult to get any meaningful rest. Every creak and rattle put me on edge, especially at night. The steady drone of helicopters, on their way to the nearby airport, was a constant torment.

I learned that my new Airbnb was located on the drive between the national parliament and the home of the prime minister of the Solomon Islands. He travelled in a motorcade, surrounded by police cars with sirens blaring. They'd drive past several times a day in a show of loud bluster. Whenever I heard that motorcade, I'd flinch, getting ready to grab my backpack and fly through the back door.

My habit of scanning for exits, developed in Indonesia, became a compulsion. I knew where each laneway and backstreet led, and which fences were scalable. Behind my sunglasses I was hotly planning my next escape.

And yet there were few ways out. With international flights out of reach, I looked for seaward routes. Of the nearby countries, I became intrigued by Vanuatu, an island chain whose northernmost reach lay just shy of one hundred nautical miles from the bottom of the

Solomon Islands. This southern edge belonged to Santa Cruz, another cluster of the Solomons, whose main island was Nendö.

On Nendö was an airstrip that resembled a golf course gone to seed, much like the grassy field in Choiseul Bay. After landing there, I could travel by sea to Vanuatu, perhaps as a deckhand on a fishing boat. It was blue-sky thinking, as I had no idea what a deckhand did, or how to find a skipper willing to take me on.

Then there was the feasibility of Vanuatu itself. For the record, it had once been an Anglo-French colony that became independent in 1980. It may have been another client state of Australia: my research had not taken me that far. Pure optimism had convinced me it might be a place where I could secure a travel document, board an international flight and get the hell out of the South Pacific, once and for all.

Arriving as a passenger made more sense. According to the Tripadvisor website, a New Zealand couple ran sailing tours in and around the Santa Cruz islands. When I emailed them, however, it was near the end of August, their off-season.

As I learned from wandering past a small building by the water, which turned out to be a hangout spot for maritimers, the Solomon Islands was a major stopover on the South Pacific sailing circuit. A steady flow of around-the-world mariners and adventure seekers plied the warm waters and restocked their supplies on the sleepy tropical islands year round. I came across websites where people could volunteer as crew members on private vessels in exchange for free passage.

That I knew nothing about sailing and was terrified of water were hopefully shortcomings that could be overlooked. A bigger problem, however, was the profile of the skippers I contacted, all of whom were either Australian or heading to Australia.

My growing fearfulness kept me from pursuing the idea further. Every promising thread I found was another strand of the web, with the fat body of the Morrison-Dutton cabal at its centre, about to pick on its next refugee victim.

My search for a place to stay, in the meantime, had better success.

The breakthrough came in the form of the website couchsurfing.com. It's a fairly well-known platform where locals offer free accommodation to the world's more frugal travellers in a spirit of grassroots support. Often the offer wasn't much – sometimes not even a room or bed of your own – hence the site's name.

After a few failed attempts at connecting with hosts in Honiara, I received a message from a man named Savang. We met over coffee near his office, and made an effortless connection. Originally from Thailand, he worked for an Australian NGO in the Solomons. As it turned out, his last job had been with the IOM, assisting refugees on the Burma-Thailand border – a responsibility that gave him a line of sight into the plight of Burmese minorities who had fled the junta.

Having worked for a time in West Papua, he was also aware of the condition of those detained on Manus Island. For the first time in a while, I felt comfortable opening up to a stranger. He listened intently and sympathetically when I spoke about the trials of life in captivity, during what should have been the best years of our lives.

And while I did not complete the confession by admitting the details of my escape from the island – in case he had qualms about harbouring a fugitive I spoke of myself as somewhat adrift in the world, and in need of a temporary haven.

'Listen, Jaivet,' he said. 'Don't worry about anything. You don't even need to pay for any food. Eat whatever you want. Feel free to hang around as long as you need to figure your shit out, okay?'

He stayed in a two-bedroom house, provided by the NGO that he worked for, in a neighbourhood called Koala Ridge. The building had a commanding view over the nearby valley, and the breeze blowing up the hill took the edge off the heat. Because Savang lived alone, he had an extra bedroom where he occasionally took in couch surfers like me.

I was deeply moved by his compassion and generosity, and amazed that I had somehow managed to connect, almost at random, with such a caring person. Savang was another point in the secret network of helpers, existing in parallel to the spiderweb run out of Canberra.

He appeared in my life when I needed it the most. And the network was about to welcome a new addition.

Finally relieved of the pressure of finding a place to stay, my mind turned with double strength to the question of how I was going to get off the island. Flying was impossible, given my lack of ID, but a sea journey seemed nearly as far-fetched. Teleporting was a great option, just not in my lifetime.

I was stuck.

One thing I had learned from my experience of depending on the kindness of strangers was this: when you did not have a ready solution to offer someone, you could recommend a helpful contact instead. Many times, the breakthrough you needed was just a friendship away.

That was the approach of Tessa, who had a long track record of solving problems. When she realised her own ability to get me out of my current bind had reached its natural limit, she offered to put me in touch with a woman she knew named Rendi, a Solomon Islander whom she had once helped in Darwin.

'I don't know if there's anything she can do, but she is someone else you can talk to,' said Tessa. 'And you can *definitely* trust her.'

She was right. A petite woman who loved to laugh, Rendi was also a natural listener – 'Keep talking' was her signature phrase – with an ability to empathise with my situation that came in part from her own biography. She had spent some time in the Wickham Point Detention Centre in Darwin, after seeking protection in Australia from domestic abuse in the Solomons. When her application was rejected, Tessa worked on her successful application to have her freed from detention and she returned to Honiara.

Our first conversation took place under the shade of a mango tree, within spitting distance of the Honiara fish market. We spent a lovely couple of hours getting to know each other. Rendi explained how life worked on the islands: 'the Solomon way', she called it.

'Things move at the speed of a snail in this place.' It was important advice for me, someone who was soon to experience a healthy dose of the Solomon way, and whose constant sense of internal pressure, if not checked by this gentle warning, might have landed me in hot water.

At our second meeting I was comfortable enough to tell Rendi nearly everything: how I'd escaped from Manus, come to the Solomons by boat, and tried and failed to secure a passport, after immigration had changed the rules a week before I applied.

'I missed out on getting it by *this* much,' I said, holding up my thumb and forefinger.

Rendi understood. Her brother worked at the Ministry of Health and he had told her about the new requirements, which were even more stringent than I knew. In addition to supplying two statutory declarations, photos and biometric data, applicants who were inelegantly termed 'mix-breed' needed to show proof of their parents' marriage or, alternatively, their own birth record from the hospital where they'd first come into the world.

Passport security in the Solomons was now in line with the rigorous standards of other countries. And the sting in the tail was that Australia had encouraged and even funded the new system. They may not have been following me in helicopters or police cars, but they were still blocking my escape at every turn.

The tropical sun that arced its way over Honiara didn't cook the blood the same way it had on Manus Island, but the weather it spawned was just as monotonous: a perpetual 30 degrees plus humidity.

Every now and then, a storm brewed, born of low-pressure systems rising from the warmth of the surrounding seas. During the summer months, any number of infant storms grow into tropical cyclones that spiral with haphazard fury across the South Pacific. In the times when these monsters swerve towards land, they leave a trail of destruction – particularly across the low-lying islands, where the locals live in huts of wood, tin and palm branches.

One unexpected upshot of such a disaster was explai∙ ʼ ᴛo me by Rendi's brother, David. Since he worked for a government agency, Rendi had recruited him to the effort of helping solve my problem of getting my hands on a Solomon Islands birth certificate.

Over *motu*, a Solomon Islands specialty made of root vegetables cooked over hot stones, David talked about some of the more epic cyclones of his experience. Back in the 1990s, the coastal town of Auki had been levelled by high winds and storm surges.

'The local hospital and health department buildings were wiped out,' David said of this provincial capital, located about 100 kilometres north-east of Honiara. 'All the records held there were completely ruined or lost.'

By laying waste to Auki, the cyclone had created a small crack in the new airtight immigration system of the Solomons. It was a crack I might be able to crawl through, and be reborn.

'There was no central system of record keeping. If you were born in Auki before the storm, your birth certificate is probably gone. That's partly why the government had to come up with the new process.'

The process sounded fairly easy, which was a red flag that it probably would be anything but. Still, what other option did I have? The cyclone, I decided, was my friend.

The next few weeks were a back-and-forth tussle with government offices as I pressed the case that I was Michael Waradi, the son of a mixed Indian-Fijian father and Solomon Islander mother, and that I had been born in Auki before the fateful storm.

I encountered a fair amount of resistance. Initially I was told I'd have to fly to Auki and present my case to the authorities in person. When I said I was unable to do that, I learned the requirement could be waived by paying a small 'fee'. With the bribe and a dozen or so documents submitted, I was mailed a genuine Solomon Islands birth certificate in the name of a fictitious man.

And now it was time to become that man.

With my language skills, outfit and backstory already in place,

ESCAPE FROM MANUS PRISON

I focused on the finer details. Many Solomon Islanders had dark reddish-brown stains on their teeth, a particular signature look in Honiara. The stains were the result of the ancient practice of chewing what was called, for convenience, betel nut: in fact a concoction of areca nut wrapped in a betel leaf with a dash of lime powder. The resulting high was similar to the one from chewing tobacco, a strong stimulant effect, with a comparable flattening of the appetite.

For me the taste was revolting and I spat out the infused saliva, rather than ingest it. I didn't want to get high – I just wanted stained teeth for camouflage.

By the middle of September I felt confident enough to lodge another passport application at the immigration office. A week after that, I was asked to attend the ministry offices in Honiara to supply my biometric data. According to the new rules, all Solomon Islands passports were embedded with an electronic chip that recorded the holder's unique features, including facial structure and fingerprints, and an iris scan.

Showing up at the appointment as an imaginary person was interesting, and worrisome. Back in my home country, I had some experience in having to mimic a young man who was Burmese in ethnicity and Buddhist by faith, in order to get past the checkpoints that screened for Rohingya and other minority tribes. Code switching was one thing. Assuming an entirely new identity was more daunting.

Despite my butterflies, I managed to get through the meeting with immigration intact, focused on keeping the tenor of my voice and the movement of my hands under control. After supplying my fingerprints and facial scans, I began to relax and even enjoy myself a little. My transformation into Michael Waradi was nearly complete.

When I was about to leave, the clerk called me back and handed me another form to fill out. Because I was of mixed heritage, he asked me to contact a separate division of the ministry to book an interview. The in-person examination was the last step before I could be issued a passport.

On the way back to Savang's place, I considered my likelihood of passing such a test. My command of the Pijin dialect may have improved with recent practice, but it was still not strong enough to bluff my way through a talk with an immigration officer, whose job it was to sniff out deception. I might look and act the part, but I was unlikely to fool a professional.

Since my method of preparation lay in thinking through scenarios, here was a new and formidable challenge to consider. I imagined how it might play out. The immigration officer, hearing my well-prepared backstory, would turn to me with a quizzical stare and state, 'If you've never had a passport before, then you've never travelled outside of the Solomon Islands, yes? Then explain to me why you can't speak your native language properly and why you have an accent.'

As usual I had trouble sleeping that night. After a while I stopped trying, and instead turned on the light and looked at the document I was supposed to fill out before the interview, scanning it line by line. Aside from the standard sections like name and date of birth, there were more pointed questions such as 'What is the purpose of gaining the passport?' and 'What is the intended travel destination?'

After what I had been through, these requirements sounded like an accusation, a demand for proof of legitimacy. As the endless night wore on, however, they took on a new light. The questionnaire could also be read as an invitation to invent any story I liked, for the sake of eluding scrutiny.

At that witching hour, the fabulist in me, so at odds with my resident logician, was let loose to play. What was my purpose in gaining a passport? I needed it to seek medical treatment that was not offered in the Solomons.

You see, poor Michael Waradi suffered from a wide range of physical and mental problems. His motor skills were diminished, he had arrested mental development from birth and – saddest of all – had lost the ability to speak properly.

The next day, I shared my woeful alibi with Rendi, who liked it so much she agreed to accompany me to the immigration interview.

Her brother joined the project, obtaining a forged doctor's certif-icate through a contact at the Ministry for Health. It stated that I required care from an overseas specialist to address my complex and deteriorating condition. The note also outlined my dependence on a full-time caregiver – Rendi – who was qualified to speak on my behalf.

Next I took a crash course in mental impairment. I read an array of scholarly articles online that described symptoms and behaviours of people with falling motor skills and serious cognitive challenges. As this was my one shot at a fake passport, I had to be convincing – as Michael Waradi, a seriously ill young man from the township of Auki.

After submitting the final form along with the statutory decla-rations, birth certificate, two photographs, a biometric data record and doctor's certificate, I made an appointment to face off with an immigration officer.

When the day arrived, Rendi drove me to the ministry offices in Honiara and accompanied me inside. The trouble began as soon as we sat down. The immigration officer turned out to be a close match with the mistrustful figure I had imagined in my fear fantasies. He was doubtful about my need to have a caregiver by my side at all times.

Rendi tried to protest but the officer was firm, 'I won't bite! I just need to talk to him on his own for a few minutes. We're going to carry on our chat in another room.'

He was onto me. Otherwise, why ask to move? Maybe there was a security guard or government agent from Australia waiting for me there.

Rendi watched in helpless distress as two officers ushered me down a hallway and into a small, austere office. Fighting an instinct to run, I scanned for exits along the way. When the officers locked the door behind me, I started to tremble.

Laying the trap, they stepped outside and left me alone for a few minutes. An interrogation about my escape from detention on Manus was about to begin.

I dug my phone out of my pocket and texted Rendi: 'Go to car.

Keep engine running. Leave door open.'

Terrified of what was to come, I was ready to make a break and run for it.

The lock on the door turned, and the officers stepped back inside. They took their seats on the metal chairs across the narrow table, and their questions came in a torrent.

'What is your father's name?'

'What is your mother's name?'

'Why are your parents not with you?'

'Do you have brothers or sisters?'

'Where did you go to school?'

'Where do you live?'

'What is the reason you need a passport?'

I replied as best I could, drawing on details from the background I had carefully fabricated for Michael Waradi. At the same time I was concentrating hard on the weird task of acting like someone who was a peg or two below the usual levels of mental acuity. I mumbled, talking in sentence fragments, and took breaks to look around the room with a startled expression. Clearly, I was at a loss without my trusty caregiver.

This was both the scene from a dark comedy and a horror movie. At any moment, someone was going to say 'Enough' and pull out the handcuffs.

After twenty spine-tingling minutes, the officers let me go. Resisting the urge to dart, I shuffled awkwardly back down the hallway, staying in character. Seeing the car where Rendi was waiting set me free and, safely out of sight of the immigration officers, I ran the last few steps and jumped through the open passenger door.

'Drive, please,' I begged Rendi. 'I don't even care if I get a passport or not. Just get me the hell out of here.'

Two days later, I received a letter stating my application had been turned down. It was almost November – the start of cyclone season.

THIRTY

'To live without hope is to cease to live.'

Fyodor Dostoyevsky

'Listen, Jaivet, the landlord is starting to ask questions,' Savang revealed. 'He wants to know who you are and what business you have staying here.'

It had been more than two months since I had surfed into Savang's spare room. The whole time he remained a supportive and obliging presence – a friend. He had offered me shelter and good company, and thanks to his cooking skills, some of the best Thai food imaginable. Were it not for his grace and generosity, there was no saying where I might have landed in my moment of crisis.

But he was staying in the house as a perk of his job, and he was answerable to the owner. While Savang never suggested I should leave – only that he was being pressed for information – I knew my time was up.

Shaken by my recent encounter with immigration, I'd given up on the passport and was thinking about retracing my steps back to Bougainville. Where else could I go? I discussed the possibility of returning in separate chats with Winiaka and Tessa, for whom my depressing situation was starting to check their usual high spirits.

The problem with Bougainville was it represented a step backward, a retreat and a defeat, with no clear next move in sight.

The options were bleak.

*

The situation back on Manus had unravelled dramatically throughout November. Hundreds of men remained holed up in the crumbling remains of the decommissioned detention centre. In the sick dilemma in which they had been placed, life in prison was seen as preferable to partial freedom in Lorengau, where they risked being attacked and murdered by the locals. They were too frightened to leave.

Each day, to tighten the screws, the authorities covered the compounds with notices that the eviction deadline was growing ever closer. Ultimately they cut off the power and water supply, and removed the food and drink from the canteens, donating them to the locals. After two days, the protesters had to dig holes in the ground in search of water. Since there was no power for the fans, the men moved their beds into the yards, where they were preyed on by mosquitos, and visited by hungry rats.

And still, they did their best to stay strong. When it rained, they stripped down to their underwear and bathed in the downpour. Phones – their only link to the outside world – were charged using batteries salvaged from an abandoned administration block. The batteries in turn were charged using solar panels taken from another demolished hut.

Meanwhile in Australia, Peter Dutton tried to salt the situation with his usual generous outpourings of doublespeak. 'The only difference in the new centre [in Lorengau] is that where we serve three meals a day at the [Manus Island detention centre], we're asking people to prepare their own meals with food supplied.' As if this were really all about different meal plans.

And yet, despite the wonders of the cafeteria meatloaf in Lorengau, or whatever nonsense he was going on about, the men stayed put, valiantly holding on for over three weeks. The Papu officials had seen enough. They overwhelmed the camp, filled in the water wells, beat the feeble, broken protesters with iron bars, and dragged them out of the camp.

For the first time in years, the Manus Island Regional Processing Centre was vacant – if you didn't count the ghosts of the dead.

It was hard to watch this happening from afar without being able to do something – *anything* – to stop it. Here I was, safe in my room in the Solomons, while the dignity of my friends was being crushed into the hard sand of Manus Island.

A silent witness to events unfolding in real time, reading the texts that the guys were writing as they were being crushed, I felt an overwhelming survivor's guilt, even if my own situation was less than ideal. The escape route I had been looking for was slow to appear, despite our combined efforts to find it, and it seemed a return to detention on Manus was inevitable. In whatever scenario I could imagine, my months-long adventure outside the walls of the island gulag was coming to an end.

Rendi, however, refused to give up. Her sense of determination was like a lava flow, slow-moving and implacable, and right now it was set on finding a way for me to travel from the Solomons. If lacking a piece of paper was the crux of the problem, so be it. As a local she knew there was more than one way to get what you needed in her home country.

She reached out through her contacts to explore the possibility of paying someone at the ministry to restart my application and have its approval fast-tracked. Although bribery had long been part of the culture in the Solomons, by early December her back-channel approaches had still failed to show evidence of progress.

Next she tracked down the immigration officer who'd said he wouldn't bite me. She paid him a private visit and explained how Michael Waradi had grown so gravely ill he could no longer leave his bed.

'If he doesn't get treatment soon, he will eventually die,' Rendi warned. 'And when that happens, it will be on your head because *you* didn't want to give him a passport.'

Cowed by the angry woman, the officer explained that the decision to reject wasn't his to make. After he interviewed me he'd presented a report to his superior, a supervisor of immigration. It was his supervisor who had turned it down.

I don't know how Rendi managed to change his mind, but the officer agreed to write a follow-up recommendation to the supervisor, stating that Michael Waradi was a special case, whose rapidly deteriorating health meant he should be granted a passport immediately. The new letter was bolstered by yet another forged document from a doctor, stressing my increasingly urgent need to travel.

Unfortunately, though, the supervisor was out of the city and not due back in Honiara for two to three weeks. That was typical of the pace of the Solomons, where all but the most pressing issues could always wait until later. There were few people in danger of having a heart attack through the pressures of work or a missed deadline. I just had to wait.

In the meantime, Savang's landlord grew more annoyed about the squatter living on his property. After three months, he had every right to question what I was doing there without his permission and without paying for the privilege.

By now Savang was well aware I was in the last, desperate stages of trying to get a passport. But there was no holding off the landlord. 'It's getting unsafe for me to host you much longer, Jaivet,' he said.

It was pressure piled on top of pressure.

As the weeks dragged on, I grew more certain of failure. We had thrown all we could at the passport idea, but the new and improved application system was proving impenetrable, just as it was designed to be.

Calling Winiaka, I let her know I had reached the end of the road in the Solomon Islands. She said she understood. Hanging up, I was crushed. Although there was a chance the supervisor might change his mind about my passport application once he returned to Honiara, that idea now seemed naively optimistic.

If I could have found a hole somewhere, I would have crawled inside it.

THIRTY-ONE

'Don't cry because it's over, smile because it happened.'

Dr Seuss

Torrential rain was falling the day Rendi answered a phone call from the immigration supervisor. It was late December. He was just back from his travels and requested to see her at his office right away.

It was a potentially alarming development. In helping me, Rendi had made fraudulent claims in official documents, which left her open to criminal charges. Still, she walked into the immigration offices that day with her head held high.

The supervisor said flat out he wasn't convinced the application was above board. He wanted to know why Michael Waradi's parents were nowhere to be seen. 'Why is it you sitting here and not his mother and father?'

We'd prepared a backstory to cover that question. 'His mother has passed away and his father returned to Fiji,' Rendi replied. 'His father is not in his life anymore. I have known Michael since he was a young boy and I am helping him now.'

'I've never heard of anything like it,' he said. 'A person who can't speak and has no parents? You do realise if anything goes wrong I am the one who will be accountable?'

'I don't know what could go wrong. He's a very sick young man

291

who needs specialised care. If he doesn't get it, he will eventually *die*. What could be more important than that?'

The appeal to the official's heart – and a potential appeal to his wallet – clinched it. He said he would grant the passport on one condition: that Rendi acted as my guarantor. If anything went wrong, it would be her problem and responsibility.

Rendi was kind enough to accept the risk on my behalf, partly because she believed it was morally right, and partly because she was ready to help a fellow ex-detainee. One more reason was in play, I suspect: it was her chance to finally give the finger to Australia.

In late December 2017 I was handed a crisp new passport. I received it with satisfaction and pride, as did Michael Waradi, by now my constant companion. The two of us were free to officially begin our shared life together, and travel anywhere in the world.

The timing could have been better. It was just three days until Christmas – peak time for travel in the strongly Christian Solomon Islands. All the international flights were heavily booked and remaining tickets were expensive.

Then there was the bigger and persistent dilemma of where to go. There were no flights to Vanuatu at that time. The three international destinations from Honiara were Cairns, in the far north of Australia, Port Moresby in PNG and Nadi in Fiji. Out of all the nations on earth, I could hardly believe these were my only options.

There was no way I could ever go to Australia or back to PNG, and Fijian immigration might arrest me the moment I opened my mouth to request political asylum. Consider the experience of poor Loghman Sawari.

My reserves of optimism, the bar graph that had once neared full capacity, was now close to zero again. Every breakthrough had brought further trouble, even in simple dilemmas that should have been easy to resolve.

Still, I had a passport and I was determined to use it. With Australia and PNG out of the frame, Fiji came into sharp focus.

Thinking things through, I realised Loghman Sawari had fallen foul of Fijian authorities because he had made a basic mistake: he had asked for help.

After entering the country just fine on a fake passport, he had ruined his chances by putting his head above the barricade and claiming political asylum. It was a request that Fiji, as a signatory to nearly every possible iteration of the Geneva Convention, should have honoured. But with Australia pulling the strings, it refused.

It was an understandable mistake for someone young and innocent enough to believe in signed agreements and moral principles. I would do well to learn from his tragic example.

If I were to fly to Fiji, it would be via a transit flight to somewhere else. Fiji was a tourist hot spot, with a reputation as an island paradise. It was also a popular stopover, and a launch pad to many other destinations.

This time, the legacy of colonialism did me a favour. Fiji, like the Solomon Islands, was part of the Commonwealth of Nations. The fifty-four member states – almost all of them former colonies of the British Empire – share an understanding, based on historical ties, by which their citizens can travel fairly easily to any country where the English monarch is head of state. I was surprised to realise half of Melanesia was in the Commonwealth, as were India, Pakistan, large tracts of Africa, Canada, Australia, New Zealand, and, of course, Britain itself.

My shortlist quickly narrowed to Canada, England and New Zealand, none of which required visas for Solomon Islands passport holders. New Zealand was dropped from the roster when I found out the flight transited through Australia. And every flight to England was booked solid, thanks to the holidays.

The normal route to Canada had a stopover in Hawaii, which was not a great option, since Hawaii, being part of the US, was subject to the Trump travel ban, and would probably place me under additional scrutiny. There were, however, some seats open on a plane from Fiji to Canada via Hong Kong, flying in two days' time. That settled it – I would make a run for Canada, a country and a culture completely unknown to me.

Occupying the full width of a continent, it was located more than 13,000 kilometres away – on the opposite side of the world. The True North, strong and free, as it apparently described itself. Time to see what it was like.

Calling back home with a new spirit of excitement, I asked Shahed to organise as much money as he could make available for the cost of my tickets. He did his best, but the well was running dry: we had enough to cover the price of a one-way fare. A return ticket was far preferable, as clearly a person without a flight back had plans to stay indefinitely. But given my financial straits, I had no choice but to roll the dice on a one-way trip to Toronto, the biggest city in Canada, and hope and plan for the best.

My confidence got a boost when I looked into the country's pre-arrival conditions. Rather than a proper visa, a foreign national from a Commonwealth nation only required an electronic travel authorisation – known as an eTA – to enter or transit through Canada.

For the online application, I checked off all the boxes that seemed most likely to produce a successful outcome, including a declaration that I was employed. A few short minutes after pressing send, my eTA arrived in an email. The speedy turnaround suggested the visa was generated by an algorithm, rather than a human being, which was reassuring. A single sceptical immigration officer was all it would take to bring my careful plans to ruin.

Once I possessed the trifecta of a ticket, a passport and an eTA, I felt like I might have a real chance of getting off the island. My flight was due to depart on Saturday, 23 December 2017.

In the days before the flight, I visited the Henderson Field airport to get a feel for it. I even surveyed the Solomon Islands Memorial park, connected to the airport on its west side, in case I needed to bypass security.

Much like I used to do in my note-taking sessions on Manus Island, I lingered for hours, my eyes open to the flow of people, the rhythm of security procedures and in particular the movements of the immigration officers. The airport was busy, thanks to the Christmas holidays. A welcome gift. When you're trying to go unnoticed, there's safety in numbers.

The next morning I bid farewell to Savang. He had thrown me a lifeline when I was nearly lost to paranoia and despair, and I needed him to know how much I appreciated it. As we shook hands, he said he was thrilled for me and hoped I would reach out again when I'd settled into my new life.

'Thank you,' I said. 'I will never forget everything you have done for me.'

As Rendi drove me to the airport, I felt a tightening in my gut. It was sadness at saying goodbye to such a good person; it was also nerves. Given my spotty track record when it came to clearing immigration, I had reason to worry. Although my observations of the previous day had indicated it should be a smooth process, there was often an unwanted surprise waiting in the shadows.

When we pulled up, I stood on the sidewalk and hugged Rendi. 'I wouldn't be getting on this plane if it wasn't for you,' I told her. 'I don't know how I will ever repay the debt.'

'You don't have to,' she said. 'In our culture, there are no debts between friends.'

With less than forty-eight hours until Christmas Day, the airport was even more crowded than it had been the previous afternoon. I walked into the departure terminal with the few possessions I had left, a personal estate humble enough to fit inside one small carry-on suitcase. Since I wasn't checking in any luggage, I moved straight through security, exchanged my ticket confirmation for a boarding pass, and approached the immigration desk, passport at the ready.

Then came the first surprise. In spite of the months spent polishing my command of Pijin, when I slipped my passport under the glass panel to the immigration officer, I couldn't understand a word he said in response. He spoke some kind of fluent Pijin that seemed free of any trace of English. He might as well have been talking in ancient Aramaic. (The roar of noise generated by thousands of excited travellers didn't help.) I stared at his face in dismay, absorbing the wreck of another of my best-laid plans.

The officer returned my stare and spoke again. This time I managed to grasp his meaning: 'Place your hand on the scanner.'

'Okay.' But as I placed my left hand on the glass screen, the officer made a gesture to indicate that I'd screwed up again. He said something that may have explained his meaning, but he had shifted back to Aramaic.

My heart pounded and my forehead itched with sweat. He pointed impatiently at his right hand and repeated himself.

'Oh, okay.' I bowed my head in shame, like the sheep I was in that moment. This time, I put my *right* hand on the machine and it made a beeping sound. The man stamped my passport, handed it back to me and waved me through.

It was around 2:30 in the afternoon when the Air Nuigini flight 84 taxied down the runway. As it hit take-off speed, its landing gear folding into its belly with a clunk, I slumped in my chair, my body accepting the permission it needed to relax.

Below the window, somewhere in the semi-urban sprawl, lay the apartment where I had stayed all this time. Back at the Airbnb, I used to wake up to the sound of airplanes passing overhead and imagine passengers happily jetting off to a new chapter in their lives.

Now, after six months as a castaway, it was my turn.

THIRTY-TWO

'Man is not what he thinks he is, he is what he hides.'

André Malraux

I'd been in Fiji just twenty minutes when the shit hit the fan. The trust I'd invested in my new passport vanished the moment I handed it to the immigration officer at Nadi Airport. He flipped through it from back to front and then from front to back, scanning each page with a laser light. I could read trouble in the lines of his brow before he spoke.

'Come with me, please,' he said in a clipped voice.

I was directed to an adjacent room, a featureless cube that had a desk, two chairs and a bench set against the wall. There I was handed over to another Fijian official – a woman. She, too, examined the passport carefully before placing it on the table and turning her eyes to me, taking in the sight with a searching scepticism.

'Are you a Solomon Islander?' she asked.

Time slowed and I found myself treading water in the deep end. She had my passport in front of her and yet was questioning my nationality. She didn't believe I was who I said I was.

'Yes, of course!' I replied with a little snort of a laugh.

'Where are you travelling to?' she continued evenly.

'I'm going to Canada.'

'Then why have you come this way? Solomon Islanders never travel through Fiji to get to Canada. Everyone goes to Australia first, and flies from there. Or they get a connecting flight out of Port Moresby. So why are you the only person from the Solomon Islands to fly to Canada through Fiji?'

It was quite an opening salvo but before I could answer she threw more grenades my way: 'Why don't you have a return ticket from Canada to Honiara? And why is it that you are flying today when your passport was issued just twenty-four hours ago?'

When she laid them bare like that, her doubts made sense, and my confidence in my own wing-and-a-prayer approach seemed foolish indeed. I had made the classic mistake of only planning for the obstacle in front of me – getting out of the Solomon Islands – without considering the bigger one that awaited me on the other side.

Without a backstory at the ready, I had to invent one on the spot.

'Normally, I wouldn't come this way but I had no choice,' I said as coolly as I could manage. 'I'm taking a vacation to stay with friends in Canada over Christmas and this was the only ticket I could find, because of the holiday rush. All the regular routes were sold out.'

Her return stare, guarded with a touch of cynicism, even disdain, showed my job was not yet done.

'The reason I had to wait until the last minute to book my flights is because I handed in my passport for renewal and it was held up by immigration in Honiara. They're slack back at home, they let things sit on the desks and only work when they're pushed. It drives me a little mad, between you and me.' I almost gave her a wink but decided better. 'So yeah, it's a fresh passport, but it's a *renewed* passport. I got it yesterday and booked my tickets immediately to make it to Canada for Christmas. To see my friends, who I miss dearly.'

Luckily I had the advantage of being able to speak in English, which allowed my mouth to keep up with the fairytale that was flying out of my brain. But the officer, whose English was as good as mine, cut me short with a new application of pressure. 'Then why don't you have a return ticket?'

'I'm in the process of getting one. Because of all the last-minute rushing around, I haven't had time to shop around for a decent return fare. If I don't get that sorted out here, I'll do it in Hong Kong.'

'This is not a matter for my discretion. If you don't have a return ticket from Canada, you won't be allowed on the plane in Hong Kong. They'll simply put you back on a flight to your last port of entry, which will be Fiji. You'll end up back here with me.' She waved her fingers in the air as if to say, 'Welcome back.'

I glanced at the phone on her desk. At any moment, this formidable border-control officer might pick it up and call immigration in Honiara – triggering a chain reaction that would quickly pull me into the abyss. Just as importantly, it might drag Rendi and my other helpers down with me too.

This uniformed woman, who in the past fifteen minutes had become my most forbidding nemesis, leaned back in her chair and crossed her arms, sizing me up again like a cop might a criminal. Her body language was clear: 'I know you've done something wrong. I know you're a fraud and I'm going to find out what you're hiding. I'm just taking my time.'

To regain a feeling of control over the situation, or at least over my own body language, I considered the arguments in my defence, with a growing sense of manufactured outrage. After all, I was no criminal – I was *Michael Waradi* from the Solomon Islands. I had a passport and a legitimate reason to be travelling on an unusual route, and what's more I had every right to do so if I wanted.

'Listen, if the problem is that I don't have a return fare then I can just get one.' My shrug indicated that doing so was as easy for me as sneezing. 'If that will satisfy you. As long as I'm in Canada for Christmas.'

'That may be, but we're going to wrap it up for the day.' She squared a pile of papers on her desk. 'At this point I can't allow you to pass. And since there are no flights back to Honiara tonight, you'll be staying in Fiji overnight. We'll take this up again in the morning.

If you can't figure it out by then, it's a return flight for you. Back to Honiara.'

Back in the transit lounge, I texted Shahed with shaking hands, telling him I had eight hours to buy a return ticket from Canada. My brother had already gone to extraordinary lengths to raise funds for my expensive voyages. He had virtually no chance of paying for more, particularly since holiday season prices for flights to and from North America were now astronomical. Still, he said he'd do his best.

As I lay on the bench, trying to sleep, I reflected upon how grateful I was to have him as a sibling. My feelings were not always like this. There were moments, growing up, when I had frankly wished for a sister. Shahed and I were just too similar, and our areas of interest and contestation overlapped too closely. If there was a ball lying on the ground, I would grab it, and so would he. We competed for everything.

Now that we were in different worlds, with different battles to fight, we were a perfect team. We shared a sixth sense, an almost tele-pathic understanding of each other. When to act, how to act, what to tell our mother and father, and what to keep strictly between us, confidences that could be shared without the need for words.

Since my days of being locked up and on the run, Shahed had taken care of me. He had saved my life, more than once. My wish now was that I could let him know what he meant to me, and one day return the favour.

Throughout the night my phone hummed with incoming text messages as Shahed kept me informed of what was happening. As hard as he'd tried, he could not raise the needed funds from the people he knew. We did not have rich friends or relatives, and the holiday pricing meant the fares were going for thousands of dollars each.

With every passing hour the window to freedom narrowed further. By 3 am, still quite awake, I'd accepted I would be returning to the Solomons in a few hours' time.

Around 4:30 am my phone hummed again. Shahed said he'd found a feature on a travel website that he thought might do the trick.

For a small deposit, the Expedia website allowed customers to book a ticket and hold it open for twenty-four hours. If you didn't end up completing the purchase, you'd lose your deposit and the ticket would go back on the market. Shahed's plan was to conjure up a bit of illusory paperwork by paying the deposit in order to generate what looked like a confirmed return ticket.

It was a clever plan that bent the rules, with a tricky flair that I could appreciate. He really was my brother.

'Once you pay, they send you a confirmation. I'll email it to you to show as proof of a ticket. They have no way of checking whether you actually bought it or not,' he explained in the Rohingya language of our childhood. 'We have to try it. It could be our last chance.'

Around 7 am the rattle of a key in the door signalled the resumption of my interrogation. The same woman from the previous day was back. She handed me a glass of water.

'So, did you manage to buy a return flight?'

Tapping into my inner Michael Waradi, I calmly showed her the booking confirmation from Expedia on my phone. 'Yeah, I bought one. You can see the details here.'

'Okay, but that's not necessarily a ticket, is it?' She cast her probing glance at my phone's screen. 'It's just a confirmation. And it's not even a return flight to Hong Kong or the Solomon Islands – it says here it's from Toronto to Manila.'

During the small, desperate hours of the morning, that happened to be the only fare Shahed could find that came remotely close to looking like a return to the Asia Pacific. It had been a case of Toronto to Manila or nothing.

This time, I was ready with a plausible reply. There was a work conference being hosted in Manila after my holiday, and I had to be there. 'As for this, yeah, it's a confirmation to hold the seat. Because it costs more than $3000, and it exceeds the limit on my credit card, I need to go to a bank and a travel agent to finish the payment. I can't do it here, on this phone.'

A pause while she took in this latest complication. To my astonishment, her hand moved to stamp my passport. There was a catch, however. Normally, people from the Solomon Islands were given no limit to their length of stay in Fiji. Since my flight to Hong Kong was leaving later that afternoon, and maybe as a warning to me that this shrewd officer could not be won over so easily, she noted 'valid for one day' on my passport.

The caveat was fine with me. Staying in Fiji had never been part of the plan. Weak with relief, hunger and prolonged agitation, I flagged down a taxi outside the terminal and fell into the back seat for the short drive to a $15-a-night motel, the Tropic of Capricorn, that I had booked days ago. Even though I was flying later that day, having spent the night in the airport I could use some rest. Plus, I did not want to be within sight of my interrogator, in case she changed her mind.

The taxi driver, mistaking me for a local, bombarded me with questions in the Fijian version of Hindi. My knowledge of Urdu, a related language, got me as far as realising he was asking me . . . something. I pretended to sleep to cut the conversation short.

At the Tropic of Capricorn, I was treated to a bunk bed in a communal room, with the showers down the hall. I spent the hours before my return to the airport texting Shahed to make arrangements for what would hopefully be the final leg of my journey. There was no point trying to sleep, given the noise generated by my two roommates, who I guessed to be tourists from Scandinavia, having sex just out of sight.

Despite running into a slew of troubles in the previous forty-eight hours, my odds of success seemed better than ever. For one thing, thanks to the interrogation, my passport was no longer suspiciously fresh. It had a history, having been used to allow me to leave one country and enter another, and its validity was established by the dated stamp on its once-virgin pages. Armed with this document, I felt better positioned to make it to Hong Kong.

ESCAPE FROM MANUS PRISON

A few hours later, the low clouds drained the colour from the landscape as the taxi took me back to Nadi Airport. Like in a film noir or a bad omen, the rain fell the entire time I was in Fiji.

Stepping into the terminal was like returning to a movie set, with all the elements of yesterday's high-tension drama still in place, and only the faces changed.

I passed through security without incident. As I approached the immigration counter, my nervous system was awash in adrenaline. My interrogator, at least, was out of sight. I handed my passport to a male officer, who took note of what was written inside and asked me to wait in a separate line. He disappeared into another room with my passport.

Something had gone wrong. The Fijian female staffer, who had all morning to investigate her doubts, must have contacted immigration in the Solomons. At this moment, the man with my passport would be reporting back to her. 'Yes, it's all over. We've got him.'

My heart was in my mouth and my knees began to shake. I steadied myself by leaning against the counter, with the practised slouch of a regular traveller.

After a few minutes the officer returned, stamped my passport and told me to have a nice trip. I smiled back at him, but on the inside I was howling, 'Holy fuck! Why did you just put me through that?'

The flight to Hong Kong was with Fiji Airways. I made my way through the international terminal to the departure gate printed on my ticket. With my mind still hot with the radioactive dust of my latest close call, my eyes took in a few details: the passengers, and the view through the large windows, the curtains of rain sweeping across the runway.

While waiting for something to happen, for a movement in the line, or an announcement over the PA, I overheard someone in the lounge talking about the flight. The man said he really wished it would leave soon, since he really had to get to – and then mentioned a city that was not Hong Kong.

303

Alarmed, I stepped out of line and headed for the check-in desk.

'Um, sir, you've been waiting in the wrong area,' said the woman on the other side.

'*What?*'

'There was a change. Your plane is boarding at a gate on the other side of the airport. It might have even left by now.'

In my foggy state, I had missed a major development. My flight had not only been subject to a change of gate, but a change of aircraft.

I have never run so fast. Every footfall was a frantic exclamation mark, a dotted line into the unknown, either out of the South Pacific for good, or back to a life of detention. A single moment, a second before or after the plane's departure, could spell the difference.

As I neared the correct departure gate I grew dizzy from lack of breath. The final push was worth it. I was among the last few people to get onboard. Any later and the door would have closed.

Twenty minutes later the plane punched through the blanket of rain clouds wrapped around Nadi, and climbed into a pale blue sky. The route to Hong Kong took us on a course past the Solomon Islands, Bougainville, Papua New Guinea and Manus Island. I was glad to say goodbye to each one of them in turn.

It had taken me six months on Christmas Island, three-and-a-half years on Manus, and six additional months as a fugitive, but I had managed to escape from Australia's 'Pacific Solution'. I had no intention of ever going back.

THIRTY-THREE

'I am not afraid of storms, for I am learning how to sail my ship.'

Louisa May Alcott, *Little Women*

I spilled out of the plane with the other passengers and into a cathedral of steel and glass at Hong Kong's Chek Lap Kok Airport. Despite – or perhaps because of – the heavy security, I felt relatively safe inside one of the world's busiest terminals. I wasn't expecting any trouble until landing in Toronto, where anything could happen. Canada was the end of the line. Make or break.

With no baggage to collect and with time to kill before the connecting flight, I passed through the shops in search of a jacket. A check of the local weather in Toronto showed a forecast of well below freezing for my arrival. This was a climate and type of cold I had only read about, and seen in the movies.

Changing money and buying a jacket left me with exactly forty-five Canadian dollars. Although my gut had begun to ache, I decided not to waste my money on food in case I had costs to cover when I arrived.

Taking a seat in the departure lounge, I phoned Nina, and then Tessa. I told them I'd made it safely to Hong Kong, and that I was boarding Air Canada flight AC016 to Toronto.

The flight was late. The first announcement was for a four-hour wait, but when that time came, there was still no sign of the plane.

The news was that an epic winter storm had convulsed the airport in Toronto, and the plane that would take us there had been severely delayed.

It was past midnight when the boarding call was announced. We were told to board in stages according to our seat numbers. I was in the last group.

'Good evening, sir, may I see your boarding pass and passport, please,' a ground staff member asked. I handed them to her.

'Thank you, sir.' She held my passport close to her bespectacled eyes. 'Where is your permanent resident card?'

By now it had been drilled into me how unusual it was for a Solomon Islander to travel to Canada through Hong Kong. I was expecting a cross-examination, and had prepared a series of replies in my defence. 'I don't have a PR card because I'm not a permanent Canadian resident.'

'If you're not a permanent resident, why don't you have a visa?'

'Because I don't need a visa with a Commonwealth passport.'

'Where is your luggage?'

'Oh, this is my only luggage.' I nodded at the small carry-on bag at my feet.

'Only that?'

'It's all I need!' Despite my jaunty tone, there was no likely scenario where I would fly across the world, from one hemisphere to another, from one climate to another, with just a carry-on bag, especially over Christmas. She asked me to step out of the line.

As I followed behind her, I pulled out my phone and texted, 'Here comes trouble.' This was to a messaging group that had me, Winiaka and Nina as members. The title of the chat, which Nina had created and named back on 25 June 2017: Prison Break.

I was led to another counter to be questioned further. Other staff joined us. The brave spirit of my doppelganger rising within me, I made my case with clarity and poise. 'I'm a citizen of a Commonwealth country. I don't need a visa to enter Canada, but I do have an eTA that I obtained through the correct channels from Canadian immigration.'

I had even memorised the eTA number in case something like this happened, or in the event my phone were lost or confiscated.

'Why don't you have any money?'

'I do have money. I've got a little cash and I have credit cards.'

They weren't really credit cards. One was the Load&Go Travel Visa, the prepaid card that Tessa had sent in the mail, and the other was a long dormant debit card attached to a Burmese bank account, which my cousin Suu Myatt had arranged for me. The credit card had about $20 on it while the other was worthless, but not when it came to putting up a smokescreen.

My research into the security of prepaid and debit cards had shown it was difficult for anyone outside the issuing bank to check whether or not they had funds in them. The mere act of possessing the cards was a way to gain legitimacy. With them in hand, I was better able to bluff my way around the world.

Every other passenger had boarded the plane but the officious Hong Kong staff still were not buying my story. 'May we see your credit cards?'

'Sure.' I handed them over.

As the staffers disappeared with my cards into a side room, I texted Shahed. 'Airline in HK thinks I'm suspicious. Won't let me board. Could be the end. If you don't hear from me, just pray.'

The employees returned and handed back my cards. 'We're still not convinced you have sufficient funds to travel to Canada,' said a thin Hong Kong official in a dark suit.

Throughout this process – as with every other interrogation – I had to concentrate on keeping my voice from shaking, both from nerves and a growing irritation.

'Listen, I have an eTA that was issued to me by Canadian immigration.' I recited the number and held up my phone, showing the email that confirmed its validity. 'I have a legal right to enter Canada and, with all due respect, you can't tell me not to board the flight because you're unhappy with the look of my luggage.'

The staff spoke in Cantonese and left me in the dark. The plane was tantalisingly just metres away. I wondered how long I'd have to rot in a local prison if everything unravelled in the next few minutes.

Finally, they told me I had to talk to an immigration officer in Canada. A number was dialled and I was handed a phone. A North American accent came down the line.

'This is Toronto Pearson Airport Immigration,' said the officer before launching into his own interrogation: 'Why is your passport so new?'

'Why was your ticket only booked a day ago?'

'Why aren't you taking the same route back?'

'What is the purpose of your visit?'

'Why don't you have luggage?'

'Why aren't you prepared for sub-zero temperatures?'

All my mental preparation – my carefully crafted excuses, attention to detail and habit of having a Plan A, B, C and D – came down to this moment. If my hard work were to count for something, it was now, at the final gate of an epic six-month jailbreak.

I took a deep breath and began a calm recital of the reasons for my unusual travel plans. Claiming political asylum was not one of them. Instead, the account took in highlights of my midwinter holiday in Canada, including Christmas events and festivals in Toronto, a couple of which I had even bothered to memorise by name. There was so much to do in this bustling city.

'I'm really looking forward to it,' I said, after a summary of the awesome time I expected to have, bouncing from one tourist hot spot to another in the company of my mythical Canadian buddies. 'It's a quick three-day visit to celebrate Christmas with old friends. Kind of whirlwind, since there's so much to see. Then I'm flying to Manila on the way home to attend a work conference. The work thing I could really do without but, you know, duty calls.'

'So why don't you have any luggage?' he cut in.

'I'm coming from the South Pacific!' I said with a chuckle. 'You can't buy warm pants or a winter coat in all of Honiara. Anyway, the guys in Toronto told me not to bother – it's only three days. One of them is the same size as me so I can borrow from his wardrobe. Though I did just buy a nice jacket this afternoon.'

The Canadian thanked me and asked to speak to the Hong Kong staff. I handed the phone to the thin man in the dark suit. I didn't understand what was said but when he hung up, he turned back. 'You can board the plane but the cabin crew will take possession of your passport. When you arrive, they will hand you and your passport over to Canadian customs. If they are satisfied, they will allow you to enter Canada. If they are not, they will put you on the next plane back here, and we will be waiting.'

'Fine by me. I just don't want to miss my flight.'

As I was the last person to board the plane, I didn't even have time to text Shahed. The flight took off and I thought of him, back in Burma, wondering if I had been thrown back into prison.

In the early hours of Christmas Day, the Boeing 777 rose over the illuminated hills of Hong Kong and banked east towards the Pacific Ocean. The flight was packed with holiday travellers, but since it was an overnight service the cabin was quiet, the lights turned low. It was my third flight in forty-eight hours and I hadn't slept for nearly three days. I was too focused on what lay ahead to bother closing my eyes.

Remembering Nina's parting advice to always keep a record, I pulled a spiral notebook and pen out of my bag and composed the note that would likely determine how the rest of my life played out. With my statement written, I took a picture of it, folded the page in half and tucked it into the pocket of my new jacket.

I had learned the hard way that my claim had to be in writing to carry any weight. In the legal process I was about to enter, like the one I had left behind, documents often mattered more than the people they represented.

For the next fourteen hours I mentally rehearsed what I'd do once we landed. My best hope for the future was to claim asylum in Canada. Yet the tarmac and the transit areas of international airports were deemed international space. I did not want to get stopped and questioned in this area, especially not while holding a fake passport. Nina advised me to move as quickly as possible to the part of the airport officially on Canadian soil. To give myself a fighting chance of success, I needed to make my claim in person, in front of a Canadian immigration officer.

About two hours before we landed in Toronto, my gut was crawling with hunger and thirst, exacerbated by regular stabs of anxiety. While they had fed us – lightly – on the Air Canada flight, it was not enough to compensate for the three days of money-saving starvation and lack of sleep that had preceded it. The pain was a problem because I needed to be able to move quickly and effortlessly when we landed. Any unusual movements would attract attention.

Although we'd left Hong Kong on Christmas Day, we'd crossed the international dateline in the prolonged dark night, which meant we landed in Toronto in the early hours of Christmas Eve. As soon as we touched down I turned on my phone and texted Shahed, and sent the photo of my note of asylum to Tessa. But neither worked: I couldn't connect to the internet.

The man sitting next to me was using his phone. 'Excuse me,' I said. 'I don't suppose it would be okay if I got on your hotspot for a moment? I have a couple of urgent messages to fire off.'

He did his best to oblige – this helpfulness was a Canadian trait, I'd soon learn – but after a few tries we were unable to get me online. Meanwhile, every second that passed brought the plane closer to the gate and whatever lay waiting for me on the other side.

I war-gamed what might happen next. If taken into custody by customs officers, I planned to hide my phone inside my underwear and tell them I needed to use the bathroom. Once there, I'd be able to send the document to Tessa, assuming the airport had free wi-fi, not always a given.

As soon as the plane rolled to a stop at the gate, I stood up and walked towards the forward door and lingered there. The door opened and I waited for the travellers to clear the first-class area, and then followed behind as if I were one of them. I had gambled that the cabin crew wouldn't expect someone whose passport was being withheld to get up and leave without it.

After everything I had gone through to get my hands on the document, the passport was now a layer of unwanted skin, easy to shed. Goodbye, Michael Waradi, whoever you were.

Trying to move quickly but without attracting attention, I made an awkward scurry through the long corridors of the airport. There was an invisible membrane that separated international airspace and Canada itself – and I had to break through it before getting stopped.

Along the way I accessed the airport wi-fi and sent the photo of my refugee claim to Tessa, mid-stride. Next I texted my Prison Break crew, who hadn't heard from me since the 'here comes trouble' half-message from the Hong Kong airport, to let them know I'd arrived. And lastly, a message for Shahed: 'I made it!'

His reply: 'Thank god, I was staying online for the last 14 hrs – standby so I won't miss ur message, in case u needed me.'

There were two queues at customs; one for foreigners and another for Canadian citizens. The Canadian one was shorter so I lined up with the locals, thinking of how the customs officers were probably searching the plane at the same moment, wondering where the hell I was.

I could feel my heartbeat in my temples as the slowly moving line brought me closer to the customs desk. Any second someone might shout, 'Stop that man!'

It was my turn to approach the counter. I stepped forward and found myself face-to-face with a fifty-something man with a long grey beard.

This was it. I handed him the signed and dated letter, scrawled in capital letters on the page torn from the notepad.

TO. CANADIAN BORDER SERVICES AGENCY

DATE. 24 DEC 2017

PLACE. TORONTO PEARSON INTERNATIONAL
AIRPORT

I JAIVET EALOM (ALSO KNOWN AS JAVET ALOM),
IS APPLYING FOR ASYLUM.

I HAVE BEEN TRAVELLING FOR THE LAST THREE
DAYS WITHOUT PROPER SLEEP.

THEREFORE, I AM ASKING YOUR KIND ASSISTANCE
HERE FOR MY APPLICATION OF ASYLUM AND
RELATED REQUIRED FORMS.

I AM A ROHINGYAN MAN FROM BURMA AND I AM
FLEEING GENOCIDE BY ITS GOVERNMENT.

THANK YOU

JE

24/12/2017

Without saying a word, the officer read it and looked at me. He
read it again, and glanced at me again. He read it a third time, stamped
something on the page, and passed it to another officer at the back
of the booth.

'Walk this way, please,' the bearded one said, and ushered me past
the booth into an area away from the other queues. By taking those
few short steps I entered the sovereign realm of Canada.

The relief was intoxicating. I didn't care if I was detained, arrested or forced to spend time in custody. I had made it as far away from Manus Island as it was possible to travel. I had entered a legal claim for political asylum in a country that recognised and understood such things, and hopefully I wasn't going anywhere.

The bearded man asked me to take a seat in a small waiting area where he and the other officers discussed what to do next. By now, Air Canada staff had come forward with my passport and offered their account as to why I'd been allowed onto the plane. Clearly I had caused quite a stir. Five officials stood around arguing over how it was possible I'd managed to make it onboard.

I overheard snippets: 'There's no such procedure . . .' 'It's not up to Air Canada . . .' 'Cabin crew don't have the authority . . .'

From what I could piece together, the airline had been under pressure to take off from Hong Kong quickly, in part to avoid additional gate fees. Allowing me to board had been an economic decision, but one Air Canada did not have the legal authority to make. I got the impression my case was an exception, even a complete accident. Fine with me. I was well overdue a lucky break.

Another official with neatly combed hair and glasses arrived shortly afterwards and asked for my name.

'Hello, my name is Jaivet Ealom,' I replied.

'Do you speak English?'

'Yeah. My English is pretty good.'

'Would you come with me, please?'

Bent at the waist to accommodate my stomach cramps, I followed him along a corridor to a small office where we sat at either side of a desk. My note was placed in the middle.

'My name is Phil and I'm going to conduct an interview with you.'

This sounded like the interrogation that had been described in Hong Kong, which could result in me being packed up and sent on the first flight back. On the other hand, it might be a proper discussion of my asylum claim, the first step in the legal process.

Phil asked me to repeat my name and date of birth. As he waited for an answer, the pain in my abdomen made me lean forward and lower my head. Although this was potentially a major turning point in my life, I was struggling to concentrate. I was in agony.

'I'm sorry,' said Phil, 'I just have a couple more of these and then I'll get you a healthcare worker, okay?'

He asked me if I needed an interpreter. When I declined, he had me sign some paperwork to show I had forfeited the service. 'So tell me, what's happening with your health situation?'

'Like it says there, I haven't eaten or slept in quite a while.'

'Well, I can't question a man who is in pain.'

A few minutes later a paramedic arrived and checked me over. He said I was most likely experiencing a build-up of stomach acid, and that the problem should diminish once I had some food and rest. He asked if I wanted to go to hospital.

'I don't think I need a hospital.'

Seeing I was not at imminent risk of dying in his office, Phil asked me to outline my reasons for coming to Canada. I explained that I had fled genocide of the Rohingya in Burma, and claimed asylum on my way to Australia, only to be imprisoned on Manus Island for years. 'After all that, they were making moves to send me back to Burma, so I escaped.'

After less than five minutes of my life story, Phil interrupted. 'Okay, listen. I am going to process the asylum claim for you right here. But first things first. Please, wait.'

Having an immigration officer tell me to wait in his office was my idea of hell. If the authorities were going to swoop in and send me back to Hong Kong, now was the time.

But when Phil returned, he was alone. In his hands: a Subway sandwich and a can of Coke. 'It's time for you to eat.'

My first meal in days, paid for by the immigration official who was in charge of deciding my fate and future in the country. None of the 'Let us mangle your name and send you straight to your cell' treatment I had come to expect. Instead, a simple gesture of kindness, from one person to another. Canada was already turning out to be a place unlike any I had known before.

Phil watched me transform the sandwich into a pile of paper scraps. There was a sparkle in his eyes, a glint of warmth or curiosity, as he made his next request.

'And now I want you to tell me your story, from the beginning.'

THIRTY-FOUR

*'One's appreciation of meagre comforts, it seems,
depends on what misery one has gone through before getting them.'*

Alice Munro, *Too Much Happiness*

By the time I wrapped up my tale, it was four or five hours since my flight had landed. It was now close to dawn. I leaned back in my seat and folded my arms behind my head to indicate I was finally done.

Phil let my words hang in the air for a moment longer, relaxed, took a breath, and at last spoke. 'You know, I have never heard something like that in my entire career. I don't know of another person who has travelled so far, through so much, to get here. And at your age!'

During the course of the interview, Phil had filled out the first of the paperwork needed to assess my claim for asylum. He handed me some forms to complete in my own time, ahead of the hearing that was to come. He even booked a hearing date: 27 April 2018. My legal journey to become part of this country had begun.

There were still many steps ahead. Because I'd arrived using a document not issued under my real name, the rules stated that I was to be sent to an immigration detention centre in Toronto until the completion of a security background check.

'But I just can't do that. What you've been through deserves a better response. I'm going to set you free, so to speak. You really need to get some sleep, Jaivet. Have you got somewhere to go?'

'No, not yet,' I replied. 'I haven't figured that out yet.'

Phil picked up the phone and called a few homeless shelters in the city. Such was my luck I'd arrived in the middle of one of the coldest Canadian winters on record, and the shelters were at capacity. He found a place in downtown Toronto called Seaton House. They could fit me in. Just.

'Do you have enough money to get there?' he asked.

'I don't know. Will $45 cover it?'

'Probably not enough for a cab. If you wait here in the airport until later in the morning, there's a bus service that runs between here and downtown.'

Phil gave me the route information and showed me where the bus would stop. Before leaving me, he stepped back to give me space to take in his words. 'Jaivet, you are not prepared for this weather. You have no idea what this cold may do to a human being. You will freeze to death if you go outside dressed like that. Stay inside the airport until the bus arrives, and go straight into the shelter.'

'Okay.'

I was ready to take him at his word. How different he was from any other person in authority I had met before, with the exception of the members of my league of helpers. In fact, he might have been a secret (and unknowing) member of that league. Despite his badges and uniform and the possibly soul-crushing rigours of his job, he was bending the rules to set me free.

The airport was quiet and largely vacant at that hour. I planted myself on a row of empty seats. Unable to sleep, I wandered the concourse until the first stirrings of life, the return of the cleaners and the airline staff.

When I was about to board the bus, I noticed a sign for a train to downtown Toronto that cost $10 less. I took the train and earmarked the money I had saved for food.

As the train swept through the suburbs of Toronto, heading for the core, I rested my head against the window and took in my first sight of snow.

I got off at Union Station in the heart of Toronto's financial district – my introduction to a major Western city. Snow carpeted the streets and sidewalks. I contemplated taking a cab but, still in frugal escapee mode, where every dollar spent now would probably be needed more urgently later, I walked the eight or so blocks to Seaton House and saved the $10.

It took less than a few minutes to realise the mistake. Having spent more than four years in the blast furnace of the tropics, I had no idea the planet could get so cold. Bone-chilling cold. Eyeball-freezing cold. The chill reached through the soles of my shoes and caused my feet to burn, and then lose feeling. With nowhere to seek shelter – the city was closed at that hour – I had no choice but to press on.

About fifteen minutes later I pushed open the door of Seaton House in a state of physical crisis, shaking and unable to speak. The staff piled blankets on me and sat me next to a heater.

When I stopped vibrating, I spoke with the woman at the reception area. 'We're over capacity because of the weather,' she said. 'The only place we've got for you is on the floor. You'll have a mattress and some blankets, but you'll be down on the ground.'

I nodded as she handed me some blankets and oversized second-hand clothes that were at least dry, and more substantial than the outfit I was wearing – the jeans that Tessa had sent to disguise me as a professional on PNG, and a brightly patterned shirt I'd bought to impersonate a Solomon Islander.

'Just some advice. You need to be aware of the people around you. Some of them are not at their best, and many are dealing with mental illness. Watch your environment and your belongings.'

Seaton House was Toronto's largest homeless shelter, located in one of the country's poorest neighbourhoods. A drab four-storey blond brick building, it resembled a prison rather than a safe harbour. It reminded me of the compounds on Christmas Island, with tables bolted to the floor, and a two-way radio squawking from the belt of every staffer.

The noise of the walkie-talkies tapped into an old and paralysing dread, and cast me back to the shadows of a past I was hoping to leave behind. At least here I was free to leave. And yet, thanks to the weather, I wasn't really. To do so would be to risk freezing to death.

My bed was a mattress recently placed on the cement floor. Some of the men in the bunks next to me were asleep, others were in a state of high-spirited agitation. The cold, which I thought I'd left outside, now reached me through the thin mattress. My first full day in Canada and I was starting from the bottom, literally: a level below some of its most vulnerable citizens.

I did not intend to stay on the bottom for long, however, and at least in this country my wish counted for something.

When my hands, pressed to my sides, were warm enough to work again, I made the belated call to Shahed. 'I'm safe. In a homeless shelter, but safe. They set me free in the airport, so I could take a bus to the city. I've even got a hearing date already.'

Shahed sounded as worn out as I was. Until I texted him after my plane had landed, he'd assumed I'd been jailed in Hong Kong. 'I thought you were done for.'

'I don't think I would have survived without your backing. It's the first time I've felt safe in years, even if it's not the safest place. I have hope again.'

'This is good news.'

'It is. And I think it's time we let Mom and Dad know.'

It is without any sense of pride or even a decent explanation that I can admit I had not called my parents since leaving Manus. Worse, I had sworn my brother to keep the secret. For four years, all they knew – and continued to know – was that their eldest son was on Manus Island. They were in the dark about my escape and my journey of the past six months, with its many reversals and close calls. And I was not quite ready to enlighten them.

'Tell them where I am,' I said to Shahed. 'Then please tell them I love them and will speak to them soon.'

With that, I was ready to sleep.

Ready, but not able. Each time the main door opened, the ground floor of Seaton House was swamped with a wave of chilly air that went straight to the level where my body lay. As I lingered in the eerie space between consciousness and a dream, the cold brought memories. I had flashbacks to the night we were close to drowning in the waters of Indonesia.

After a near sleepless day and night I asked the woman at reception if there was a chance I could move to the quieter area upstairs. When I swallowed my pride and admitted I was a refugee who'd just made the journey from the other side of the world, she took pity on me, and found a space on the second floor.

Here, in a room shared with five other men, I had a bed and even a locker. The air was properly heated and there was a washroom, where I took my first shower since leaving Honiara. This time, when my head hit the pillow I blacked out.

I woke the next morning with no idea what to do. The emptiness and lack of urgency were strange. There were no escape plans to hatch, backstories to spin, or documents to chase down. For the first time in years I could exert my precious freedom and enjoy the luxury of an unplanned day, rich with hope and possibility.

The weather had warmed, by the standards of Canadian winter, so I dressed in my baggy new clothes and set foot outside. A few doors down from the shelter, an elderly couple was chatting by the front gate of a townhouse. The sight of them might have been mundane to anyone else, but to me seemed profoundly memorable and reassuring.

I was definitely no longer on the run, or in a prison or interrogation room – I had found myself in a community.

When I returned to the shelter the woman from reception asked me to follow her to her office. 'Here,' she said, handing me a large brown paper bag. 'This is for you.'

Inside was a pair of mittens, a sweater and a scarf.

'Oh, thank you, that's very kind.'

'It was Christmas, and everyone got a gift. You arrived a day late. I didn't want you to miss out, but this is all we have left. It may not be the right size, but there you go. Merry Christmas.'

When I had arrived, cold and battered, on the doorstep of Australia, they had refused to grant me even a pillow for the first six months. Here, I had been in the country for two days, and this overcrowded, under-resourced homeless shelter had dug deep to give me a Christmas gift.

The next day, after lunch at the shelter I pulled on my new sweater and ventured out further, leaving behind Seaton Street and George Street, and explored the nearby neighbourhoods. They were remarkably neat and attractive, given their proximity to the shelters.

There were shops and houses adorned with Christmas trees, and strung with colourful lights. Children tumbled in the snow in parks, and couples walked past holding hands, too engaged in their chatter to notice me. I was just another person on the street, with as much right to be there as anyone else.

There was still work for me to do. In a local branch of the public library, I spent hours at a computer: filling out and submitting the asylum claim forms I'd been given at the airport, plus a few additional ones.

There was something called the Interim Federal Healthcare Program that asylum seekers were encouraged to apply for. If I got sick, I could access the public health system free of charge under the IFHP – another stunning contrast to the barbaric treatment meted out by Australia. Canada was a country that even took care of the wellbeing of those who had yet to prove their right to be there.

On the way back to the shelter I passed markets and restaurants brimming with people. How quickly I began to feel part of the crowd, just by walking through it.

The night-time was when the past came back to stake its claim. About 5 am I was awoken by the terrible clatter of a two-way radio. The shelter staff were doing a headcount; the crackling airwaves took me straight back to Christmas Island and the early morning visits from Azrael, the angel of death.

The rest of the day was short. I didn't eat or go out, but stayed in my room and watched steam from a vent on the next-door rooftop fill the air, rising against the falling snow. That night, the clouds cleared enough to reveal the moon, my old companion. She looked different here, so small and faraway, a white dot in the cold northern sky.

The sinister radio noise resumed at 5 am. The day after that, I came down with a fever. Staying in the shelter was starting to undermine both my physical and mental health, but I didn't know where else to go. I had no money or means of getting a job, as far as I could tell. While there were thirty-seven million people in Canada, I didn't know a single one of them.

Through Facebook, I contacted some Burmese and Rohingyas living in Canada, but they didn't reply to my messages. With help from Shahed, I managed to speak with a man named Saiful, who was well connected to the small but growing Rohingya diaspora in Canada.

'We have a little bit of a community here,' he said over the phone. 'If you're in trouble, let us know.'

'I am in trouble, actually. I'm sick and think I need to see a doctor.'

'Toronto's a big city and there's often a long waiting time at the hospitals. I think you should come and stay with my family. We might be able to get you in to see our family doctor.'

'I'm going to be honest with you,' I said. 'I don't have the money to even buy a bus ticket to the end of the street.'

'Don't worry about that. Just get a cab and we'll pay the fare when you arrive.' He told me his address, in a place named Kitchener-Waterloo, which I wrote down in my notebook.

Downstairs, I thanked the woman who'd given me the Christmas presents and told her I was leaving.

'What's wrong?' she said, concerned.

'There's nothing wrong. Quite the opposite. There's a family I'm going to see. And I wanted to thank you for your kindness. Maybe you don't know how important it is, but it is.'

'You're welcome,' she told me. 'If anything changes or something happens, just come back or give me a call.' She pressed her business card into my palm. 'I wish you the best of luck.'

It was only after I entered the cab that I discovered that Kitchener-Waterloo was more than 100 kilometres west of Toronto. The fare ran into the hundreds of dollars.

When I arrived, Saiful came out to the kerb and paid it in full.

THIRTY-FIVE

'Every moment is a new beginning.'

Elie Wiesel

For the first time in years, I wanted to talk to my parents again. In part because the dark clouds of shame had slightly lifted, and I had some decent news to share. And also because staying with a family that was kind beyond words, but which was not my own, had made me miss my own parents more.

The first thing I heard was my mother crying – a startling sound. This was a woman who I had always considered to be made of pure confidence and strength. Hearing her at her most vulnerable undid a hardness in my own soul, a stone placed to keep the dam from breaking, and her tears were answered by my own. Suddenly I realised how dearly I had been missing her over the long period of our separation.

When her words came out, they were equally unexpected. 'How are your teeth?' she asked, between sobs.

Of course. She had no idea I'd had the braces taken off in Port Moresby, a good six months earlier. We had a lot of catching up to do.

We shared our stories. While I was making my own odyssey across the seas, my parents had been on their own path toward self-preservation, travelling deep into the jungle of Burma. With their sharp planning and acute survival skills, they had managed to endure what was now being referred to in the news as the Rohingyan genocide.

Our lives were still linked, even as we had fallen out of touch. When I was first taken into detention on Christmas Island, before I had learned to fully distrust the system and those who ran it, I had listed my mother as my emergency contact, along with her phone number in Burma.

Later, when I was moved to Manus Island, the Australian authorities reached out to their peers in Burmese immigration to tip them off that they had one of their countrymen in their grasp, someone who had managed to get away. They were instructed to tell my mother that her son was in detention in PNG and should call him back.

This was at the height of the reign of terror in Burma, after my parents had moved to a different side of the country, where no Rohingya was permitted to settle, to ride out the violence. The phone call from immigration put her and my father in great danger, and it was on account of the conniving Australians.

Fortunately, my mother had some manoeuvres of her own, and managed to finish the call without arousing questions about her current whereabouts. She also admitted, quite honestly, to having not spoken to her son for years, defusing the risk that she would be summoned to immigration to help convince me to come back home. Through a mix of truth and evasions, she saved her own life, as well as mine.

There were other links between the two ruling regimes. For one thing, Australia was the only Western country that continued to train the military of Burma throughout the years of the genocide. The Australian defence department spent $400,000 on this effort in 2017–18 alone.

The family with whom I now stayed were survivors in their own right, like nearly everyone who was part of the Rohingya diaspora. Saiful was a student, with a wife and daughter – and another daughter to come.

They were grateful to be in Canada, where they were doing well. They lived simply, but their hospitality made their apartment more welcoming than any mansion.

Soon after my arrival at their home, Saiful arranged an appointment with his family doctor. The GP let me know my feet were frostbitten – a memento of my first outdoor walk in this country. Thankfully, my flesh survived the ordeal, but I had painful and swollen toes for a while. I also had a bad cold. While I didn't require hospitalisation, the doctor put me on a busy schedule of follow-up appointments.

With my health improving, I readied myself for the upcoming hearing with Canadian immigration. I passed a mandatory medical examination and secured a lawyer, paid for by the state, to help me present my case.

After four weeks with Saiful's family, I began feeling guilty for overstaying, not that they ever gave me cause to. They treated me as one of their own. I was so thankful for their hospitality but couldn't stay any longer.

By that point I qualified for rent support, and I found a cheap basement room to rent in Waterloo. It wasn't much, a bed and a desk crammed next to a water heater and furnace: my first private space since my university days in Rangoon. A room of my own.

'Oh no, no, no, Jaivet!' said Saiful when I showed him around. 'This is no place for you to live. It's practically a boiler room, and there's no light coming in.'

He was right about the lack of light. The room had just one small glass pane window high on the wall. 'Please just come back and stay with us. We feel like you are part of the family.'

Saiful was a good man and a wonderful host, but I had been in Canada for more than a month and feared inertia. I was eager to stand on my own two frostbitten feet and walk my own road.

My new room sat beneath the modest home of a gruff older man named Joe. A retired truck driver, he was somewhere between seventy and eighty years of age. Joe lived alone and he adored Donald Trump.

Despite our differences, he was a decent guy, if prone to grumpiness, and we struck a deal that allowed me access to his living space upstairs. We were the ultimate odd couple.

I spent hours up in Joe's house, sitting at the dining table, preparing for my hearing and speaking to my legal aid representative, an affable lawyer named Ebrahim. He was based in Scarborough, two-and-a-half hours away by bus on the opposite side of Toronto.

A few weeks after our first phone meeting, on a snowy day, I took the bus to Ebrahim's office to sign some papers. On the return trip I had a four-hour stopover in Toronto. It was bitterly cold and still snowing, but the brief visit to the city put a glow in my heart.

Leaving the warmth of the bus station, I pushed my hands deep into my pockets and headed north toward the gullies of concrete, glass and steel. After half an hour I found myself in a neighbourhood of old stone, looking up at a sprawling gothic building crowned with spires and parapets. It was as if a piece of Hogwarts School of Witchcraft and Wizardry had been dropped in the middle of the modern city.

There was a group of people who did not look like they belonged together, standing on the steps outside the unlikely castle. I fell in behind them.

What I first guessed to be a tour group was in fact a gathering of new students – including international scholars and their parents – on an orientation visit to campus. It turned out the splendid building belonged to the University of Toronto. 'Okay then,' I thought to myself, 'I guess this is how I'm spending my afternoon.'

Over the next hour or so I strolled the grounds and took in the ornate high ceilings, lavish woodwork and sturdy masonry of the Victorian-era construction. I only half-listened to what the university guides had to say about the history of the place, and the courses offered. I was too awestruck by the architecture. When the tour finished, the guide handed out a selection of brochures and application forms.

I took a handful, just in case.

*

In our meetings earlier that day, Ebrahim had assured me I could expect a favourable outcome when my case went before the refugee board. 'After what you have been through, I'm pretty sure you'll be fine. It won't even take long.'

His optimism struck a chord. I was impatient to regain control of my stolen life and begin shaping my future. With my twenty-sixth birthday looming large, it was depressing to think I'd been forced to spend a quarter of a century in a state of busy stasis, constantly moving but never getting my start.

On the bus back to Waterloo I thumbed through the university applications and wondered if I had a chance in the gothic wonderland of academia. It might be wiser to take the practical path of looking for a job.

Back at Joe's, the choice took on a painful edge. There was not just my welfare to think about, but that of Shahed, who had sacrificed his own comfort to rescue me, repeatedly. He had taken on serious debt, and I owed it to him to repay it. I needed to find a job as soon as possible.

Over the next few weeks I applied for countless positions, from restaurant and bar gigs to professional roles in pharmacies. I scoured Craigslist and other websites for any job, from the trades to data entry, that paid a wage. Each time I was either turned down or ignored. Meanwhile the cut-off date for applications to the University of Toronto was approaching.

Researching the school further, I discovered that in addition to being architecturally elegant, it was a prestigious seat of learning, the best-known university in Canada and among the top twenty globally. Something my mother said to me, a piece of advice from the past, sounded in my ears: 'Jaivet, you need to be the best you can possibly be in order to survive.'

If I found a regular job to pay the bills, and offset my debt to my family, who knows, maybe I would end up stuck in the same state of wage slavery years from now, with no hope of advancement. It took more time and effort to build a career by first gaining a Canadian education. But a bigger investment promised a bigger reward.

For my parents, I needed to try harder. They had taken risks and made sacrifices to give their children a fighting chance, and the least I could do was honour their efforts. I also needed to do it for my own sake. Otherwise, all that I had been through, setback after setback, challenge after challenge, added up to little.

Also in my mind were the guys still in detention, or stuck in refugee limbo in the countries I had passed through to get here. Whether they thought of me, or even knew I was still alive, I owed it to them to do my best. There were opportunities available to me that they could only dream of, and for their sake, as much as mine, I should make the most of them.

As usual, my peculiar legal status made the challenge more difficult. Even in a country like Canada, which prided itself on being welcoming to newcomers, it was unusual to apply for a top university before having any confirmed legal status. To navigate the system, I would need help. I booked an appointment with an academic advisor at U of T only to learn that the deadline for online applications had passed.

By now I knew there was likely to be a loophole, a hole in the fence. After some prodding, the advisor admitted there was still time to submit a paper application to the university.

She told me this in late February or early March. By May, to have a chance at being accepted, I needed to complete the application – no easy task – as well as obtain my original academic transcripts from Burma. I also had to pass the academic English test – more demanding than the one required by immigration – with a score of no lower than 6.5 on all four dimensions: reading, writing, listening and speaking. All while completing my preparation for the hearing with the refugee board, which would make or break my chance to stay in the country.

The memory of my recent past, the sinking boats and the missed flights, played in a continuous loop as I undertook one of the most gruelling efforts of my life, this one of the intellectual kind.

There was not enough light or space in the basement, so I used the kitchen table, spending so much time with my books and paperwork that it angered my housemate. 'You go to bed so late and then in the morning the first thing I see is you sitting at the table studying your ass off,' Joe snarled one day. 'When I rented you the room, I didn't know you'd be occupying the rest of the place too. I know I said it's yours to share, but do you have to be in here all day every day?'

It was a fair point, so I started studying at the local library instead. First up was for the IELTS, the standardised English test. Most people studied for it for months, if not years, under a teacher. I had less than four weeks and no instruction.

The test was held at 8 am at the university. I woke up at 3 am to make sure I did not miss the two buses to get there. I ended up receiving a score of 7.5 across the board. My mother would be proud. She *was* proud, when I told her.

Just as I was ready to relax again, I received some distressing news, in the form of a letter from the Canadian Immigration and Refugee Board. The same month it was due to take place, my hearing was postponed indefinitely, with no reason given.

That term – indefinitely – was anathema to me. The salt in the wound during my years in Manus was the open-ended nature of indefinite imprisonment. The loss of hope, of not knowing when the hurt would stop, had often been harder to bear than the hurt itself.

The rote procedural letter from the Canadian government plunged me into a depression. I could hardly sleep and, when I did, I had recurring nightmares about being back in detention. Guards shouted and chased me through the ghastly dreamscapes until, cornered, I woke in a sweat in my bed in the basement.

Once again, I was stuck. Despite all the risks I had taken, and the sacrifices I had made – and the ones that had been made for me – it felt like I was back at the start, still trapped, in my mind at least, in one of the most cursed places on earth.

THIRTY-SIX

'What is to give light must endure burning.'

Viktor Frankl

'I think you should see a psychiatrist,' said Saiful's doctor. 'You may be experiencing post-traumatic stress.'

Great. Post-traumatic stress. Another souvenir from the Australian government, to go with my chronic stomach problems, aching teeth, and inability to sleep for more than two hours at a time.

A few days later I met with a psychiatrist named Nicole at her practice in Waterloo. Remembering the appointments with the robotic shrinks on Manus, I was wary to begin the session, but soon warmed to the occasion. I spoke of my time in detention and the psychological blight that had resulted from the ordeal.

Nicole diagnosed this as a case of acute PTS, and suggested I focus on the experiences that triggered me. Along with uniforms and two-way radios, the sound of sirens was on the list of things that could easily light a fire of panic. The closer the siren, the more intense the dread I was about to be arrested and locked in a cage.

'Whenever you hear sirens from now on, I want you to imagine an ambulance rushing to help someone, not a police car coming to get you,' Nicole said. 'In those moments, when you picture an ambulance, remind yourself that you haven't done anything wrong: the sound of a siren poses no threat.'

She also advised me to get out of the basement where I was staying. It was too similar to the shipping containers and the windowless solitary blocks of Chauka.

As much as her advice made sense, I couldn't move so easily. Joe's was the cheapest room I had found, with a built-in discount since I was responsible for shovelling the snow from the walkway: I was not in a position to afford a brighter, more expensive place. Besides, with my hearing delayed and my application to university in process, I had little better to do than hang out with old Joe.

He was originally from Liverpool, England, and had come to Canada for work. We had led different lives, and although we saw the world in predictably different ways, I had a soft spot for the guy.

A lifetime of experience had taught me to become accustomed to living under the boot of people whose values and beliefs were very different from my own. I'm not sure that Joe had faced the same ordeal. It seemed to me that everyone who came to visit him was white, old, male, grumpy and conservative. Sometimes I'd overhear their conversations and picked up on a common theme: all Muslims are bad.

Although he'd been prickly to begin with, over time Joe softened toward me too – particularly now that I'd stopped studying at his kitchen table. I had regular conversations with him, partly because I like to hang out with older people and partly out of boredom. I offered to help him with the groceries, and before long it became a ritual for us to go out shopping together every weekend.

'You know what, Jaiver?' Joe suddenly offered one day. (For some reason he was never able to pronounce my name.) 'I never knew a Muslim could be so nice.'

I had to smile. 'Okay. But I'm not a Muslim. Not anymore, anyway.'

'Well, then you're the nicest brown person I've ever met.'

'Thank you, Joe. It means a lot.'

And it did. Our relationship was evidence that if someone is brought close to a person they have learned to hate or fear – and get to know the person behind the deception – their racism may wash away.

Through this process Joe and I ended up becoming friends. He'd call me over to the couch to watch a soccer match – he was a hardcore Liverpool FC fan – or arrive home from the grocery store with something he knew I liked. He even invited me and Saiful's family to go fishing on a boat he kept at the marina.

In spite of all this I never told Joe about my past or my escape from detention. I didn't know how he would take it and was wary of jeopardising my chances of gaining legal status in Canada. The Australian government had a history of pulling the strings of foreign governments for its own political ends, and the five countries that made up the Five Eyes alliance – Australia, Canada, New Zealand, the US and the UK – had an agreement to share intelligence. With a single phone call to local immigration, I could be arrested and put on a plane back to PNG before getting the chance to attend my hearing.

For this reason I never told the guys on Manus Island where I was. Of the Australians, Tessa was the only person who knew I had made it to Canada.

I was still keeping an eye on the private chats of the guys in detention, and reading the public headlines to stay on top of the latest developments. Some of the news was terrible. Australia had built a new prison, an extension of the notorious Bomana. It was the destination for the guys in Hillside Haus who had been deemed non-refugees, but who, for the sake of staying alive, had refused to return to their home countries. Two of my friends from Burma were put in that prison, where I heard they had been beaten and tortured.

More positive was the mysterious deal with the US. During the presidency of Barack Obama, the country had agreed to take some of the guys in detention – based on an opaque selection process – and resettle them on its own soil. And the resettlement continued, even under Trump. While the guys who made it to that country were largely left to their own devices, with meagre funding and few local contacts to offer them support, most of them preferred their new life to the hell they had left behind.

This was also the time of the first payouts to the guys in detention, the long-delayed result of the class-action lawsuit launched back in 2014 by the firm Slater and Gordon. The lawsuit took aim at the Australian government and the companies operating its offshore processing centres.

The government had made many attempts to block the trial. It placed a travel ban on the detainees to keep them from testifying in court, and pushed for the hearings to be held behind closed doors. (Just as, for years, it had made it difficult – and expensive – for journalists to visit Manus and Nauru, with only the cheerleaders from Murdoch media given easy access.)

When the court refused to accept the government's bag of dirty tricks, and ruled instead that the trial would be broadcast on Australian media, there was a rush to settle out of court. This was the scenario that the politicians feared the most: a long line of detainees and security and immigration staff called to the witness stand, giving voice, in the most public forum imaginable, to what had taken place, and was still taking place, in the processing centres. As always, the PR game, and the need to preserve the lie-making machinery, was the top priority. More than the financial losses involved, and certainly more than the lives of the affected refugees.

The collective payout was considerable, but not all the guys received a piece of it. And no amount of money could compensate for the pain they had experienced, and continued to experience, at the hands of their jailers. While it was small comfort, at least the fact of Australia's egregious treatment of its asylum seekers was now on the public record.

Reading about all these developments wasn't great for my PTS. What could I do? Those poor men were family, my brothers-in-arms. My survivor's guilt grew in tandem with my inability to help make things better.

Also dismaying, on a much smaller scale, was my own state of legal limbo. A deep dive into every website concerned with the status of refugees in Canada showed the reason for the delay in my court process. It turned out the refugee board had decided to clear a two-year backlog. It was a relief, in a way, to know my case hadn't been singled out, since all the hearings had been bumped to a later date.

My research also unearthed a key fact, a clause that applicants who had faced persecution or genocide could ask to have their cases expedited. Mine checked both boxes: ethnic cleansing in Burma and persecution by the Australian government.

I discussed this with Saiful, who said he had a contact in the office of the local member of parliament who might be able to help me push the issue. We made an appointment and were referred to the MP's legal counsel.

The lawyer helped me draft a letter to the refugee board asking that my file be expedited. A month later I wrote a follow-up letter stating that the uncertainty over my legal status was affecting my mental health. Neither letter received a response.

At an impasse, I was relieved to receive notice from the University of Toronto that my application had been accepted, and that I was due to start in the fall semester, in a few months' time.

My program was political science with a side order of economics. Things had changed since the last time I was enrolled in university. The study of pharmacy no longer seemed relevant to the future I saw for myself. Since graduation, and even before then, my life had been tossed on the swells of geopolitics. Now I wanted to understand that maelstrom, where greed and power collided and combined to destroy the powerless.

The past few years had brought me close to the daily face of suffering, to both the tormentors and their victims. That experience had shown me that statelessness, poverty, persecution and inequality were human-made problems. They must, therefore, have human-made solutions.

In Burmese, we have an expression, 'A thousand cuts from a knife are not as lethal as the stroke of a pen.' Most of the bills related to offshore detention were rushed through parliament, or passed in the middle of the night. And each one of them altered the quality and course of our lives forever.

I needed to gain a sharper sense of the machinery of power, if I hoped to nudge it in a more positive direction. By learning about the causes and methods of persecution, of cruelty and torture carried out through legal means, I could hopefully make a difference, however small. Who knows, maybe a career in the law or policy making lay in my future.

The acceptance letter from U of T was a sign that I was on the right course: it represented the best piece of news I'd received since arriving in Canada.

The excitement didn't last long. Because I was a refugee *claimant* – and not yet accepted as a refugee in Canada – I was expected to pay tuition fees of $50,000 a year, the rate for international students. The $5000 fee for domestic students was the one I had been counting on, and even that was at the limit of what was financially possible.

As far as I could see, my only option was to postpone my studies for a year, by which time I would have a better chance of getting legal status in Canada and gaining access to loans. Had my hearing not been postponed, I would likely have had my claim processed in April 2018 – and none of this would have been a problem.

A year is a long time when you've already lost four years of your life. I wasn't willing to wait. Instead, I bombarded the refugee office with phone calls and emails that went unanswered, and hassled Ebrahim to push for my case to be expedited. He drew a blank too.

My breakthrough came in the form of a kind man at the refugee board who showed me the courtesy of chatting over the phone about my dilemma. 'Your only chance of an earlier appointment is if there's a cancellation,' he explained. 'I can put you in touch with the person who handles scheduling. At least that way you have a chance.'

Half an hour later I was talking to the woman who booked the hearings. The delay was going to be even longer than I'd imagined.

'I'm sorry, but how long am I looking at?' I asked.

'The average wait is twenty months.'

Two more years in more legal limbo. I watched my acceptance to the University of Toronto disappear over the horizon.

'What if there is a cancellation? If someone drops out, is there some way I could take that place on the schedule?'

'There's no waiting list for cancellations. If someone backs out, then the person behind them on the list moves up.'

I was about to say thanks and hang up when I realised this was the opportunity I was looking for. I asked her to explain further.

'In the unlikely event of somebody cancelling at very short notice, that cancellation slot *might* become available,' she admitted. 'The problem is we are legally required to give people seventy-two hours' notice to appear in court.'

'Short notice is just fine with me. If I can make a request, it's this. If there is a cancellation any time – even in the middle of the night – please dial my number. I'll come with ten minutes' notice if I have to.'

With a reluctant sigh, she agreed. 'If a situation like that arises and it is feasible, I'll give you a call.'

A month passed without a word. With the financial deadline for university fast approaching, I contacted her every two weeks to check if there had been a cancellation. Nothing.

Then, on the evening of 10 September, I was sitting at home with Joe when my phone rang. 'A family just cancelled, and there is a slot open tomorrow morning. You have one night to come to Toronto from Waterloo to present your case. If you do decide to come, we have to look for an interpreter. There's no guarantee you will get one. Can you do it?'

'Yes. *Yes!* I don't need an interpreter, forget about that. I'll do it myself. And thank you! Thank you! Thank you!'

I hung up and called Ebrahim at his home in Scarborough. 'We're on for tomorrow morning. I've been given the slot for my hearing. Can you be in Toronto first thing?'

Ebrahim was stunned that I'd managed to cut my waiting time by some eighteen months. We spent several hours on the phone preparing for what he said would be a two- to three-hour hearing. He promised he'd meet me at the session room in the morning.

'Goodnight, Jaivet,' he said. 'Everything is going to be alright.'

I gathered my documents and boarded the night bus to Toronto.

THIRTY-SEVEN

'Come into my eyes, and look at me through them,
for I have chosen a home far beyond what eyes can see.'

Rumi

At 10 am, I stood alone before a judge in a sparse and low-ceilinged office space in downtown Toronto. The hearing had been underway for fifteen minutes and Ebrahim was nowhere to be seen.

'Mr Ealom, if your lawyer doesn't present himself in the next five minutes I'm going to adjourn this hearing,' said the judge.

'If he doesn't arrive in time, is it possible for me to present the case myself?'

'Yes,' she replied. It was a reluctant yes, far from a word of encouragement.

'Okay. I will do it myself.'

I'd spent years sitting alongside some very accomplished lawyers like Nina and Winiaka as they worked through the legal issues of Manus Island. That experience had given me a glimpse of what was involved in mounting a case.

While I had received some help from Ebrahim, I had done much of the heavy lifting to prepare for this hearing and had some confidence in my efforts. Still, I was no lawyer and my future was on the line. If I made even a small technical mistake, it could spell the end of my stay in the country.

Five minutes had passed without a sign of Ebrahim. I stood up and took a deep breath. Formally introducing myself, I began to make my case. 'Good morning, your honour. My name is Jaivet Ealom. I am a Rohingya man, born in Burma on . . .'

A door opened at the back of the room and Ebrahim bustled in, files and folders in hand, offering excuses about a long commute and terrible traffic.

After Ebrahim outlined my refugee claim, the judge turned to me and asked some gentle follow-up questions. To my surprise she was most interested in what had happened to me on Christmas Island and Manus, rather than in Burma.

Forty minutes into the hearing, the judge said she had heard enough and would retire to make her decision. Ebrahim had explained that the ruling would be made in writing and would likely be handed down in a few days.

Thirty minutes later, the judge called us back into the room. She told me to rest assured I had the legal right to stay in the country as long as I wanted.

It was all I needed to know. My journey was coming to an end. I had travelled around the world, through seven countries, without the advantage (thanks, Burma!) of a single legitimate passport, and yet, here I was, being offered the chance at a new start in Canada. This fugitive was keeping his freedom.

The ruling, when I read it later, was kinder and more humane than I expected from such a purely legal piece of paperwork.

'Your case is extremely well-documented Sir . . . You provided [an] extraordinarily detailed account of what happened to you since the extreme military groups have started [to] ethnic cleanse the Rohingya people.'

The document went on to talk about my time in offshore deten-tion. 'You as a young man have endured physically, mentally, and emotionally in your young life [. . .] You have tried over and over again to obtain refugee protection in Papua New Guinea, in Australia but were unsuccessful [. . .] You were not allowed to make a claim because of the new laws of Australia since you arrived by boat. You were then taken to Papua New Guinea to a refugee detention centre at Manus Island. You were held there for almost four years. During this time at Manus Island, the conditions were unconscionable. There was poor food. They were forced to sleep in shipping containers that were unbearably hot [. . .]'

A few more lines, and then the magic words: 'Based on the totality of the evidence, I find you to be a Convention refugee.'

On a personal note, I found the final farewell most touching of all: 'Sir, I wish you the best of luck.'

After years of being the invisible man, this felt like my first step into a new legal existence, both a stamp of legitimacy and a kind-hearted endorsement.

Freedom – at last! We had chanted this word so many times at the protests on Manus, and talked about its meaning, in quiet conversations in our shipping container cells. And now that I had won my freedom, what would I do with it?

There was little time for big questions. In a pattern of high-altitude drama that I should have been used to by now, the refugee hearing happened to coincide with the final day I could enrol at U of T. This was the second time in my life when my entry into university depended on a document that was withheld until the last moment. My future, once again, was on a tightwire.

I took the subway across town to the university registration office. 'I have just come from a hearing where my legal status as a refugee was confirmed,' I breathlessly announced to the woman at the front desk.

'That's great. Do you have proof?'

'The paperwork takes a few days. But I just came from the hearing and it's been confirmed by a judge. So I can enrol now and give you the document when it arrives.'

'We really do need it now, otherwise I can't process the registration. If you don't have the confirmation today, there's nothing I can do.'

By now I should have learned this lesson. For something to be real, it needed to be written down. The records we generate over the course of our lives will outlive us all.

My eyes on the clock, I headed back across town to the refugee board office. At the reception area, I asked to see the judge who had handled my case.

'I'm sorry,' said the office manager, a woman whose blouse matched the off-white walls. 'Unless you have an appointment you can't just turn up and ask to meet with her.'

'This is not an average situation. It's an emergency.'

'Excuse me, you can't just . . .'

'Listen, you know what?' I said, cutting her off. 'I really must stay in this office until I get a chance to talk to her. It's a very simple request which means *everything* to me.'

As the realisation dawned that I was not going away, and that, at her end, another Canadian apology – or a show of officious strength – was unlikely to defuse the situation, she relented, and gave me the Judge's email address.

Taking a chair in the lobby, I pulled out my phone and tapped out a message explaining my dilemma and asking for help: 'I have been admitted to study at the University of Toronto and today is the deadline for enrolment. In order to start as a domestic student I need written confirmation of my legal status as a refugee. I would greatly appreciate it if you could give me some kind of written official confirmation that your ruling today was positive . . .'

About an hour later my phone vibrated with an incoming message from the judge. She had contacted the school in her official capacity and gave her assurance that the paperwork would be forthcoming. In the meantime she confirmed I had the full legal status needed for my admission as a domestic student.

I raced back to the university to finish the registration process.

'Yes,' said the woman at the front desk. 'There's just one thing – you haven't paid yet.'

I knew this was coming. Students of modest means tended to apply for government grants and loans months ahead of enrolling at university. But as someone who had spent the past months in legal limbo, I didn't have that luxury. The rules were clear: either I paid up before the end of the day or I would miss out.

Once again, it was time to call a friend. Stephen Watt worked at the University of Toronto, as a marketing manager at the business school. We had met through the most unlikely and roundabout of ways, a thread that extended around the world and back again to the U of T campus.

As well as being a university staffer, Stephen was active in Canada's private sponsorship program. In his capacity as a volunteer, he had raised the needed funds and completed an application to bring Amir, the Iranian soccer player who had once been my neighbour and friend on Manus, to Canada.

It was Amir who first put us in touch, almost by accident. 'Someone I know might be in Canada,' he had said to his sponsor, while waiting for his own chance to come to the country.

At that time, I had a profile on Facebook, while mostly flying under the radar. Stephen had searched my name, sent a message, and was pleased to learn we were indeed in the same part of the world, and often in the same city.

We met at the cafe on the ground floor of the building where he worked, and hit it off. It's a friendship and volunteering partnership that continues to this day.

'Hello, Jaivet,' he said, sounding a bit surprised to hear from me. 'How are you doing?'

'I'm good. Listen, this is really awkward, but I need $5000.'

This was a man I had only known for a few months and had met just twice in person. I couldn't believe I was cold-calling him to ask for such a sum of money.

It was a quarter past four in the afternoon. The university closed at five. This late in the day, everything was on the line.

'I will pay you back, of course, but I need that amount.'

'When do you need it?'

'Right now.'

'I'm at work!' he laughed.

'If it's at all possible, I would like you to somehow find the $5000.' As I made the request, it sounded too outlandish to be taken seriously. But I was desperate.

'Okay, but I have maybe a $2000 daily withdrawal limit on my card.'

After all I'd been through, I couldn't believe my hopes of getting into university depended on the daily withdrawal limit of a friend's credit card.

'Trust me. I need this. Go to the branch and see if the manager can make it happen.'

And miraculously he did, riding his bike to the nearest bank branch and making his case. For the next half-hour, I kept my eyes trained on my phone, watching the time pass, minute by minute, as I waited for the all-important message.

Then it came. Stephen texted me a photo of the receipt showing the funds had been deposited into the U of T account. I emailed the image to the registrar's office and was admitted to the school with barely a moment to spare.

'Thank you, Stephen.' I could have cried for joy. 'I owe you one.'

Through our shared interest in helping others, we have been owing each other favours ever since.

In May, I took a bus from Waterloo and moved into a decently sized room, filled with sunshine, on the top floor of a big old house near the university. It was just a short walk from the magical-looking building in the middle of campus.

My first day at university felt like the beginning of a new journey, one that I was proud and relieved to take. Each new arrival was given a school ID card. This time, my name was spelled properly.

I was twenty-six years old: getting on a bit for a first-year student but not unusually so. In my heart and mind, though, I felt older than my years, and often noticed a disconnect between myself and the other students my age.

There was too much in my past to ever forget. The reign of terror back home marched onward, with little sign of slowing down. While my friendship with Saiful had allowed me to shift into advocacy work on behalf of the Rohingya and other minority groups in Burma, the genocide and the refugee crisis it had spawned might take generations to fix.

Meanwhile, the guys I had left behind on Manus were still in detention, on the island and in the new prisons that Australia had constructed across the region and on its own soil, in a bitter shell game of hide-the-refugee. The luckier detainees would be released into Australia on 'renewable bridging visas', with no path to permanent settlement in the country.

Their misery and persecution were to continue, in new and ingenious forms, with the long-promised political solution delayed another week, another month, another year. One day soon, I hoped to draw attention to what the guys had been through, and help them find a measure of the justice and mercy they deserved.

Closer to home, there was my own life to rebuild. With stability and a sense of possibility once more within reach, and my family doing okay back in Burma (my brother employed, my parents relatively safe), I was able to focus on the basics.

I began to meditate, and to write down some words about my life so far. After years of chasing down documents for other people, other authorities, it was time for me to write a testament of my own.

I bought furniture for my spartan room near the university. I got my teeth fixed by an orthodontist. I watched videos to learn how to cook. I began dating women again.

And on Saturdays, when my classmates were going for coffee or recovering from their hangovers, I was in the university pool, finally learning how to swim.

EPILOGUE

It has been a little over three years now since a judge at the Canadian Immigration and Refugee Board restored my existence on paper by granting me refugee status. As moments go, it felt nowhere as sensational as that bus trip out of the Christmas Island dock after days onboard the *Emelle*, with the sea breeze and a sense of possibility and safety in the air.

But, this time, the promise was real, and I was able to stop running and start living. A hope for the better future that I had longed for during those dark Manus days finally returned, one I had not felt in years. And the hope has stayed alive. In 2020, I became a permanent resident of Canada, the country I now call home. A sense of relief rushed through me again. Becoming a person of legal standing in this great country felt like an incredible milestone for someone who crossed three continents – without papers – in search of a sanctuary.

Since arriving in Toronto, I have tried my best to discover who I am outside my status as a stateless person and former Manus refugee. Sometimes at the University of Toronto, I felt like a bit of an imposter, going through the motions of normal student life while knowing my unusual past set me apart. Certain sights and sounds – like the sight of uniformed officers or the noise of a passing fire truck – would set my nervous system ablaze. In my first year, I attended a seminar on trauma, and was re-traumatised myself when, for lunch, we were asked to line up for sandwiches. Even to this day, I suffer the stomach pains that are a puzzling legacy of the Manus plumbing, shared by many of us. Whether they are a result of the atrocious washroom facilities, the rotten food, or the years of grinding hopelessness, we may never know.

Over time, though, the patterns of work and life started to come more naturally, bringing me a little closer to your average twenty-something young man, if there is such a thing. Keeping busy can be good therapy. Through some of my original connections in Canada, I ended up meeting and getting hired by a start-up that brings tech solutions to humanitarian crises. The job felt like a good fit for someone like me, and it was inspiring to join a team of other moti-vated people, each trying to make a difference in their own way.

I started to feel normal again: judged for my work and ability to contribute, rather than my immigration status. One amazing thing about Toronto is most people are from somewhere else. Over lunch one day, my boss pointed out how no one on her team was born in Canada. This was typical. You could go to a party and the topic of your national origin might never come up. Or if it did, it was in an equitable, getting-to-know-you way. Like, 'Oh, you are from Burma? My parents are Polish.'

These are examples of Canada's famous multiculturalism in action. While it is most prominent in the bigger cities, the commitment to diversity is widely distributed. In fact, it's core to the values and laws of the country. While there are many reasons this culture sprang up in the first place, it is not upheld by chance. Indeed, it is kept alive and well through deliberate government policy.

That is not to say Canada has not committed great misdeeds as well. Although historians have made the case that the country has more than just two founding cultures – the French, the English, and Indigenous peoples – the relationship between them was hardly equal or peaceful.

The French and the British were famously in competition and even at war with each other in the centuries prior to Confederation. At the same time, they were also making cruel strides to colonize Indigenous peoples. Canada only emerged as a nation by building a railroad – the most dangerous section of which was built by Chinese immigrants who were paid significantly less than their white counterparts – bringing in the Mounties, and pushing out everyone who got in the way.

And not just pushing them aside: in the first century after Confederation, the project included taking Indigenous children from their families, forcing them to adopt the culture, religion and language of their abductors, and beating them or letting them die of neglect if they refused – or even if they did not refuse – the force of oppression. The more I read about Canadian history, the more I see a history of land theft and genocide familiar from the history of both my homeland and that of Australia.

Despite these terrible and calculated misdeeds, which have created a legacy of shame and destruction that continues today, there are elements of Canadian culture that are deserving of respect – and indeed, serve as an exemplar for nations around the world.

Maybe because the country evolved out of its relationships with its imperial masters, rather than refusing them outright (as the Americans did, for example), there developed a tradition of compromise and finding common ground in Canada that has served it well, and got it through some tough scrapes and moments of crisis. This is a place where it's understood that you can only survive with the help of your neighbours, and that those neighbours might be quite different than you.

That appreciation of strangers continues. For decades, Canada has invested in bringing newcomers to the country, and making sure they have the opportunities and resources to fulfil their potential. Even refugees are given attention and financing to help them get the language and training they need to get a foothold in the economy.

Contrast that with Australia, which dedicates vast resources to keeping newcomers out of the country and punishing those who do manage to get in by placing them in boxes. The government has spent $7.618 billion on regional processing since Manus was reopened in 2013, representing $2.44 million to torture each of the 3,127 people sent to offshore detention. This is likely to be an underestimated figure as it does not include other deals such as $40 million in foreign aid to Cambodia where seven refugees were resettled. The pure waste of money and human potential is staggering.

And to what end? To keep a bunch of nativist politicians in power? To shore up the profits of a media company? Whatever the reasons or motivations, like the results, they are unjust and sickening.

At the time of writing, the injustice continues. There are still about 200 guys from Manus trapped in Australia's refugee detention system, many of them getting close to their ten-year anniversary of detainment, with no end in sight.

Some of the lucky ones have been settled in third countries, like Shamindan in Finland, or Amir in Canada, or the dozens of single men and families who have been settled in the US under a deal struck by President Obama and carried out, miraculously and somewhat remarkably, under Donald Trump. Each person reacts differently to this second chance at life.

Consider Amir, the friend who once helped me hide my cell phone – not just in one secret place, as he took pains to remind me during the writing of this book, but dozens. He finally arrived in Canada in 2019, through a sponsorship application submitted by Stephen Watt. The media spotlight shone bright on Amir's arrival, and while he was reluctant to be cast as a public refugee, he agreed to talk to journalists in the hope that the coverage might bring more help and attention to the guys he left behind.

Once the media spotlight moved on, to his relief, Amir kept busy making up for lost time. It has been a pleasure to meet with him again in our new adopted country, and watch him use his gifts of intelligence and charm to carve out a new and fulfilling space for himself.

Another story needing no introduction belongs to Behrouz Boochani, who went from shouting his rage from the top of a tree to sharing his story with the world, through his book *No Friend But the Mountains*. He was the first to open the eyes of the reading public to the grim facts of offshore detention, from the perspective of one who lived and suffered through it. His book won prizes and opened doors, and he continues to raise awareness of refugee issues through his work as a journalist in New Zealand.

Other men who walked the pages of this book have found their own happiness, albeit in a less public fashion. Zakaria, my stalwart friend and leader of the Rohingya crew who talked me through the escape from the hotel in Kendari, wound up in the US where he became a car mechanic. In his career choice, he carried on a proud family tradition. His family was full of mechanics, down through generations, which is why I will always associate him with the military jeep that I used to see parked next to my grandparents' house.

There have been dozens of guys like Zakaria, who journeyed through the fire and somehow made it to the other side. I have been delighted to reconnect with each of them from the safety of my new homeland. Like me, they are happy and grateful to be free and pursue their own paths. Their achievements, large and small, pay tribute to the amazing resilience of the human spirit, once the weight of oppression has been lifted.

However, not all have done so well, post-detention. One of my Manus bunkmates who was resettled in the US continues to experience severe trauma, to the point where he is unable to carry on with daily life. Another bunkmate from MA2-09, Haroon, the older man who was with me during the attack that claimed the life of Reza Barati, was also resettled in the US. A year after he arrived, he died alone in his apartment of no known cause.

And everyone I continue to talk to seems to suffer the same mysterious stomach pains that I had once believed to be my own unique memento from the tropical island prison.

This is what living in a cage does to a person. No matter your powers of resilience, detainment changes your sense of the world – and yourself – forever. When the forces of society, the media, political and legal systems come together in a conspiracy to rob you of your freedom and define you as less than human, it is not easy to resist. You start believing their lies.

For the most part, those who have been released are the lucky ones. There are still hundreds of people caught in the web of the 'Pacific Solution'. They are stuck perpetually indoors in the 'hotels' in Australia, or still reside offshore, shifted from one facility to another by authorities who believe, against years of evidence to the contrary, that they will one day lose their resolve and agree to return to their countries of origin. Over the years, Australia has sent a total of 3,127 people to Papua New Guinea and Nauru. Despite the fact that 86.7 per cent of this population has been recognised as refugees, almost half of them (1500 individuals) continue to languish in limbo.

Further from the colonial core, there are many more thousands of refugees stuck in Indonesia's detention and refugee centres, caught in 'green hell', as they often call it. A decade after arriving, they are still there, legally unable to work, open a bank account, go to school or get married. They spend their days learning English and trying to reach out to someone – anyone – who might care, as their youthful promise fades, along with their hopes of resettlement. All the while, Australia, of course, continues to pull the strings and pay the bills.

The fact that this system has existed for so long, and *continues* to exist, demonstrates that the humanitarian disaster on Manus Island was far from a one-off mistake. It wasn't a policy blip nor a rogue political misadventure that the government can now downplay, blame on someone else or pretend never happened. The illegal imprisonment we endured for years was part of a large-scale and well-planned abuse of human rights and human lives that has deep and tangled roots in the Land Down Under.

Offshore processing and the violence it involved was overseen by no fewer than six prime ministers since the 'Pacific Solution' was first announced by the government of John Howard back in 2001, with strong bipartisan support. In the fast-spinning rolodex of Australian leaders, three of them – Kevin Rudd, Tony Abbott, and Malcolm Turnbull – each managed to sit in the big chair during the four years I spent detained, with no detectable change to the brutal policies that kept us caged.

You might think public opinion would have shifted once the facts of our suffering managed to squeak through the Murdoch media wall. Any reasonable scenario would suggest that eventually, the state-sanctioned detainment and torture of men, women, and children might turn from a political winner to electoral poison. Not so! For decades, Australian voters have rewarded political candidates for possessing a coldness of heart. The way they deny the truth is so precise it seems provocative, a form of Double Speak. The phrase 'saving lives at sea' was first used in Operation Sovereign Borders – and then became a rhetorical weapon of the entire ruling Liberal regime – to justify, of all things, *losing* lives at sea. A border protection policy that is considered a horror by many legal scholars and refugee advocates around the world, and a national shame even by some Australians, was proclaimed by Malcolm Turnbull to be 'the best in the world.'

Against this rhetorical backdrop it was no surprise when, in 2018, Scott Morrison assumed the prime ministership. This was the faux-pious immigration minister who helped design and lead Operation Sovereign Borders, driving it forward with the zeal of a tank commander. Now in the general's seat, he led the Liberal-National Coalition to a memorable victory at the polls the following year. Believing he had been called by a higher power 'to do God's work', Morrison described his unexpected election as a 'miracle.'

Many believe Morrison's career benefited from a power of a darker sort. His government and its policies certainly received a warm reception from the Murdoch media conglomerate and the other right-wing news properties of the nation. And he repaid their kindness by serving more red meat to the beast. True to his shameless character, Morrison made a point of placing a shiny steel trophy on a display table for all to see. Cast in the unmistakable shape of an Asian fishing boat rolling on waves, the strange-looking totem is emblazoned with bold black letters reading 'I Stopped These'.

For all I know, the trophy is still there, since at the time of writing, Morrison still sits in the prime minister's chair. I wonder if he ever walks past his prized possession and gives a moment's thought to the terrible damage done by his pet policy. There's no way of knowing just how many people died as a direct result of Operation Sovereign Borders, but the numbers would not be insignificant.

There are many unknowns. We can never be sure how many detainees were murdered or killed themselves after being deported or forced to repatriate to lethal homelands. We can't put a figure on the souls lost in the UNHCR's sprawling system of suspended animation, where lives drift into emptiness and suicide is a popular option. We'll never find out how many people have drowned since Scott Morrison asserted control over the waters beyond Australia's 'sovereign borders' and strongarmed them into refusing refugees. And that is to say nothing of the thousands of survivors who will carry sickness, trauma, and scars – both in mind and body – for the rest of their lives.

My own survivor guilt came in waves, even as I tried to leave the past behind. The awareness that others were continuing to suffer left a stain on my enjoyment. The situation back in Burma was impossible to avoid (and remains so today). I knew from my volunteer work as a researcher and an advocate for the Rohingya, and more intimately, from my phone calls to my parents back home, things were just getting worse.

In 2021, the country endured another coup d'état, triggering unrest that quickly dragged the entire country into a state of civil war. The trouble came from the usual source: the Burmese military, which deposed the country's elected leader, Aung San Suu Kyi, and then put her back under arrest.

The resulting uproar across Burma was dealt with by the usual heavy hand of the military, only this time, it was not just the Rohingya and other minorities who were subjected to violent persecution, but the entire civilian population. Thousands have been detained and hundreds killed. The economic impact of the crackdown has been compounded by the effects of COVID-19, which have joined forces to cause the country's health and education system to collapse. It's a catastrophe nowhere close to finding resolution, with the darkest days still to come.

One insight that I had glimpsed on Manus was reaffirmed by my tenure as a student at the University of Toronto: that documenting a crisis, making careful note of its causes and implications, can actually alter its course. Many policy decisions, including the successful effort at the United Nations to declare the genocide against the Rohingyans in Burma just that – a genocide – started in obscure research think tanks, which added documentation and legitimacy to the basic truths being lived by those suffering under tyranny.

The genocide motion at the UN was first launched by Canada, and I am pleased to note how the country's support of multiculturalism has translated well into bringing light to refugee crises the world over. On a similar note (though on a much smaller scale), in 2020, I was proud to accept an invitation to join the Refugee Advocacy Network (RAN), which officially launched on World Refugee Day. Itself an offshoot of a 'policy dialogue' at Carleton University in Ottawa, RAN has been endorsed by Immigration, Refugees and Citizenship Canada, and is the first refugee-led advocacy group to officially advise a national government. It's a model that has attracted the notice of other countries, with New Zealand and Germany launching their own versions in 2021.

As I learned all too well on Manus, government policy is not just something that should be left to the politicians and ignored by everyone else. Policy changes lives, in profound and sometimes devastating ways. At the Canadian Rohingya Development Initiative, and other projects, like Northern Lights Canada, I have done my best to combine my energy with that of other volunteers to bring a little more fairness and hope to this often cruel and callous world.

It is in the same spirit that I agreed to write the book you are reading now. When first approached by the publisher, who had seen news stories of my journey from Manus to Canada, my reaction was, 'Please no. I can't return to those days.' Talking to journalists after years of deliberately flying under the radar was hard enough. Now I was being asked to dig deep into the details of those years and share the most intimate and painful experiences with a reading public that mostly consisted of complete strangers.

It seemed impossible, and unwise, given how much tough emotional work I had to put into leaving that past behind. And yet, like my friend Amir before me, I felt like I owed it to the guys who were still being held in detention, who might never have a chance to share their own accounts of what we had been through together.

So, with some very considerate and helpful friends acting as listeners, I began to open up about those days, and the tale began to take shape. And as the narrative unfolded, it brought with it the memories of those old horrors. At night, I was convulsed by nightmares. I would wake up in terror, thinking I was back in solitude, with no way out.

My book has an ending, but the story does not. In Australia, at least, nothing much has changed, despite all the madness and suffering. While 'Manus Prison' is gone, the offshore detainment system continues. Together, the terrible forces of government, ideology and media march in lockstep to trample the lives of the world's most vulnerable (and often most talented and resourceful) people. My wish is that this book, while keeping the reader interested, will draw some attention to this evil system, with the hope of one day bringing an end to it. My own journey to freedom was made possible by quiet individuals who took a chance on me because they believed that doing so – helping even just a single person get to a better place – was worthwhile in itself. My ability to write this book is a testament to their courage, and to the small actions that came together to point my way to freedom and save my life. A single person can make a difference through the smallest act of goodness, because small actions can come together to make great ones.

This is my hope, at least. Whether it's Burma or Manus, or some other totalitarian regime, the past does repeat itself, and the same narratives of oppression occur in different times and places. At least if the facts are properly recorded, there's a chance that someone will stumble across them at some future moment in history and say, 'Not this time. Not again.'

IN MEMORIAM

There's no way of knowing just how many people died as a direct result of Operation Sovereign Borders. At the Manus Island detention centres alone, seven men perished by either murder, suicide, accident or medical negligence. I feel it's important to name them here:

Reza Barati, from Iran, was beaten to death by G4S employees in Mike compound in February 2014.

Hamid Kehazaei, also from Iran, was twenty-four when he was medevaced from Manus. After a poorly treated infection on his leg had turned septic, Hamid suffered a heart attack. He was flown to Port Moresby and then Australia, where his life support was switched off on 5 September 2014.

Faysal Ishak Ahmed was a Sudanese man who died in Brisbane on Christmas Eve 2016 after the repeated seizures he suffered on Manus were ignored.

Kamil Hussain was a thirty-four-year-old from Pakistan who drowned while swimming in a waterfall in Lorengau in 2016.

Hamed Shamshirpour was an Iranian national who died of suicide in 2017 despite multiple warnings that he was dangerously mentally ill.

Rajeev Rajendran from Sri Lanka also died of suspected suicide. His body was discovered near the hospital in Lorengau in 2017.

Salim Kyawning was a stateless Rohingya man like me. He jumped from a moving vehicle on Manus Island in 2018. It was considered a suicide.

I knew most of those guys: they were never far from mind as I sat down to write this book.

ACKNOWLEDGEMENTS

To my family, who made me the person I am today. To the helpers, who took a chance on a stranger. I hope I can one day repay your generosity of spirit. To Craig Henderson and my publishing team, who turned my words into a story. To Stephen, who worked hard with me over long nights to bring that story to life. To those around the world who had to leave their homes in search of a safer future: that future is still to come.

Above all, to my brothers in detention, who continue to bear the certainty of uncertainties.

© Saiful

JAIVET EALOM was born in Myanmar and now resides in Toronto, where he has become a prominent spokesperson for the Rohingya community. He is studying at the University of Toronto and works for a company that provides software to non-profit organizations.